ACCEPTABLE MISCONDUCT

LAW SCHOOL HERETIC SERIES

ACCEPTABLE MISCONDUCT

MARIA RIEGGER

For information, contact
Maria Riegger
P.O. Box 90541
Alexandria, VA 22309

Print ISBN 978-0-692-80795-8
Ebook ISBN 978-1-5323-2420-8

Printed in the United States of America

First edition 2016

10 9 8 7 6 5 4 3 2 1

ACCEPTABLE MISCONDUCT

FOURTH WEEK: **SUNDAY (FALL 2010)**

I woke up too early on Sunday morning, wondering what the hell was wrong with me. I started thinking about the previous night, revisiting every detail in my head.

My friends and I had gone out dancing. Tarek had come with us.

Meeting Tarek Cordiez at the beginning of the law school semester had been a coincidence, a coincidence for which I was grateful. My friend Josh said that Tarek was almost like a male version of me, but nicer.

Indeed, Tarek and I had many things in common. We both spoke French (he had grown up in France, with a French father and a Lebanese mother); I had lived in France for a while. He loved listening to my stories about my Latin family (my father was from Spain; indeed, my last name, Vilanova, is Catalan; and my mother is Argentine). And, amazingly, we had similar political beliefs, which, for me, instantly set him apart from most of the other men in the Washington, DC area.

After this year, he and I would have one more year of school. Tarek was in the full-time law school program, while I was in the evening program while working a full-time job during the day, an undertaking that sometimes made me question my own sanity.

I had decided that meeting him had been a positive thing. I enjoyed spending time with him, and sometimes thought about him when he wasn't around. But our relationship up to this point had been strictly platonic.

Until, perhaps, last night. Last night we had almost kissed, and he told me things that made it sound like he was interested in me as more than a friend, but hadn't been totally clear on that, either.

So was it up to me, then? Why couldn't I have just kissed him last night?

Ugh, I would think about it later.

I rolled over on my side and went back to sleep.

I slept in that morning as late as possible, but it wasn't late enough. When I woke up, my stomach was basically eating itself. I cooked a huge brunch, eggs and toast and bacon and fruit and coffee.

As I was finishing brunch and slurping the last dregs of coffee, my phone rang. It was Lara. I had never been so glad to hear from my middle sister.

"Oh my God, do you have time to talk?" I said to her.

"Yes!" she exclaimed. "I got your text from last night. What happened?!"

Lara was a medical resident. Because of her crazy schedule, I was lucky to get to talk to her at all.

I proceeded to tell her everything that had happened the previous night, in a whirlwind, blow-by-blow retelling.

"Slow down! I can't understand you," she told me several times.

I took several deep breaths and continued.

"Wait," she said. "Eric likes you?"

Eric was a good friend of mine, a fellow law student. He was several years younger than me, and I had never considered him as a romantic partner, but Tarek thought that he liked me.

"I don't think he does. But Tarek thinks so."

"He's probably jealous."

"I don't know."

When I finished telling her everything, she excitedly said, "Oh my God, Tarek is totally into you!"

"I'm not sure."

"How can you not be sure?"

"Dude, how long has it been since I dated someone?"

"How long *has* it been, Isabel?"

I exhaled a long sigh. "A long time. So, what do I do now?"

Lara laughed. She always found my ignorance in this area amusing.

"What do you mean?" she asked me.

The pitch of my voice noticeably went up a notch. "I mean, what the hell do I do? What's the protocol? Help me out here! You're a Millennial! He's closer to your age than mine!" Indeed, it was true. I was thirty-four years old, technically a member of Generation X. Tarek was twenty-nine.

"Oh my God, Isabel, you are totally lost!"

"Yes, I am! And I'm not too proud to ask for your help!"

"All right, calm down."

"So what do I do?"

"So you like him, right?"

"Yes!"

"You want to date him, right?"

"Yes."

"So ask him out."

"Jesus Christ, he's the man. *He* can ask *me* out."

"Didn't he do that already?"

"He said it wasn't a date." I paused. "Ariel said he may be interested in a friends with benefits situation. That's common among you Millennials, right?"

Ariel was my youngest sister. She worked in finance in Manhattan, and had clued me in on modern Millennial dating habits.

"Well, I've never done that but there are people who do. Anyway, Ariel's not right about everything."

"I can't do that. And I can't—Lara, I can't stand the idea of not seeing him again. If we hook up then—if it's too awkward then, if we don't see each other anymore—"

"Hey, it's all right. Then you know what you should do?"

"What?"

"Wait a little bit. If you're uncomfortable about it, just wait." She paused. "If he really likes you, which it sounds like he does, then he will let you know."

Maybe he *was* letting me know, but maybe I was too dense. Or maybe there were too many innuendos. Maybe he and I were both at fault for that.

But there was something else, too. Last night I hadn't had the energy to give it too much thought.

"Hey, Lara—how long does it take to get over someone?"

"What do you mean? Who are you not over?"

"No, I mean—how can you tell whether you're just a rebound for someone or not?" Then I explained to her what Tarek had told me about the Dominican girl he used to date. He said that they had broken up about three years ago.

"You don't know why they broke up?"

"No, I didn't want to ask." I had known that if I had asked and he had told me, he would've asked about my past, *quid pro quo*, and I wasn't ready to share that.

"Three years is long enough. I wouldn't worry about you being a rebound for him." Lara was always so practical.

"OK," I answered. But telling me not to worry was like telling the Pope not to be Catholic.

"Thanks for listening, Lara."

"Anytime. You know that."

I asked her about work, and she filled me in. She was incredibly busy, but I could tell that she loved it. We talked excitedly about getting together for dinner over the next couple of weeks.

When we hung up, I suddenly felt alone. This was why I hated Sundays. There was usually nothing to do but be alone with my thoughts. I normally went to campus and studied, or stayed at home with my head buried in my law school textbooks. But with my mental confusion, there was no point in even trying to study today.

I sat back into the sofa and turned on the TV, hoping to find something enjoyable. I rejoiced when I finally found a Western.

I continued snacking, thinking that I should probably cook something.

I was chopping up ingredients for homemade *tuco*, Argentine tomato sauce, while waiting for another pot of coffee to brew when my cell phone rang.

My heart jumped when I saw that it was Tarek. It took me three rings to answer it.

"Hello?" I answered, pretending like I didn't know who it was.

"Hey, Isabel," he said. Did he feel as nonchalant as he sounded?

"Hi," I said. "What's going on? Did you just wake up?"

"No, I—I've been up for a while." He paused. "I was calling to see if you've recovered from last night." I could tell he was smiling.

"Recovered from what? You mean because I'm old?"

"No, no, no," he said quickly. "That's not what I meant."

"Tarek," I said, chuckling, "I'm kidding."

Then he was laughing nervously.

"I'm almost recovered, I would say." I tried to control my palpitations.

There was silence for a few moments.

"Isabel," he began slowly, "I was calling to see if—to make sure that you and I are OK. I mean, I hope you don't think—after what I said—like I said, I don't expect—" My heart went out to him as he struggled. Strange, I thought. My heart hardly ever goes out to anyone. It was usually locked up and only made an appearance when I saw my sisters.

"Hey," I said, "Tarek, it's OK. Everything's OK."

"Are you sure?"

"Of course." I weighed what to say. "I told you last night, I really enjoy spending time with you. That's the truth."

He appeared to relax, but it was difficult to tell over the phone.

"OK, good."

"It's very sweet of you to call me." Then I added, "I'm glad you did." I could feel the heat in my cheeks, and was glad that he couldn't see me.

I thought about inviting him over for dinner but decided not to complicate my life further for the moment. At some point I would have to decide, but didn't have to decide now.

As if he read my mind, he asked, "What are you doing today?"

"Um—I thought about studying but it's pretty much no use so—I'm doing a little cooking. And I'll probably go to bed really early."

The thought of Tarek and my bed at the same time suddenly made my pulse race. I wanted to see him but didn't trust myself. It was like the previous night had depleted all my reserves and I needed to rebuild them in order to be able to resist him again. I felt like the more I saw him, especially in a situation like last night, the weaker I would get, until I would wilt.

Thinking about all of that, I decided to cut the conversation short. "Look, I'll see you tomorrow. And next weekend you can help me with Property, if that's OK." He had a real knack for that class.

Tarek and I coincidentally had all of our classes together. Since he was in the full-time law program, he had one more class than I did.

"Of course. I'll see you tomorrow."

"OK, bye."

"Bye, Isabel."

I hung up, sat down, and put my hands over my face. What do I do now?

FIFTH WEEK: **MONDAY**

As usual, on Monday morning I hit the ground running. Shower, coffee, granola, in that order. I grabbed all my stuff and headed to the metro.

I was still going over the events of Saturday night, and had difficulty believing that it had all really happened.

I got to work at about 8:15. I worked full-time for a company contracted by the federal government, like so many people in this area. My job consisted of translating documents all day at my desk, usually between Spanish and English. It suited me as I could work in relative isolation; superficial interactions with others exhausted me.

As soon as I walked in, I noticed that something was different. As I passed my coworker Abdul in the hallway, he looked at me with playful eyes.

"Hi Isabel, how was your weekend?"

"It was fine," I said, confused.

"Did you have a good time Saturday night?"

Aw, *fuck*. Miguel and his huge mouth. I was going to kill him.

"Yeah, I—I guess," I stammered as I continued past him.

Miguel, one of my coworkers, had run into Tarek and me on the metro. I had left Miguel with the impression that Tarek was my boyfriend. That had undoubtedly been gossip fodder at work.

I dropped my stuff at my desk and proceeded to the kitchen to put my lunch in the fridge. This day was going to be hell.

Peter McBride, my one friend at my day job, was in the kitchen making his instant coffee. Peter was only about ten years older than me, but was protective of me in a fatherly sort of way. Well, he had four children; it must be difficult to turn off the paternal instinct.

"Dude, no self-respecting Spaniard I know drinks instant coffee. *No jodas,*" I teased, smiling slightly.

"*Hola, nena!*" Peter said in his usual cheerful voice. "Well, you know I'm only half-Spanish, and half-Irish." Then he leaned toward me and lowered his voice. "Hey, everyone is talking about your Arab boyfriend."

"*Jodeeer,*" I said with exasperation. Then I told Peter that Miguel had seen Tarek and me Saturday night.

"*Por cierto,*" I told Peter, "he's not my boyfriend. Miguel just assumed that he was."

"Sooo," Peter said with a twinkle in his eye, "he's a guy you went to dinner with late on Saturday night?"

"Yes, dinner and dancing." I smiled in spite of myself.

"Oh my God," Peter said. "So you like him?"

I exhaled. "Yes." Then I looked at Peter. "*Pero no digas nada.*"

"Hey, don't worry, I won't say anything; I'm your friend," he insisted, putting his hand to his chest. "How do you know him?"

"We're in school together."

"Ohh, I see." Then we smiled at each other conspiratorially.

After lunch, I was working on translating a contract, and one of the Spanish translators came by my desk. I always got the feeling that this particular woman didn't like me. But then, I had that feeling about most people.

"Isabel," she began, sitting down on the chair next to my desk.

"Hey," I said. "What can I do for you?"

"The other day you reviewed a translation I did of this commercial text, from English to Spanish. But there's something I don't agree with."

Great, I thought, feeling my shoulders become tense.

"What's that?" I tried to remain friendly.

"Here," she said, pointing.

"*Producto interior bruto,*" I read, then shrugged. "OK, what's wrong with the change?"

"Shouldn't it be *producto interno bruto*, like I had originally said?" she said in her thick accent.

"No," I shook my head.

She was staring at me, as if she expected me to say more. I waited for her to speak. She had come to me and had to tell me what she wanted.

She finally spoke. "*Producto interno bruto* is the more common term."

"OK," I began, sighing, "what is the purpose of this translation?"

"It's a commercial document."

"Right. Who's the client?"

"A U.S. consulting firm."

"Right. But what is this translation for?"

"It's for—" She didn't see where I was going with this. "For the client's overseas branch."

"And where is the branch located?" I asked her.

"In Madrid."

"Right. And in Castilian, the term *producto interior bruto* is used. *Producto interno bruto* is more commonly used in South America."

"*Pero así se dice en el mundo,*" she began to protest.

"*No en todo el mundo,*" I corrected.

She pursed her lips, frustrated. She obviously was not convinced, but didn't put up a fight about it.

After she left, I exhaled slowly. I was getting too old for this shit.

After work, I got to the law school campus pretty early, with over half an hour before class. I sat downstairs at one of the small tables and pulled out my textbook for my Criminal Procedure class to begin reviewing cases, trying not to look around nervously for Tarek.

Would everything be the same between us? I thought. Well, why wouldn't it?

Because when you were dancing with him, you held onto him like you were drowning, and you almost kissed him . . . twice.

Did he notice that I had tried to kiss him, but decided not to? Stupid question. Of course he did. He wasn't an idiot. I, on the other hand, was starting to think that *I* was.

I had been staring at the same page in my textbook for at least five full minutes, my head reeling as I was trying to think about how to act around Tarek, when my friends Josh and Eric showed up together. Eric had a weird expression on his face.

I had known both of them since practically the beginning of law school. Josh was the same age as me, thirty-four, and was also in the school's evening program. Like me, he had a full-time job. Unlike me, he had a scientific mind, with a doctorate in Biomedical Engineering as evidence of that. In spite of his Anglo name, 5 feet 10 inch stature, and blond hair, he spoke Spanish; his father was Venezuelan.

Eric was only twenty-five years old; he was slim with thick, dark brown hair and blue eyes. He was in the school's full-time program, but had had a few classes with Josh and me. Eric had grown up in Brazil (his father was Brazilian), and he possessed the fluid, effortless manner of movement that I often associated with Brazilians. He was also an incredible dancer.

"Hey," I inclined my head.

Josh sat down but Eric remained standing.

"What's up, Isabel?" Eric asked. They were both looking at me. I suddenly felt like I was about to be interrogated.

"How was Saturday?" Josh asked.

I cocked my head and furrowed my brows involuntarily. "Uhh, I was with *you* guys Saturday. Don't you remember?"

"Not the whole time," Eric said.

I looked from Eric to Josh and back to Eric. Realization dawned slowly. "Holy shit." I leaned all the way back in my chair and crossed my arms. "You guys are a piece of work, you know that?"

"Why?" Josh asked.

"You two think I slept with him, don't you?"

"Did you?" Eric asked.

"*No,*" I said with emphasis. "Not that it's any of your damn business."

I looked dead into Eric's eyes, suddenly remembering what Tarek had said on Saturday, that he thought Eric was crazy about me. That couldn't be right, I thought.

"Really?" Eric was relentless today.

"Look," I said, my face hardening. Eric was pissing me off. I leaned forward and lowered my voice. "I don't know what the hell your problem is, and this has nothing to do with you, but nothing happened." I looked at Josh again. "This conversation is officially over, you guys."

Eric scoffed, apparently unconvinced. "I'm going upstairs," he said, and left.

"What's with him?" I asked Josh.

"Who knows?" Then Josh looked at me, leaning in. "So you really like him."

I stared at Josh. He was smiling from ear to ear.

"Are you crazy? I don't *like* Eric. I mean, only as a friend—"

"I'm not talking about him. I'm talking about Tarek. You're crazy about him. That's why you didn't hook up with him."

"Oh, so you think you know me?"

"I know you better than you think." Josh raised his eyebrows, looking very sure of himself. But then, he was always a bit arrogant.

"Whatever, dude."

"Isabel, I don't understand why you're so hard on yourself."

Because it's the only way I know how to be, I thought.

Then I saw Tarek. He had walked in talking to Dalia, a girl in our Property class. She was actually nice, for a Millennial. She and I had previously had a couple of classes together. She was cute, with long brown hair and brown eyes.

I noticed then the intense way she looked at him. She was also holding her book very close to her chest, as if she were nervous. Tarek was looking at her face as he talked to her.

I suddenly became exceedingly jealous, the color rising in my cheeks. I wanted to stomp over there and push her out of the way and tell her, "You can't have him! He's mine!"

But he wasn't mine, not really.

All the emotions I ever felt were intense. It was a Latin thing, most people said. It was the Arab blood on my father's side, my mother said. It was the Italian blood from the Argentine side, my aunt had said.

Only my father had it right. "It's OK to feel that way," he would say, "as long as at the end of the day you can think logically about things. Emotion is OK, but emotion without logic is meaningless. And you have to find a way to deal with your emotions when they get to be too much."

Here I was again, thinking about my father, and his death, and how I hadn't been able to prevent it.

I saw Tarek and Dalia say goodbye to each other and quickly buried my head in my book, pretending to be oblivious. Josh had been watching me, and he chuckled.

"*Te lo dije,*" he said.

"*Que te calles,*" I retorted, hoping he would really shut up.

But I was dying inside. In that moment I began to doubt everything I thought I had known about Tarek up to that point. I thought he was beginning to like me. I thought that maybe he wanted to be romantically involved with me. But now I wasn't sure. Maybe he acted that way with every girl.

How could I have been so stupid?! I never, *never* succumbed to some guy's charms. He spent time with me, offered to drive me home, took me out to dinner, danced with me, and maybe all he wanted was sex. I was totally doubting my radar. So foolish.

And I was sad.

"Hey," Tarek said as he approached us.

"Hey," I answered, looking up. I meant to be aloof but couldn't help giving him a warm smile. His expression was so open and welcoming. He smiled back.

"How are you guys?" he asked us, but he was only looking at me.

"All right," I said. Josh didn't answer, I noticed.

The three of us walked upstairs.

Class that night was uneventful. Later, Eric, Josh, Dinesh, Tarek, and I were on the metro on the way home. Dinesh was another friend of ours; he laughed all the time and had an easy smile.

I had hardly said anything the entire evening, too wrapped up in my own thoughts. They were taking me down the rabbit hole.

"Are you all right?" Tarek asked me. We were both standing up. The metro was pretty crowded tonight. Josh and Dinesh were deep in conversation over patent prosecution. They both worked as patent agents for law firms.

"Yeah," I shrugged.

"You haven't said anything since we left campus." He had a concerned expression on his face. Or maybe he was curious. I could care less what he thought, I told myself.

"Yeah, well, sometimes I don't feel like talking. I'm not here to entertain you."

"I don't understand. Did something happen?"

"Shit happens every day," I said, nonchalantly. That was the story of my life.

But I was like a bubble waiting to pop. As he was standing there, wondering what to say, I opened my mouth.

"I didn't know you knew Dalia," I said, trying not to look at him.

"She's in our Property class," he answered, as if that explained everything.

"I know; I've just never seen you talking to her before."

He looked at me then. I looked away, but not before catching his expression of realization. He wasn't dumb.

"She's really nice," he said.

"Oh, I'm sure she is," I said sarcastically. Then I paused. "Do you want to date her? *Are* you dating her?"

His expression now was amused. It seriously pissed me off.

"No." He paused. "How would I have time to date anyone when I spend all my free time with you?" He smiled knowingly.

"No, you don't," I retorted. "I work all day, and who the hell knows what you do? You probably sleep until 11am and then have your girlfriends over."

He chuckled. "That is *exactly* what I do."

I started to smile. I couldn't help it. Damn him and his sexy goatee and gorgeous eyes. I bit my lip on purpose.

Tarek sighed, as if he were about to explain something basic to a small child. "Dalia missed class the other day and she asked me for my notes."

I turned on him then. "You're not giving her our outlines, are you?"

"No," he shook his head firmly. Tarek and I studied together regularly, and took copious notes.

"Because I'm not helping you so that you can share my hard work with other people." They could do their own damn work.

"Relax, Isabel. I just gave her my class notes for one day."

Oh, and in a class of about fifty people, there was no one else she could ask?! I thought.

Josh was staring at me, wondering what was going on. I glared at him, telling him with my eyes to stay out of this.

I looked at the floor, slowing my breathing to relax.

The train was stopping at Pentagon City. I decided not to say anything else.

As Tarek grabbed his stuff to exit the train, he reached his hand out and squeezed my forearm. I smiled weakly.

"See you tomorrow," he said as he left.

Josh sighed a sigh of exasperation. Dinesh was looking at me curiously. I tried to hide my face.

"Isabel," Josh said carefully, his voice low, as if he were afraid to startle a deer. "If you like him, you have to tell him."

"You like him?" Dinesh's eyebrows shot up.

I put the back of my hand against Dinesh's shoulder. "If you tell anyone, I'll deny it. And don't tell Eric." Then I turned to Josh. "If he likes me, then he can tell *me*. I'll be damned if I set myself up like that."

"That's illogical," Josh said calmly.

While I appreciated Josh's attempt to appeal to my sense of logic, I disagreed. "No, it's the prisoner's dilemma. If I tell him, and he doesn't feel the same way, I will have humiliated myself."

"But if you don't tell him, and he *does* feel the same way, you'll never get together. So, according to you, it's better for you not to get together with him than risk humiliation."

"Yes," I said. But I sounded more certain than I felt. I wasn't sure which was worse.

"You're crazy," Josh scoffed.

"No, I'm—" I thought for a second. "I'm saving myself."

"From what?" Dinesh asked.

I looked at him with my chin raised. "From everything." From falling for Tarek, from sleeping with him, from having him possibly regret sleeping with me, from not seeing him again. From everything.

Josh shook his head. "You know, I should tell him myself." I put my hand up but Josh stopped me. "I won't, though, because this is a lesson that you need to learn. See how long it takes for you to realize it."

"Realize what?" I said.

"That he's crazy about you."

After Josh and Dinesh left the train, I sat by myself and thought about what Josh had said. I still wasn't sure what, if anything, to do.

I looked at my phone, to have something to do. I had a message from Tarek.

Please call me when you get home.

Like hell I would, I thought. He's not the boss of me. I was slightly amused, though, that he had said please, as if that would move me somehow.

When I got home, I kicked off my flats and left them by the door. I couldn't be bothered to put anything away. Then I nuked some leftovers and sat on the sofa, thinking. Thinking like this always got me into trouble.

It really was the prisoner's dilemma. Once I spilled, I wouldn't be able to take any of it back.

When I finished eating, I put my dishes in the sink. I wasn't going to call him. I would let him stew in his own uncertainty, as I was stewing in mine.

But I should have known by now that he never just let things go.

About forty-five minutes after arriving home, I was getting ready for bed, and my cell phone rang.

It was Tarek.

Jesus, I thought.

I answered on the fourth ring. "Hello?" as if I didn't know who it was.

"Hey, it's me."

"Me who?"

"Oh, you're funny." His French lilt seemed stronger somehow, and incredibly sexy.

I paused, figuring I would wait him out. *He* had called *me*; *he* could tell *me* what he wanted.

"I told you to call me when you got home," he said.

"Dude, I'm not your girlfriend. I don't have to do what you tell me to."

He chuckled. "So if you *were* my girlfriend, you would do what I told you?"

I huffed, then smiled a little. "Maybe," I said.

"Well, that's an incentive for me then."

I ignored his comment. "So what's up?"

"Isabel, I don't like it when you're upset at me."

"Well, I'm upset at everybody all the time, so, don't take it personally."

"Tell me why you're mad," he said softly.

Because I'm afraid that Dalia likes you, I thought. And there are probably tons of other girls who like you, too. Girls who are younger and skinnier than me. How can I compete with that?

"I'm not mad."

"Yes, you are."

"I may have been—slightly—discombobulated before, but I'm not now."

"Why not?"

"Because I'm talking to you." It was true. Talking to him, even just being with him, had kind of a soothing effect on me. Sometimes being with him bothered me physically, but it also toned down my anger somehow.

But I wasn't going to say anything else.

"I think I said enough to you on the metro," I told him.

"OK." He paused. "Are you sure you're all right?" I guess he figured there was no point in pushing me any further.

"Yes. Don't worry."

There was silence for a few moments.

"Isabel, is there anything you want to tell me?" Tarek's voice was very calm.

Not now, I thought. Not over the phone. But yes, there is something I want to tell you. I like you. I think about you all the time. I can't wait to see you again.

But of course I didn't say any of that.

"No." My voice was barely above a whisper.

That had been my opportunity and I had let it pass. I rationalized my decision by telling myself that if I did tell him how I felt, it would be better to do it in person.

"Well, there's something I want to tell *you*, " Tarek said then.

Oh my God. What?! I thought. But I simply said, "OK."

"I got a callback for the New York firm. I'm going next week for the interview."

My heart dropped. Tarek, don't go to New York this summer, please, I thought.

"That's great. I'm happy for you," I choked out.

"The interview's Tuesday. I'm leaving Monday. I won't be in class next week until Wednesday."

"I'll send you my notes," I said.

"OK, thanks."

"Look, I need to get to bed," I said. "Some of us have to work tomorrow."

"OK, good night, Isabel."

"Good night. I'll see you tomorrow."

We hung up.

All in all, it had been a bad day.

I was on the metro on my way to class.

The day before had passed relatively without incident. Work had been quite busy so, luckily, no one bothered me or made fun of me.

The problem was that my mind raced constantly. To avoid the pitfalls that that would inevitably lead to, I concentrated on reading and taking detailed notes on all of the cases for class. That way I would be better prepared for our study session on Saturday.

I still couldn't believe my bad luck that Tarek had an interview in New York.

Why are you surprised? I thought. That's the kind of luck you always have. *Mala suerte.*

Yesterday, I had gotten to campus early and had been sitting downstairs, with my back to the hallway so that I wouldn't be distracted looking for Tarek.

I had been lamenting the current state of my life, and of humankind in general, when I had felt a hand on my shoulder. It had been him, of course.

"Hey," he had said.

"Hi," I had smiled.

He had sat down facing me. Then I remembered the first day we had had a real conversation. It had been at a small table like this one. I had kept trying to chase him away, but he wasn't having any of it. I chuckled. That had only been like four or five weeks ago.

"What's so funny?"

"Nothing," I said, remembering. "So tell me about the firm in New York."

It was a large firm, he told me, one where his accounting expertise would definitely be appreciated (I still couldn't believe he was a CPA; he didn't appear nerdy enough). I also knew that it paid exceptionally well, which was necessary to attract attorneys since it was located in New York. New York was tax hell and pretty much the most expensive place in the country.

"That firm has many offices," I had said. "So would you definitely be in the New York office?"

"The way they're talking, probably, but I'm not sure. I'll have to find out."

"Is it your first choice?"

He hadn't answered right away. "I don't know," he had ended up saying.

"Well, good luck. I mean that."

No, I didn't. I felt bad at being so selfish. Just when we were really getting to know each other. Just when I was starting to really like him.

Then I actually had a positive thought. The associateship would be for next summer. A lot of time would pass between now and June of next year, and a lot of things could happen.

"I don't believe it," I said to myself then.

"What?" Tarek was curious.

"I'm going to kill you."

"Why? What did *I* do?" He leaned forward and touched his chest.

"Sometimes I think I'm becoming an optimist." I looked directly at him. "Tarek, if you turn me into an optimist, I'll never forgive you for it."

He had laughed then, a deep-throated laugh. It had put a stupid grin on my face.

Today, I smiled while thinking about that conversation. In the end we were OK. I hoped that in the end we would always be OK.

As the train was arriving at the metro station, I got a text message from Tarek.

I'm downstairs. And I got your coffee.

Thanks, I texted back.

I got to campus and joined Tarek. I took my coffee, thanking him as always, and took a big sip. Wednesdays and Thursdays were long days for me. Four hours of class in a row with Tarek next to me. How was I possibly expected to concentrate on Property that way?

As usual, he wouldn't let me pay him for my coffee. As usual, I felt bad about that, thinking about how he didn't have an income since he wasn't working like I was.

"Isabel, about this weekend—" he started, trailing off.

I looked at him. "What? Are you too busy to study? Have hot dates lined up?"

He smiled. "No, I—I have a meeting here at school after lunch so—could we meet in the morning? We can meet at my house."

"Sure. What meeting is it?"

He didn't answer right away, which made me curious.

"For like the—the—"

"The what?" I made a motion with my hand, the Argentine sign for impatience. "The Anarchists' Club, what?"

He smiled. "No, the Arab law students group."

"Oh, I see." I raised one eyebrow.

He was still smiling.

"So are you a member of the French students group, too?"

"If there were such a group, I would be." He paused. "By the way, I know you're in HLSA."

HLSA was the Hispanic Law Students Association, and I attended their meetings with Josh.

"How did you know that?" By the end of my question, I knew the answer.

"Josh told me."

Jesus Christ.

I wagged my finger in the air. "There's something you need to know about Josh."

Tarek waited expectantly.

I continued. "He gossips worse than an old Spanish woman."

Tarek chuckled.

"So what else has he told you about me?" I narrowed my eyes.

"That's it, I promise."

There was silence for a few moments.

"Well, thank you for getting my coffee today."

"You are most welcome."

I hesitated, weighing something. "So when does your meeting end?"

"Probably at like 3 or 3:30."

What the hell.

"If you want," I began slowly, carefully choosing my words. I nervously played with my hair and avoided looking at him directly. "If you want I can pick you up after your meeting and then drive you home. And we can study after—I mean—if you want."

Tarek smiled a broad smile. "That would be great. And we can order dinner."

"OK," I said softly.

Then we went to class.

After Property class, Josh was chatting with some of our fellow students. Dinesh left in a hurry. I told Josh we would wait for him downstairs.

Eric, Melanie, Tarek, and I went downstairs. Melanie was my only female friend at law school. She spoke with a smooth Texas accent and didn't seem to be phased by my personality.

After class ended at 8 p.m., the lower floor of the law school building was like social hour. There were a ton of people around. We were all standing at the main entrance, chatting while we waited for Josh.

"Isabel, you look great today!" Melanie told me. Her eyes went down to my chest.

She meant my *boobs* looked great today, but she wouldn't say that in front of the guys.

They *did* look good. I was wearing a wrap top that showed just enough cleavage.

"Yeah, you *do* look good!" Eric said then, his eyes dropping to my chest.

I backhanded him on the shoulder. "*No me mires las tetas!*" I could feel my face going flush.

Melanie was *uber* social. She knew everyone, including the girl whom I referred to as Sorority Girl. SG (whose real name was Alyssa) was a short, skinny blonde. I had no idea why she was studying law, as she appeared to have no interest in anything other than chatting up men. SG came up to us now and started chatting with Melanie, but not before throwing me a vicious look.

Screw you, I thought, glaring at her.

Melanie was talking to SG about some meeting she had gone to recently.

"Oh, Isabel! That reminds me. I met this guy I think you would really like." Melanie looked at me, but not before stealing a quick look in Tarek's direction.

Oh God, I thought. This could get interesting.

Then she spoke quickly. "I was at this meeting for this political group.

This guy, he's a Republican, and he even worked in the last presidential campaign. He's really nice. He's an attorney, and I'm pretty sure he's single."

Melanie and I were forever bemoaning the lack of quality available men in this town. And I was always telling Melanie how difficult it was to find men here who I would date, who shared my beliefs. I felt like the number of available men who fit that description in this town, I could probably count on one hand.

"I appreciate the sentiment," I told her truthfully.

"What does he look like?" SG asked Melanie all of a sudden.

Wait, what the hell did she care? I gave her a crazy look, but she was looking at Melanie.

Melanie also seemed surprised at SG's question. I felt uncomfortable talking about this in front of Tarek.

"Um—he's good-looking, light brown hair with blue eyes—" Melanie started.

SG cut her off. "No good. Isabel doesn't like blonds."

I stared at SG, open-mouthed. What the fuck—?

"He's not blond," Melanie said. "Is that true?" She looked at me.

SG continued, with a smug expression on her face. "According to the Gospel of Isabel, anyone lighter than she is is blond."

Holy shit, I *had* said that.

"How the hell do you—" I started to say to her.

"You don't think I listen to you? Oh, I listen. You told Josh one day how you're not attracted to blond men, and by 'blond' you said that you mean anyone lighter than you. Really narrows down the pool, doesn't it?"

"Screw you," I told her.

"Dark men, that's who you like. Like that guy last year—" Then she looked at Tarek, so quickly that I was sure she didn't think I had noticed.

The guy she was talking about was Saul, someone who I had hooked up with—three times—the previous year. It had been strictly casual. I tried to leave my past with men in the past, but I had found out recently that Saul and Tarek knew each other. It made me feel awkward and uncomfortable. On the one hand, since Tarek and I seemed to be growing closer, I felt that I should tell him about it. On the other hand, it was my personal business and it was in the past.

I wanted to protest but was too shocked at Alyssa's comment. I was deathly afraid that she would say Saul's name and then Tarek would know.

She had been there that night, the night that Saul and I had first hooked up. She and Josh and Eric had been at the club.

But she inexplicably suddenly stopped talking.

"Anyway," she said, by way of conclusion, "I do listen."

I finally found my voice. "I'm not waiting for Josh anymore, you guys. I'm going."

Thankfully, Josh showed up just then.

"Come on, let's go, we've been waiting for you," I said with frustration. Now everyone knows my goddam business, I thought, because you constantly run on Venezuelan time.

I was silent on the metro ride home, but was fuming inside. How could she say that? Wait, why was I surprised? She had told Tarek once that I "slept around." Why wouldn't she out all my past indiscretions that she knew about?

But there was something else that puzzled me. She knew Saul. She knew his name; she had had classes with him. She knew that he and I had hooked up. I felt like almost everyone must know because he hadn't been able to keep his damn mouth shut.

So why hadn't she said, "Just like Saul?" I hadn't stopped her.

I replayed the entire scene in my head.

Did she know something that I didn't know? Or did she somehow know that I liked Tarek? If it were the latter, why wouldn't she use that against me? Nothing like that had ever stopped her before. She had had the ability to royally screw me over right then and she hadn't. Had that been a conscious choice? Did she actually have a conscience? Or did she think I would kick her ass if she did?

I was growing more confused every day.

Tarek sat down next to me on the metro. Josh was sitting across from us, talking to someone in our class, but not anyone I knew well.

I needed to say something. The silence was killing me.

"Some people told me once that law school was like high school. I didn't believe it, but now I do."

Tarek smiled. "Well, you've got a bunch of narcissistic, somewhat antisocial overachievers together in one place. There's definitely going to be trouble."

I chuckled slightly. "You're calling me narcissistic?" I looked at him.

"No, you are *not* narcissistic."

"You don't know me that well."

"I'm getting to you know, though. I know enough to know that you aren't." He was still smiling.

Would you care if you knew that I slept with Saul? I thought. Would you be pissed off or would you not care?

The train was stopping at Pentagon City. I gave Tarek a weak smile. "I'll see you tomorrow."

Then he reached out and touched my hair, brushing it away from my face. I smiled a bit more.

After he left I noticed Josh looking at me from across the aisle. He was grinning.

"*Te lo dije*," he said.

"*Que te calles*," I scoffed at him.

FIFTH WEEK: **SATURDAY**

Saturday, as usual, came more quickly than I had expected. Work on Friday had been crazy. Everyone had a deadline, and everyone had needed my help with something.

Of course, I had thought. You guys all rag on me all the time, but when you need my help, you come running.

I had treated everyone in an aloof, businesslike manner, but hadn't turned anyone away; I had entertained all of their questions. But I hadn't been friendly, either.

I didn't give a rat's ass. I had more important things to worry about, like whether Tarek was going to go to New York next summer. Then, in a moment of rationality, I wondered why I cared about events that might or might not happen several months from now.

This morning I had woken up relatively early and had done a ton of reading. I was sore from weightlifting the day before, so I stretched a little bit.

Tarek had told me to pick him up at 3 p.m. from campus. I left at 2:30, hoping that traffic would be light. There was nothing going on in the city this weekend, no parades, no fairs, etc., that would bring the dreaded street closures and *desviaciones*.

More and more, I felt like I was losing a little bit of control over my life. I felt like the duality of opposites. I both liked and didn't like how Tarek made me feel. I wanted to tell him how I felt and desperately wanted to keep it a secret.

I was failing miserably at keeping it a secret from everyone else. My sisters knew, but that wasn't a big deal. But now Josh and Dinesh knew too, and if Eric didn't know for sure, he would soon figure it out.

I thought again about what Tarek had said the other day, about how he thought Eric liked me. There's no way that can be right, I thought. I'm like an older sister to him. I decided not to think about Eric now.

Luckily, the traffic *had* been fairly light, and I arrived at campus at about 3:05. Tarek had sent me a text message to say that he was waiting outside. I would double park long enough for him to get in the car.

I'll never forget the scene when I drove up that day. The weather was crisp; autumn had definitely arrived. I had the windows rolled down and was singing along to Daddy Yankee.

A ella le gusta la gasolina, dame mas gasolina, le encanta la gasolina, dame mas gasolina . . .

I was wearing dark jeans and a long-sleeved black top, with minimal makeup and dark red lipstick. It was bright outside and I was wearing my sunglasses.

I pulled up in front of campus and stopped the car, putting it in park. I looked around and suddenly felt like I was in the Twilight Zone.

There were five or six people standing around outside, all talking amongst themselves, all Middle Eastern. I saw Tarek and recognized Zara and Sameer. Zara was a very sweet girl in one of my classes. Sameer was a friend of Saul's, and an acquaintance of Tarek. I did a quick scan and didn't see Saul, thank God. I didn't know if he was part of this group or not.

They all turned around and looked at me. My first instinct wasn't to be embarrassed. It was to stare back, which I did, shoving my sunglasses up on my forehead.

I inclined my head at Tarek in acknowledgement. He smiled at me, but not before I realized that he had been in a heated discussion. His jaw had been set tightly and his eyes had been on fire. I wondered what was going on.

Everyone was looking at me as I continued to stare. When my eyes met Sameer's, I smiled, with one corner of my mouth curling upward. His expression was one of shock. I didn't understand why. Was it so weird that Tarek and I were friends?

Tarek said goodbye to everyone and promptly got into my car.

"What's up?" I asked him, finally turning the music down.

"Not much." He was smiling.

"Are you all right?"

"Yes. Why?" He looked at me.

"It looked like you were kind of having an argument with them."

He paused. "You're very observant."

"I'm a loner. That's what happens when all you do is watch other people."

He chuckled. "It's just—I don't agree with them on—almost everything."

I sighed. "Welcome to my city, Tarek."

"I know, you warned me."

Then I smiled at him. "I guess it's you and me against the world then."

He was looking at me again. "I guess so." Then he was laughing, as if he were thinking about something.

"What's so funny?" I asked him.

He was still laughing as I looked at him. He was trying to speak but couldn't.

"What the hell?!" I said, smiling myself. "What happened?"

Tarek was starting to calm down. I rarely saw him laugh that hard.

"Sameer was talking about you."

Great, I thought sarcastically. This couldn't be good.

"I can only imagine what he said." Then I added without thinking, "He hates my guts."

"Why?" Tarek's expression was curious. I was trying to pay attention to the road.

"Nothing. Go on. I'll tell you later." Sameer hated my guts because he didn't like the type of person I was. Unfortunately for me, he also knew that I had hooked up with Saul.

Tarek hesitated for a second and then continued. "Well, Zara was asking about you. That's how it started."

"I don't think Zara likes me either," I said then.

"What makes you say that?"

I laughed. "What are you, a shrink? Tell me, how does that make you *feeeeel*?" I said, making fun of him.

There was silence for a few seconds.

"Soooo," Tarek said, "why don't you think they like you?"

"Tarek, please," I began, "look at me. You know they don't approve of a woman like me with an NRA sticker on her car, who occasionally wears a low cleavage, and who curses all the time."

Tarek smiled. "Zara likes you."

"I doubt that. She never talks to me."

"She's really shy," he said by way of explanation. "She's probably a little bit intimidated by you. But she asked about you."

I was surprised, and I was rarely surprised. "So what did she say?"

"She asked me where you were from. She also said you were really smart."

"What did you tell her?"

"I told her the short version, Argentine mother, Spanish father." He paused. "Anyway, as I was saying—"

"Sorry for the interruptions."

"No, you're not." He was chuckling.

I smiled. "You're right, I'm not. And you're in a damn good mood today." My smile evaporated. "You must be excited about New York," I added, trying to sound nonchalant.

He ignored my comment and continued, but not before sighing with a bit of exasperation. I had that effect on people.

"She asked about you, and then Sameer started talking about you. He said how crazy it was that the sexiest girl on campus—"

"Wait," I said firmly. "He did *not* say that."

"Isabel, I wouldn't lie."

I looked at him briefly, before returning my eyes to the road.

"I don't believe it," I said under my breath.

"Anyway, he said that he couldn't believe that the sexiest girl on campus was so—" he stopped.

"So what?" I prodded.

He was thinking of how to say it in English.

"Like—so tough, so—"

"Rough around the edges?"

"Yes, something like that. And then—" Tarek started laughing again.

"I'm starting to think you smoked some *maria* at this meeting," I said, smiling.

"I didn't, I swear. It's just, then like ten minutes later I told them I was going outside to wait for my ride, and they were outside too, and we were talking about politics, and then you showed up, blaring your *reggaeton* like always."

"Hey, I don't apologize for that."

"I wasn't asking you to."

I sighed. "OK, so that explains Sameer's expression."

"Yeah, he was a bit surprised."

"He's a jackass."

There was silence for a couple of seconds.

"So how do you know Sameer?"

Oh no. This route may lead to a conversation about Saul. I needed to derail it.

"We've had classes together."

"Have you—"

"Have I what?"

"Never mind."

"Tarek, what?"

"Nothing, it's too personal of a question."

"Were you going to ask if I slept with him?"

"No, I was going to ask if you dated him, specifically, if he was who Alyssa was talking about the other day." Then he went on quickly. "But it's none of my business, so I'm sorry for asking."

I sighed. "It's OK. But no, I have never dated him, or slept with him."

"Not that it's any of my business," Tarek added.

"You're right, it's not." But I smiled. I guess I had had that coming.

We studied at Tarek's place for a couple of hours. He spent at least an hour explaining recording statutes to me. It was freaking annoying but would most definitely be on our Property exam.

I had brought a thermos of coffee with me, because Tarek didn't have a coffee maker, or coffee, and occasionally sipped from it.

I was going over Criminal Procedure notes when I caught him looking at me. He was sitting next to me on the sofa, but a few feet away from me, a fairly comfortable distance, although I was never 100% comfortable when he was around. I was relaxed but always a little turned on, like someone with generalized anxiety disorder on a low dose of Xanax, barely enough to make sure my symptoms were controlled. I constantly tried to channel that tension into studying. It had been several days since we had gone out dancing that Saturday, and I figured I had recouped enough of my energy to be able to resist throwing myself at him. But the desire was always there, lurking in the background.

"What?" I asked.

He looked surprised, like I had caught him unawares. "I was going to have tea. Do you want any?"

"Sure."

Tarek went to the kitchen to put the kettle to boil as I watched him. Try as I might, I couldn't tell what he was thinking. I went back to my notes.

"OK, so I have a question," Tarek said.

About what? I thought.

"Shoot," I said.

"It's about automobile searches."

Thank God it was a law school question and not a personal question.

"OK, what's the question?"

"What part of the car can the police search if they arrest someone while driving?"

"OK, let's back up," I started. "The general rule is that the police, when they arrest someone, get the automatic right to search the entire person of the arrestee—"

"The entire person?"

"Meaning the person's body. It's more than a frisk, remember? It's pursuant to an arrest, not a stop. To arrest someone, the police need probable cause that the person has committed, is committing or will commit a crime."

"And the police don't have to show anything?"

"Right. They don't have to show that there's the probability the arrestee has weapons or anything like that. It's an automatic right to search when they arrest someone. So, for the auto search, if they arrest someone, they can search the entire passenger area of the vehicle. That's the so-called 'grab area,'" using my air quotes, "of the car."

"That's the *Belton* case."

"Right, *but—*" I emphasized, "*Belton* is old law, it's not valid anymore. So forget about it. The current rule is *Arizona v. Gant.*" Then I read from my notes. "The police can search a car incident to arrest only if the arrestee is within reaching distance of the passenger compartment at the time of search or it is reasonable to believe the car contains evidence of the offense of the arrest. If those justifications are absent, then police need a warrant or another exception to search the car."

"But they can't search the trunk without a warrant, right?"

"Right, or unless another exception applies, like the arrestee opens the trunk himself and something is in plain view, or exigent circumstances, for example."

"OK, I think I got it," Tarek said.

"It's easier than Property," I teased.

"No, it's not!"

I chuckled.

"You should do criminal law," Tarek told me.

"It's too—oogy." I reconsidered. "I would do white-collar defense, medical malpractice defense, something like that." I sighed. "But the pickings are slim right now."

Tarek nodded. "I know, but don't worry, Isabel."

Easy for you to say, I thought. You're not a woman in your mid-thirties fighting law firm stereotypes. And you've had two callbacks already. I've had *nada*.

I lay my head against the sofa, thinking.

"When do you want to order dinner?" Tarek asked.

I looked at him. "Whenever you want."

We ordered Chinese and drank tea while we waited for the food to arrive. I was leaning over his kitchen counter, since I needed to stand up and let my blood flow a little.

"You're leaving Monday, right?" I asked him hesitantly.

"Yes."

"What suit are you going to wear?" I was picturing him in the suit I had seen him in for the DC interview.

"Actually," he laughed softly, "do you mind if I ask your opinion on something?"

"Sure. I mean—I don't mind."

"I kind of narrowed it down to two suits, but I'm not sure."

He led me into his bedroom. Oh, geez, I thought. It occurred to me that this may be a pretext, but he didn't seem like that kind of guy. Besides, he really didn't need a pretext with me. I had the growing suspicion that if he propositioned me I would melt.

I noticed that his bed was made, and laughed inwardly at the fact that *my* bed at home wasn't made. It was pretty much never made.

He had a full closet of clothes.

"So I see that Miami has rubbed off on you," I said, smiling.

"Really?"

"Absolutely. I hear that the men down there dress really well. You're no exception. Also, most of this stuff is for summer weather."

He showed me two suits, one that he wore to the DC interview that I had seen him in, and one dark gray one.

"I like them both," I said honestly. "But this firm is a high-flown New York firm, and I think the tiebreaker is the fact that you should err on the conservative side, so go with the darker suit."

"OK, that's kind of what I was thinking. With a white shirt?"

I clicked my tongue, thinking. This was the kind of thing I used to help my dad with.

"Hmmm, let me see what you're thinking about."

He showed me a white shirt and a light purple one, both with long sleeves. He also had a light gray one and a dark blue one. He had other shirts, but these were the ones that he was considering.

"OK, technically, these all go with the suit." I held them up individually next to the dark suit. "Who's interviewing you?" I said.

"I don't remember the names offhand."

"Men or women?"

"It's a mix. The partner is a woman."

I smiled. "I would go with the light purple one. But—" I tempered my answer a little. "If you're unsure about the color, go with the white shirt. But then you should wear a tie with some color in it."

"Not a problem. Why the purple one?"

I looked at him. "It's conservative enough. And you'll look incredible in it. The women will be salivating."

He smiled. "I think the partner's like fifty years old."

"Doesn't matter." My smile this time was coy, then my expression turned more serious. "But what tie would you wear with it though?"

He showed me his ties. He had a *ton*. Of course, I thought, he used to work in consulting.

I picked out a deep purple one. The purple tie was so dark it was almost black. "I like this one."

"Oh, you're good at this," he said approvingly.

"Tell me something I don't know," I said with some attitude. "I can dress myself, you know?"

"I've noticed."

I ignored him. "The dark purple tie will work with the white shirt too, but take something else in case you change your mind. It's always good to have options." I picked out a couple more ties to go with the white shirt. "OK, those are my suggestions," I said with finality. Then I thought of something. "Do you have tie clips?"

He rolled his eyes, as if the question were an inane one. "Of *course*."

He showed me what he had and I picked out a couple that were conservative enough.

"Thank you, Isabel." He smiled at me so that his eyes lit up.

"Anytime." I smiled back.

The food arrived, and we were dipping it up onto plates in the kitchen. I was smiling again. It was really difficult not to smile around him.

"Kung pao, huh?" I said then. "So you like spicy food."

"I like spicy everything."

"Well, you did have a Dominican girlfriend, so—you must like spicy."

I wasn't sure if he remembered telling me that, that night we went out dancing, and I had commented that he danced very well, and he had mentioned that it was because he had had a Dominican girlfriend.

Tarek signed. "Yeah, well—that was crash and burn."

I stopped what I was doing and looked at him. "I'm sorry, Tarek. And I'm sorry for—bringing it up."

"It's OK. It—it didn't end well."

"You don't have to tell me about it; it's not my business." I looked at my plate, aimlessly separating the rice and the meat with a fork.

The silence was almost too loud. I counted silently to compose myself. One—two—

"She cheated on me with a supposed friend of mine."

"Wait—what?" I shooked my head to clear it, as if the statement were incomprehensible.

Tarek looked at me, sighing again. "It's true."

"I'm sorry."

"She said it wasn't a big deal, and she insisted that it only happened once, but then I found out that it had been going on for months. I found out through another friend. I felt like an idiot."

"You're not." Then I said without thinking, "*She* was the idiot."

"And to top that off—" he continued. "She wanted to get back together with me, but—I mean, I could maybe forgive the truth, if she had been the one to tell me, but I can't forget the lies, you know?"

I nodded.

"And who knows what else she was covering up. I mean, in the end I didn't know what to believe."

"I am so sorry." I shook my head slowly.

"It's OK." He paused, then looked at me. I waited for what was coming. "When was the last time you were in a relationship?" he asked.

"I think you'll be shocked." I smirked.

"You must have confused me with someone who shocks easily." He smiled and turned toward me, expectantly.

"Well, I mean I've gone on dates over the past few years, like maybe gone on one or two dates with a guy, before deciding that I didn't want to see him anymore. But over the past few years, I haven't 'dated' anyone," using my air quotes. It really depended on how you defined "dating" someone, but I wasn't going to go Socratic right now.

"So when was the last time you were in an actual relationship?"

I couldn't believe I was going to tell him this. I did the math. "Twelve or thirteen years ago."

Tarek sucked in his breath quickly. I suddenly realized that I had been holding my breath, and exhaled. "Yeah, so I'm—kind of—out of practice." My situation was kind of an anomaly, I realized. Statistically, a woman my age should have had at least a couple of long-term relationships by now, and later in her life as opposed to when she was in college.

"So, wait, you were like, around twenty-one?"

"Right." I dropped my utensils on my plate, giving up the pretense of rearranging my food, and turned to face him. "Tarek, I don't—I don't remember, you understand? It was a long time ago, and I don't really remember what it was like, just that it was really nice. That it was a good thing."

"Well, that explains a lot," he said pensively.

I wasn't sure what he meant by that, but I looked away, totally embarrassed now. Maybe divulging that hadn't been such a good idea. I didn't do a good job of talking about my feelings, anyway.

"But," Tarek continued, "you told me before that you've had, I mean—"

I waited expectantly, not understanding his question.

Now *he* seemed embarrassed. "Do you remember when we were talking about this on the metro a while ago, about your—?"

I suddenly understood. He was talking about sex, as in, whether I had been celibate for twelve years.

"Oh, right, no, I—I've had plenty of that. It's just been—"

"Casual?"

"Right. But I mean, I haven't had any, like—I mean, I don't regularly—I mean, not recently. It's been well over a year." Suddenly, I was thinking about Saul and didn't want to. "Look, can we please not talk about this?"

"I'm sorry. I don't care anyway, Isabel. But I'm sorry I asked."

"It's OK." I began to pick at my plate again, still standing in the kitchen.

"So who was he?" Tarek asked cautiously. Maybe he was afraid I wouldn't answer.

I was instantly sad. Every time I thought about Santi I was sad.

I took a deep breath.

I told him about Santi, how I had spent the summer before my senior year of college in Madrid, taking some classes there to occupy my time. Santi was the friend of a cousin of mine. He and I had clicked instantly, and we had been practically inseparable since we met. This despite the fact that my father was from Barcelona and Santi was from Madrid. He always called me *la catalana*. Technically, I was only one-quarter Catalan but the fact that I spoke Catalan was enough for him to so brand me. We spent the entire summer together. His parents lived on the outskirts of Madrid, in the suburbs, but he had been renting his own apartment in Madrid that he shared with a friend. At the time, he was studying at one of the main universities there. He had been studying microbiology and had stayed over the summer to work in the university lab and finish his research projects. I remembered him complaining all the time about having to count the seeds for his project. It was mind-numbing, he had said.

We had gone out dancing, walking around town, to bars, to museums and tons of other places. I had met his parents when they were in town.

Santi had never told me that he loved me, and I had never told him. But we both had known that we felt that way about the other. He was really good to me, selfless, in fact. He cooked for me, accompanied me home at night (the few nights that I didn't sleep at his apartment) and comforted me when I missed my sisters. He loved his family, and I loved that about him.

I told Tarek that at the end of the summer, Santi and I were talking about me going back home. I had a year of university to finish and he did too. I told him that I would go back to the U.S. and that he would stay in Madrid, and that thinking about anything else beyond the summer was not "realistic." The future was too speculative, I had told him. We didn't know where we would end up.

I told Tarek that Santi had grudgingly agreed with me, saying that I was right. But years later, I thought about what I had said to him, and the fact that maybe he hadn't wanted that, that in actuality he had wanted to stay together, to wait out the year and then see whether we could be together. That realization had eaten me up, since I thought that maybe he had only agreed with me because he had thought that was what I wanted. But it really wasn't. What I wanted at the time was to stay with him, or at least to try.

"And the worst part of it," I told Tarek, "was that he ended up marrying someone else a few years later."

"I'm sorry, Isabel." Tarek looked sympathetic. "I'm so sorry."

"It's OK." Then I added, "I saw him, a few months after I moved to Barcelona. I went to Madrid to see my cousins, and he and I met for dinner. But—it was different." I took a breath. "And to be honest, I'm not sure that we would have ended up being compatible. I'm a completely different person now, anyway." A bitter, surly, horny person who can't get any satisfaction.

"You can never know what will happen in the future," Tarek said then. "It's better to live in the moment."

I looked at him and couldn't help smiling. "Maybe."

We looked at each other right then, with about a foot of distance between us. I almost leaned in to kiss him. I was waiting for him to look away but he didn't. I used almost all my energy to look away and busy myself with my plate.

"Thank you for getting dinner," I said, feeling my face turn red.

"Anytime."

I could see from the corner of my eye that he was smiling. I needed to change the subject. I hesitated a second, then asked him something I was curious about. "So where are you staying in New York?"

"With a friend of mine from undergrad. You would like him. He's Cuban."

"*Por Dios.*" I rolled my eyes.

"We'll probably go out Tuesday night."

"Oh my God, don't go out with him. He'll have you out all night." The Cubans I knew definitely knew how to party.

Tarek laughed. "Is that an order?" We were standing right next to each other now. Had I moved closer to him or had he moved closer to me?

"Yes," I said firmly. I couldn't stand the thought of him hooking up with some hot New York model.

"Hey, I'm not your boyfriend. I don't have to do what you say."

I put my hands on my hips and looked directly at him. "So if you *were* my boyfriend, you would do what I say?"

He smiled slyly. "Maybe."

"Well, I'll remember that." I could feel myself starting to blush again. Then I took my plate and sat on the sofa. Tarek joined me.

"So," he began in a low voice after he sat down. His expression was kind, and cautious, like he was trying to help a small wounded animal. He must be about to ask me a question that he knew I wouldn't like. "So you dated someone last year?"

I had been right.

"Where did that come from?" I was surprised.

"Alyssa mentioned it the other day."

"Yeah, well, Alyssa says a lot of shit about me. Most of it isn't true." I was annoyed with her for bringing it up and with Tarek for asking about it now. I took a bite of my chicken with cashews.

"I understand," he said. "When did you break up?"

We didn't really "break up" because I never dated Saul; I only slept with him. But I didn't say that.

"Please, Tarek, I really don't want to talk about this." I couldn't look at him. I couldn't believe SG had brought that up in front of him. I vowed to get her back somehow.

"Look, I'm sorry. I just—" his expression got serious, "like I told you the other day. I just want to get to know you."

I exhaled slowly. "Tarek, I don't see the point if you're going to New York." I put my plate on the coffee table.

Tarek did the same and then turned toward me, leaning his elbow on the back of the sofa. "Isabel," he began, "first, it's not anywhere near certain that I'm going to New York. Even if they make me an offer, which they probably won't, I may not accept. Second, it would only be for the summer. And third," he smiled at me, even though I could barely look at him. "A lot can happen between now and next summer."

I shuddered all of a sudden.

"Are you cold?" Tarek asked me. "I can turn the heat up."

Oh, the heat was turned up enough, I thought.

"I'm OK," I lied. We were staring at each other. Again, I thought about kissing him, but resisted.

After dinner we had more tea. We chatted for a long time afterward, about politics, things to do in DC, our families. I talked mostly about my sisters. It was difficult for me to talk about my relationship with my Mom. I couldn't do it without thinking about my father, and that always made me sad.

At one point I closed my eyes and leaned back on the sofa, stifling a huge yawn.

"Hey, don't fall asleep," Tarek said, touching my arm, "you have to drive home."

"Oh, yeah, I forgot."

He laughed.

I checked the time. It was 11:00.

"I should go."

"I'll walk you to your car." Of course he would.

I had actually had some luck that day and had found parking on the street, not far from his apartment building. When we got to my car I opened the driver's side door and then turned to him.

"Hey, good luck on the interview. Let me know how it goes."

"I will. I'll see you Wednesday in class."

"OK, I'll send you my notes for Crim."

"Thanks."

I blushed and looked at the ground. I felt fairly certain he couldn't see the red of my face in the dim street light.

"Monday and Tuesday will be horrible without you," I said, looking up at him. Then I realized what I had said. "I mean, I'll have no one else to keep me sane at school. But—I managed for a long time without you so, I'll survive for two days." I smiled at him and then looked down again.

"Isabel," he said softly.

"Yeah?"

"Come here." He took my arm and drew me to him, hugging me. I put my arms around his waist and rested my head on his shoulder, with my mouth away from his neck. Then I started to get a little carried away and began rubbing his back, which was quite muscular. I thought about him with his shirt off.

Then I pulled away from him all at once. "Have a safe trip, OK?"

"Thanks." He let my arm go and I got into my car quickly, closing the door. I waved to Tarek and pulled away.

When I got home I had a message from him.

Did you get home OK?

I wrote back.

Yes. Good night.

He answered within a minute.

Good night, Isabel.

I decided that I was in so much trouble.

SIXTH WEEK: **MONDAY**

My alarm went off on Monday morning and I pounded the snooze button, rolling over onto my back. I needed to get up. I needed to get to work early because I needed to leave early. I had made an appointment at the Career Center before class. I figured that since Tarek wasn't around, I should distract myself with something. And what better to distract myself with than figuring out what the hell I was going to do after law school?

But to get there on time I had to get up. Get up, get up, Isabel. I put my arm over my eyes and started to daydream. Invariably, I thought about Tarek.

No, come on, you have to get up. You have to figure out your future. OK, one . . . two . . . three . . .

I sat up on the edge of my bed, put my feet on the floor, and then stood up.

My Mom always said, whatever happened the day before, today is a new day. It's fresh. Take each day as it comes.

Why was it turning out that she was right about so many things?

I switched the coffee maker on, showered and, a little while later, was ready to go.

The morning had been fairly uneventful, thank God. I kept my head down and tried not to listen to the workplace chatter. I had a French-to-English translation to do. It was large and would take me most of the week to do. It was accounting-related, which made me think of Tarek.

Everything had been going all right that day. I ran on the treadmill at the gym, and nuked my lunch without incident.

Then, late in the afternoon, when there were fewer people in the office, Miguel stopped by. I groaned inwardly.

"Hi, Isabel."

I gave him a forced smile.

"I'm curious," he began.

Jesus, I thought. What does he want to know now?

"Where's your boyfriend from?"

"Miami. Didn't he tell you?"

Miguel smiled. "No, I mean, where is he *really* from?"

"Where is anyone really from?" I asked rhetorically.

"Hmm. Does he speak Arabic?"

"Why do you want to know that?"

"Just curious."

I couldn't think of how to get out of his question. "Yes, he does, and other languages."

"French?" Miguel asked quickly.

I saw exactly what he was doing. He was doing the same thing that I had done initially, when I had figured out where Tarek was from, piecing the evidence together.

Again, I saw no way out.

"Yes. Look I have work to do—"

"Where's he from then? Morocco?"

I was silent.

"Like I said, I have work—"

"Well, it doesn't matter," Miguel interrupted me. "He's only with a girl like you for one thing—"

What the fuck—

Miguel smirked and shrugged.

"Thanks for your unsolicited opinion," I couldn't resist saying, "but not all men are assholes like you."

Miguel's smiled disappeared. "I'm going to tell Martin you called me that." Martin was our boss.

"Tell him," I challenged, standing up. "I'll tell him that you talked to me about inappropriate things at work."

I was wrong to call him that, though. Not because Miguel may tell Martin, but because it meant that I had cared about what he had said.

Miguel left in a huff and I put my earbuds in and continued working.

I left work and rushed to campus, lugging my backpack and purse upstairs to the Career Center.

In a good legal market, the Career Center counselors didn't have to do too much, since jobs for students were much easier to come by. However, since the economic bust that had begun in 2008, the chips were down and the market had headed south. I wasn't sure the counselors could help me, but was going to talk with one anyway.

I arrived a few minutes early and waited outside the counselor's door. The door was ajar and someone was in there with her. I immediately recognized the voice. It was SG, but her voice was different somehow. I leaned toward the door, trying to listen without making it obvious.

"I mean, my plan was to work for a firm when I graduate, but now I'm thinking maybe the government would be better for what I want to do," SG was saying with determination.

The counselor spoke next. "Well, you have great grades, and you have some past experience working as a paralegal for a firm—"

Wait, I thought. She has *great grades*? How was that? She never spoke in class, and when she did she said completely inane things. Was the curve that generous? Well, then I should be getting A+++s if that were the case.

"I'd like to apply for the DOJ internship," she was saying now.

Like she had a chance, I thought.

"It's very competitive," the counselor responded.

That's putting it mildly, I thought.

The counselor continued. "Go ahead and apply for it. I also recommend applying for internships with judges. That will be good experience for you."

Did SG have the stuff to do a clerkship with a judge? I hadn't thought so.

They were wrapping up. I moved away from the door, pretending to be busy with my paperwork that I had in my hands.

SG stepped outside the office and about had an epileptic seizure when she saw me. I smiled at her slyly.

"Hey," I said.

"Hey," she huffed, then left in a hurry.

There was something weird about that. She never missed the opportunity to say something snide to me. Was she in a hurry to get somewhere, or in a hurry to put distance between her and me?

There was also something odd about her conversation with the counselor. She apparently had great grades, and she had sounded smart, like she knew what she wanted. That was never the impression I had had of her.

I entered the counselor's office and greeted her. She was in her forties and was nice enough. I had met with her at least once before.

"So what can I help you with?" she asked professionally.

"Well, here is my updated resume for reference," I began. "I've had a few initial interviews with firms, got rejections from two and am waiting to hear back from two, but I'm not optimistic."

"OK. With your grades, I'm surprised you didn't get more interviews. You participated in on-campus interviewing, right?"

"Yes, I did." I paused. "I'm convinced that firms aren't interested in me because of my age."

"What do you mean?"

"Well, how many women in their mid-thirties get entry-level associate attorney positions at top firms?"

"There are some." She didn't sound convinced, however.

I decided to unload. "Well, I'm starting to feel like firms are interviewing me only to be able to say that they interviewed a minority candidate. And then I get that form from them to fill out, declaring my minority status. It's insulting."

She stared at me, not knowing what to say.

"Well," she started, "firms are committed to diversity."

"That's BS, with all due respect. Look at my resume and tell me any firm wouldn't be happy to have me. Someone with a 4.0, fluent in several languages, including Spanish, with consulting and international experience. But they would rather have a 25-year-old with no real work experience who they can work to the bone without complaint. Isn't that the reality?"

She continued to stare, so I went on, more diplomatically this time. "Look, all this is a lot of work for me, with a full-time job on top of everything, to prepare for all these interviews that come to nothing." That was about the end of my diatribe.

"Well," she began slowly, "that's what happens. You have to do a ton of interviews to get some offers. But I think there are firms that would hire you, or at least consider you as a serious candidate."

"So what do I do now? Assuming the other two interviews don't pan out, I won't get a summer associateship for next summer, and if I don't, it will be basically impossible to get a full-time offer with a firm after I graduate, isn't that right?"

"Yes, it will be very difficult." At least she was honest about that.

"So where else should I be looking?"

"Are you interested in government work?"

"Yes, I'm looking at that too."

"Are you applying for government internships?"

"I'm considering that, but I have a full-time job and bills and rent to pay, and I'm not sure that I can take time off of work to do an unpaid internship." I wasn't sure that my boss would let me.

"But the internship may lead to an offer."

"It would be imprudent of me to gamble on an offer that probably will not happen by quitting my job." I sighed. "But I'll see what I can do."

We talked for a bit more. She gave me some resources for my job search, most of which I already knew about. I was realizing that the Career Center was no substitute for doing my own legwork.

I looked at the time, and got up. "I need to go. I have class. Thanks for your time."

"You know," the counselor said, "you should be happy that you have a job. At least you won't be desperate for one when you graduate, like other people are."

"Yeah, well, I will be in the same situation as before, except with six figures of law school debt to repay, and those people you're talking about are younger and have ten more years than I do to repay it. It was my decision to go to law school when I did. I get that. But I also think that the law schools are making it seem like it's very easy to get a job after graduation, that they're hiding the ball, and not making the realities clear to students. For example, the fact that firms only hire younger attorneys as first-year associates. And that if you don't get a first-year associate job right after you graduate, it's basically impossible to get one later." Indeed, no firm would hire a first-year associate in 2012 who graduated law school in, say, 2009 or 2010. And if that person didn't get a law firm job when he graduated, he was basically screwed. Law firms were extremely regimented in their hiring.

As I turned to leave I added the *coup de grâce*. "For a profession where most attorneys say they're so liberal, in reality they are complete reactionaries." Then I left.

I was pissed off, more so than usual. But it didn't matter. Nothing about that conversation had changed my plan of action. I was going to have to prepare a complete resume blitz. I would make a list of every place I was interested in, private or government, and send applications. Someone, at some point, would have to bite.

I made it to Crim a few minutes before six. Everyone was already there. Eric was looking at me curiously.

"Where's Tarek?" he asked me.

I turned around and looked at him. I was having trouble reading Eric lately. This was a new phenomenon. His expression was neutral, but there was a hint of a smile on his lips.

"He's interviewing in New York tomorrow; he left today," I said. My voice was much more aloof than I felt.

"Really?" Josh asked then.

"No, dude, I totally made that up." I screwed up my face. "*Yes*, really."

"God, you're in a crap mood when he's not around," Eric said then.

I glared at him, then turned around to face my laptop screen. I opened my Crim Pro book. Eric was right. I might be physically bothered on some level when I was with Tarek, but I was also happier when I was with him.

"Isabel." The voice was so soft that at first I thought it was my conscience talking to me. I figured that sooner or later I would go completely nuts.

Then I looked up and saw Dalia standing in front of me on the other side of the long desk.

I didn't know how to address her. Should I be mean or nice or aloof? Then I looked at her face and saw that she looked intimidated. In fact, she looked almost scared. Her big, brown eyes were wide, like a deer in the headlights. I felt a little bad. My reputation definitely preceded me.

"Yes?" I said, as calmly as possible. I had no idea why she would talk to me. Everyone knew I didn't give my notes to anyone except my boys and Melanie.

"Um—" she began, leaning forward a little, "do you have Tarek's email address?"

"Why?" It was my first thought, and hence the first thing out of my mouth. There were lots of reasons someone would want someone else's email address. But of course I always thought the worst. Maybe there *was* something going on between them. Then I logically dismissed that thought. If that were the case, there was no way she would be asking me for his email address. She would have it already.

"Um—I told him I would send him notes from tax class." Bless her heart, she thought that that was a rational question and she actually answered it. It made me soften a little.

I kept forgetting that Tarek had another class that wasn't with me.

"I mean," Dalia went on, "I could email him at his school address, but I don't know if he checks it."

"He does," I said, "but I'll give you his personal one." I figured he wouldn't mind.

Dalia carried a notepad and pen and I motioned for them with my hand. She gave them to me and I wrote Tarek's email address down for her.

"Thank you, Isabel."

"Sure," I told her.

She hesitated for a second and then left. I was sure that she liked Tarek. She must be crazy if she thought she was going to compete with me. Then I immediately had the thought that that was harsh of me. If she liked him and he didn't like her, then I would feel bad. No one likes to have unrequited feelings for someone.

"Wow, Isabel, your group of friends keeps growing. What—do you have like five now?" Eric asked sarcastically, interrupting my thoughts like a derailed train.

Dinesh laughed so hard I thought he was going to bust a gut.

"Six, not including you," I threw over my shoulder.

Class started and I sighed. These would be a very long couple of days.

I had gotten to campus early again before Crim at 6 p.m., and was sitting with Josh and Eric downstairs, trying to explain stop and frisk to them. I wasn't sure how much attention Eric was actually paying to me.

"Dude, you're distracting Josh!" I told him, annoyed. "And he actually wants to learn this stuff, so could you please shut the f—"

"I am *not!*" he protested, interrupting me.

"Then stop making jokes and looking behind me at any hot girl who walks past!"

"I wasn't!"

"Then what the hell are you staring at behind my back?!"

I turned around and was looking right at Sameer. He had approached and was directly behind me. He walked around to stand next to our table. I stood up and faced him, crossing my arms.

"May I help you?" I asked him. He had a sly smile on his face. It pissed me off.

"Can we talk?" he said, looking at Josh and Eric.

"Sure." When he didn't say anything, I said, "Whatever the hell you want to say to me, you can say it in front of them."

He again looked from Josh and Eric to me. The three of us were staring expectantly at Sameer.

"All right," he said, then lowered his voice. "He's not going to date you, you know? And even if he did, it wouldn't be for any length of time."

"Who the hell are you talking about?" I shrugged.

Sameer smiled. "Don't be dumb, Isabel. You know."

"Oh, you're the boss of him?"

Sameer chuckled but not in a friendly way. "Men like him wouldn't be with women like you."

"Fuck off," I told him. Unfortunately, I knew exactly what he meant. Women like me. Promiscuous, in his mind. Whatever that meant.

Sameer leaned in a little bit. "Just because he likes to screw Latin women doesn't mean he wants to be in a *relationship* with you," he said with a sneer. He emphasized the word "relationship" with a mocking tone.

I couldn't take it anymore. I took a step forward and backhanded Sameer in the chest, without thinking about it. His eyes widened and his mouth parted. Eric and Josh stood up immediately. Eric came to stand right beside me.

"You know shit about Latin women, and you know shit about *him*," I said angrily.

"I know enough to know he won't end up with you." He looked at Eric, who had crossed his arms.

"Really brave of you, to say this to me when you know he's not here, damn coward." I raised my chin.

Then Sameer played his trump card. "Does he know about Saul?"

"You're an asshole," Eric said to Sameer. I gave Eric a look that said it wasn't worth getting worked up about.

"Pssh," I said as nonchalantly as I could manage, raising and lowering my shoulders, "that's old fucking news. Of course he knows. Like anyone cares."

I was completely bluffing but figured if Sameer thought Tarek didn't know, he could hold it over me indefinitely, and I couldn't bear the thought of that. There was still the chance that Sameer would tell him, but I couldn't prevent that either way.

"Anyway," Sameer said by way of conclusion, looking again from Eric to me, "I think it would be best for you if you left him alone."

"Well, thanks so much for considering my welfare." I uncrossed my arms and flicked my right wrist. "*Aire*," I told him, a Castilian way of saying, "Get lost."

Sameer left but not before giving me a dirty look. What the hell did he care about who Tarek went out with anyway?

I looked at Josh and Eric. "Interesting," I murmured.

"He's an idiot," Eric told me.

"How so?" I agreed, but didn't know what Eric meant.

"Telling you not to be with Tarek is a foolproof way of making sure you *do* end up together, because you're that *cabezona*."

I looked at Eric curiously, then gave him a huge smile. I hugged him, squeezing him tightly. "You made my day, you know?" I said into his ear.

"Anything for you, you know that," he said back to me. I released him and he was smiling.

I put a hand on each of their shoulders. "Let's forget about this."

"Does he know, though?" Josh asked then.

"Does who know what?" I was confused.

Josh leaned in, and Eric and I did too, with our heads together conspiratorially. "Does Tarek know about Saul?"

"No, dude," I whispered, "I was totally bluffing."

"You should tell him at some point," Josh said. "I mean, if they know each other and—if you're going to be—"

"I get it," I put up a hand. "I will."

Eric was shaking his head and smirking at me.

"What?" I asked him defensively.

"You are so weird."

"Why?"

Eric leaned toward me. "If you like him, then be with him."

I opened my mouth, then closed it and sighed.

Eric chuckled.

"It's not that easy!" I protested. "We're friends right now."

"*Friends*," Eric scoffed.

"OK, you guys, please don't say anything to Tarek, or anyone. I need some time to figure out how to tell him."

"Well, if he hurts you, then it's game over for him," Eric said with a tight voice.

I smiled. "You're a good friend, Eric." I sighed again. "OK, let's go. We're going to be late."

The three of us went to class, and I couldn't stop thinking about whether or not to tell Tarek about the confrontation with Sameer. I was also bothered by the fact that Sameer had told me that just when I was starting to have serious doubts. Maybe Tarek wasn't for me, but I refused to believe that.

After class, I was on the metro alone after Josh, Dinesh, and Eric got off at their stops. Wondering how Tarek's interview had gone, I took out my phone and sent him a message.

How did it go?

Once home, I was a little too wired to sleep. I nuked some leftover *tortilla de patatas* and put together a salad with avocado and *queso fresco*. I sat down at my dining table with my plate and opened my laptop. I created a spreadsheet in Excel and started to list all the places I wanted to apply to for jobs and internships. I also wanted to find out about any possible minority or diversity career fairs, even if they were outside of the DC area. I couldn't afford to be picky. The fact that Lara was nearby made me want to stay, but there was no guarantee that she would stay in DC after her residency anyway.

About half an hour later my phone rang. Who would call me this late?

It was Tarek.

"Hey," I answered.

"Hi, Isabel. Thanks for your text."

"So how did it go?"

"I think it went really well. I wore the purple shirt like you recommended."

I smiled. "Awesome. I'm sure you looked great."

I heard rapid-fire Spanish in the background.

"Sorry," Tarek apologized. "I'm at my friend's place. He's talking on his phone. We're about to go out."

"You're flying back tomorrow morning, right?"

"Yes, I should be there in time for class."

"Well, don't get too crazy tonight."

He chuckled. "Don't worry, we won't."

"OK, I'll see you tomorrow, then."

"See you tomorrow. Good night, Isabel."

"Good night."

I always felt a thrill whenever he said my name.

I took a cold shower and went to bed.

All day at work, I tried not to think about seeing Tarek later. I had dressed for the occasion in a black pantsuit and sleeveless fuchsia blouse, with low black heels. After the gym, I had moussed my hair and left it wavy. Even though he had never expressly told me, I had the feeling that Tarek liked my hair wavy.

Not that I cared what he liked, I thought then.

Oh hell, I *do* care what he likes. Why should I deny it anymore?

I rushed out of the office early to be able to get to campus on time for my 3:50 International Law class.

Right in front of the campus' main doors, I ran into Saul. Seeing him was like someone dousing icy water over my good mood. I quickened my pace to pass by him all the more rapidly.

When we were about to pass by each other, he stopped.

"Isabel, I haven't seen you in a while."

I slowed a bit but didn't stop walking.

"Hey," I said quietly, afraid that if I ignored him he would make a scene. He was good at that.

"We should go out sometime," he said as I walked past him.

You mean we should screw sometime, I thought.

"I can't," I said.

Then I was like lightning, getting away from him as quickly as I could.

Man, I just dodged a bullet, I thought.

Once inside the main law school building, I left my sunglasses on and tried to scan the place without seeming to do so. I walked past the elevator and the staircase and into the lounge area. I saw Tarek sitting at a table with Eric.

My heart leaped.

They saw me as soon as I turned the corner. I walked over to them and Tarek stood up.

"Hey, stranger," he said.

"Hi." I could feel my mouth curving into a smile. I tried to make sure that my movements slowed down, because when I got worked up I started to move fast and talk even faster, and that usually led to me falling over my feet or tripping over my words.

He was wearing jeans and a T-shirt. I felt my chest rise with a deep inhalation. I grabbed his shoulder and kissed his cheeks, alternating, one, two, three, four, as was our usual practice.

Eric had stood up too. I gave him his kisses.

I looked at Tarek. "So how did it go?"

"I was just telling Eric. Really well. I should hear something soon."

The three of us sat down. Tarek handed me my coffee and I thanked him.

"Would you be in the corporate practice there?" I asked him.

"Most likely."

"Ooo, corporate practice in New York. I hope you don't plan on having a life anytime soon."

He chuckled. "Yeah, I would have to clear my schedule." Then he added, "Thanks for sending me your notes from class."

"Anytime."

Eric spoke up then. "I would send you mine too, but compared to Isabel's, they're something a first grader would write."

I gave Eric a smile. "What class do you have now?"

He told me. It was about 3:40 so we grabbed our stuff to go to our respective classes.

Then I saw Eric's devious smile. Oh no, I thought.

He looked at Tarek. "Thank goodness you're back, man. Isabel's been in such a horrible mood with you gone."

Tarek looked at me. "Is that true?"

I sighed, a little embarrassed. "Yes, but not because you weren't around. Well—a little bit because of that but that wasn't the only reason."

Tarek smiled. "You can tell me all about it after class. By the way, what's the occasion today?"

I was confused. "What do you mean?"

He touched my arm. "You look great."

I shrugged, then the words left my mouth. "You're back."

He smiled broadly, and I thought he blushed but I really couldn't tell because of his dark skin.

The rest of the evening went by pretty quickly. During breaks from class, Tarek told me about the interview. As I had expected, he had been wined and dined by the associates and a couple of the partners. The firm was a white-shoe, Big Law firm, so the minimum billable hours per year were about 2200, but of course associates were expected to bill more than the minimum. Our conversation reminded me of a story about one of Lara's friends, who worked at a firm in Chicago. By May, he had billed all his minimum hours for the entire year. Mathematically, there was no way to bill that amount of hours without double- and triple-billing time. I also knew that, according to Lara, her friend was routinely at the office until around midnight, and was of course expected to also work from home.

Tarek was young now, but at some point that type of lifestyle would burn someone out. Eventually, most people married and had children, and staying long hours at the office became a real drag. If you made partner, then you could relax somewhat. But making partner meant drudging it out for a minimum of seven to eight years.

I had been thinking a lot about that this past week, ever since my meeting at the Career Center. I really had no interest in making partner. If I did find a job with a firm, then I would be, at a minimum, forty-five when I made partner. That was almost too old to begin to have children. Not like I had any prospects in that area, anyway. I had decided that if I did end up working for a firm, it would be only for a couple of years to pay off my law school debt and get some experience before going somewhere else, maybe at a government agency or as corporate counsel. I would try to figure it out.

When we were on the metro later that night, I was thinking about my confrontation with Sameer. I felt bad keeping it from Tarek; after all, he should know Sameer's intentions. Maybe Josh or Eric would mention it to him and I wouldn't have to.

I felt conflicted, because I didn't like keeping secrets from him, although I was keeping my past with Saul secret. But if he didn't know about Sameer, he might think that Sameer was his friend, when it appeared that he was anything but.

"Hey, are you all right?" Tarek asked. He was sitting next to me on the metro.

I looked at him. "Yeah, why?"

"I was asking you a question, and you were totally zoned out."

"I'm sorry. I was distracted."

"Yeah, I can tell."

I smiled. "What was your question?"

"Are we studying this weekend? I need to catch up."

"Sure. You can come to my house if you want, Saturday afternoon."

"OK."

I hesitated for a moment. "Tarek, I have to talk to you about something. Can I call you later tonight?"

His look turned serious. "Of course. Do you want to come over?"

I thought about how it would look if I left with him at Pentagon City in front of Josh and Dinesh. I didn't really care.

"No, that's OK. You had a late night and were up early this morning. You're probably tired. And I have to work tomorrow. I'll call you when I get home."

"OK."

We talked the rest of the way about his Cuban friend and how he liked New York. I sensed that Tarek hadn't totally made up his mind about whether or not he would take an offer with the firm, if he should get one. He told me how politically liberal New York was, which I knew, and how expensive. DC was *uber* liberal too, but not nearly as expensive. And in DC, at least I could drive an hour south to my hometown and recharge my batteries by talking politics with my family.

At home, I nuked some leftovers and sat on my sofa. I ate for about ten minutes, then picked up my phone and called Tarek. He answered after one ring.

"Hey."

"Hey," I said. "Did you eat dinner?"

"I ordered out. Mexican."

Thinking about Mexican food made my mouth water. That sounded better than the leftovers I had had. "If you're still eating, I can call you later."

"No, no, it's fine. I'm already done."

I paused. Just do it, I thought.

"Look, Tarek, I have to tell you about something that happened, but I honestly don't think you'll like it."

"What's going on?" His voice grew serious. I hoped he didn't get mad.

"I don't think that Sameer is your friend."

"Did you talk to him?"

"He and I kind of had an argument." I proceeded to tell Tarek about what had happened. Tarek wanted to know every word that was said, and I told him most of it, but didn't tell him about the part where Sameer told me that Tarek would not have a "relationship" with me, whatever the hell that meant. I also held off telling him that Sameer said he liked to "screw Latin women."

"He basically told me to stay away from you," I summed up.

I heard nothing but silence on the other end of the phone.

"Tarek, are you mad?"

"Isabel, of course I'm mad," he said tightly.

"Please don't be angry with me," I pleaded. I was having second thoughts about telling him.

"Oh my God, why would I be angry with *you*?!"

"I don't know, but I can tell you're angry."

"I'm angry at *him*." He sighed. "You didn't do anything wrong." His voice was calmer now.

"I don't know, I feel bad telling you but felt horrible *not* telling you."

"You were right to tell me. None of this is his damn business."

I wondered what he meant by "this." My second thought was that he must be really pissed off, because that was the first time I had ever heard him utter a curse word.

I decided then to tell him something else, even if I thought it would make him more upset. My curiosity got the better of me.

"Sameer also said that—that you like to—" My voice halted.

"What?"

"These are *his* words, OK—to 'screw Latin women.' " I held up my hands in air quotes even though no one was there to see them. Force of habit.

"Oh my God, that's—" I had never seen Tarek angry, but was starting to think that his temper was almost as bad as mine. Then he seemed to calm down a bit. I was starting to wish that I was with him to be able to read his expressions. "I'm sorry, Isabel. That's so insulting."

"Tarek, what does that mean exactly?"

"I mentioned to him that my ex-girlfriend was Dominican. And he probably assumes—" he paused.

"Yeah, I got it." Sameer assumed that Tarek and I had slept together.

"Tarek, I didn't tell you to make you angry."

"I know, Isabel. It's OK. I'm going to talk to him."

"It's not worth it. This is nothing. Seriously. I've honestly had to deal with a lot worse than that. Besides, his efforts are going to totally backfire." I thought about what Eric had said to me.

"What do you mean?"

"I don't give a shit what Sameer says, Tarek. It's not going to make me stay away from you."

I heard him chuckle.

"Good. That makes me happy, then."

I wanted to diffuse his anger as best I could. "And that wasn't even the strangest thing that happened while you were gone."

"Oh, really?" He was interested now. "What else could have happened?"

I told him about running into Alyssa at the Career Center.

"You know, I always had a weird feeling about her," Tarek told me, "like she was hiding something. I've seen her like, totally into her books and outlines, like she was studying really seriously."

"But that's not the impression she makes on you."

"Exactly," he agreed.

"But why would she do that? Actively hide the fact that she is studious or ambitious?"

"Why does anybody do anything, Isabel?"

That was true enough.

"So," Tarek began, "how was *your* meeting at the Career Center?"

"Pretty unproductive." I told him about it, and also told him about my plans to do an all-out resume blitz.

"So you're willing to go anywhere?" he asked me.

"*Almost* anywhere," I emphasized, "within reason." I sighed. "But for now I have to plan to stay in DC since that seems most likely at this point."

"Everything will work out, Isabel."

"I wish I were as optimistic as you."

"Really? I thought you liked being a pessimist." He was almost laughing.

I smiled. "Even that is a drag sometimes." I paused. "Look, it's late. I know you're tired. We'll talk tomorrow. And we're on for Saturday. I'll cook something for dinner, if you want to stay for dinner," I hastily added.

"That would be great."

We said goodbye and hung up. I wasn't sure if I had done the right thing telling him about Sameer. But it was too late for regrets now.

SIXTH WEEK: **SATURDAY**

The rest of the week went by fairly quickly. The French finance project I had been working on for my day job wasn't finished yet. It was more complicated than everyone had thought, and it was going to go until next week at least. Before I knew it, it was the weekend.

I read and took notes on cases in the morning, then made a *tortilla de patatas* for dinner. After putting that in the fridge, I showered quickly, moussing my hair and leaving it wet. After that, I straightened up my apartment as best I could.

I had had lunch but was still really hungry. No surprise there. My mother was always making comments about how much I ate. I looked at the time, noticing that it was almost 3:30. Tarek would be here any minute.

I threw together a protein shake, with a bunch of blended fruit. Tons of protein and antioxidants. It turned out this blue-green color; it was much tastier than it looked.

So when I opened the door to my apartment for Tarek, he saw the rest of my shake on the counter.

"What are you drinking?" he asked as he put his backpack on the floor and took out his laptop.

I told him. "Try some," I said.

He looked at me suspiciously, but took it and tried it.

"It's not bad." He seemed genuinely surprised.

"It's a protein shake with some blended fruit. I usually drink them after weightlifting."

"Oh, that explains a lot."

Now *I* was suspicious. "What do you mean?"

"I meant that's why your arms are so toned."

"Well, that and lugging all my bags and law school books around."

He smiled. "I don't weight-lift that much. I mostly run."

"Yeah, I know."

"How would you know that?" He was curious.

I chuckled. "Dude, you totally underestimate me. Because you're scrawny, and you have the body of a runner. Kind of wiry with little bulk."

"Scrawny? Well, thanks."

I was a little embarrassed. "Sorry, I meant,—you don't have a huge upper body like some men." I paused, feeling like I was digging myself in further. "But it's OK. I actually don't mind scrawny men."

Tarek smiled. "Well, that's good to know."

I wanted to change the subject. "I run too, you know? In fact, I'm going to run tomorrow. The weather's supposed to be nice."

"Really?" Tarek grinned. "I was planning to run tomorrow too."

We looked at each other for a moment. I had an idea but I was sure he would say no.

"I'm going to run near Old Town Alexandria. There's a path that goes by the Potomac River to National Airport and even further."

"Really? Sounds awesome."

"You haven't been there? Do you want to run there tomorrow?"

"Sure. What time?"

Wait, did he just say yes?

I hesitated. "I usually go at about 10 or 10:30 in the morning, but I'm flexible."

"OK, then." He smiled. "We can get something to eat after."

"Oh, I'll definitely need something to eat afterward." I smiled, then hesitated. "All right, now that our workout schedule is set, let's do this. Studying, I mean."

Our studying session went well. We were already working on our class outlines, although for most students it was a bit early in the semester for that. Generally, November 1 was the unofficial date to start class outlines, which would be used to study for exams. Most law school exams were open-book, so you could use any materials at your disposal, including textbooks, class notes, your own outlines that you created, commercial outlines you could buy from law bookstores and basically any other material.

Thankfully, I would have open-book exams for all my classes this year. My outlines were uncharacteristically long. It was not unusual for me to have a sixty-plus-page outline for a class. Most students had outlines that were about twenty-five to thirty-five pages long. That got me to thinking.

"Hey," I said, looking up. "How long are your outlines generally?"

"Hmm," he murmured, "it really depends on the class."

We were both sitting at my dining table. I was sitting at the short end and he was next to me at the long end. Tarek was looking intently at his laptop screen, writing notes.

"Well, how long has your longest outline been?" I was curious.

"I think—like about seventy pages." He was smiling.

I chuckled. "My outline for Crim is going to be at least seventy pages. I figure between the two of us, we'll have everything covered."

"I hope so."

"Is your tax exam open-book?" I asked him.

"Yes, thankfully. I don't know about that class, though. The professor goes through the material so fast."

"Oh please, you're a CPA. You'll be fine." That reminded me that I wanted to ask him something, but was too distracted with something else.

"I hope so," he half-smiled.

"So who are you studying with for tax?" I asked him, trying to sound as if I didn't care about the answer.

He raised his head and looked at me. I continued to look at my screen. "Why?" I looked at him out of the corner of my eye. He had a curious expression on his face. "You're not in that class."

"Sorry. Guess I was out of line. Forget I asked."

"I didn't mean that," he said.

I saw from my peripheral vision that he was still looking at me. I didn't say anything at first. Then he looked back at his computer screen. I tried holding it in, but couldn't resist. Think about something else, I told myself. But it was no use. I blurted out, "So are you studying with Dalia?"

Tarek chuckled. "You're cute when you're jealous."

I burst out laughing. "Oh my God, that is the lamest thing any guy has ever said to me!" We looked at each other then.

"Oh, so you think I'm lame?" Tarek said, but he was still smiling.

"No, I said that what you said is lame, not that *you're* lame." Good, I thought, let's move away from what I just said.

But he wasn't having it. "Ah, but you're not denying that you're jealous."

I figured I would hit this head-on, since I was already halfway in. What the hell. "Of course I'm not denying it. And you didn't answer my question. It's making me insane with jealousy," I said with much more sarcasm than

I felt. I looked at my laptop screen again. "Maybe I'm so jealous I won't let you leave tonight."

"Well, maybe I won't answer your question then. Maybe I don't want to leave tonight." He raised his eyebrows suggestively.

This was too much innuendo. I thought about throwing my books and my laptop to the floor and pulling him on top of me on my dining table, right here. I had a mental picture and everything. I exhaled.

Instead, I said to him, as seriously as I could manage, "You didn't answer my initial question, Tarek. Answer it—please," I added as an afterthought.

He looked up at me again and I looked away quickly.

"Oh my God," he said, his voice rising a bit at the end.

"What?"

"You *are* jealous. I can tell."

"Am *not*."

"Yes, you *are*." He paused for a moment. I closed my eyes and rubbed my forehead, thinking of how to turn this around. But he had me and he knew it. *Shit.* I had royally screwed myself.

All of a sudden he furrowed his brows. "I'm not studying with anyone for tax, Isabel. Not with Dalia. Not with anyone."

"But Dalia gave you her notes when you were in New York." I suddenly realized how juvenile that sounded. *Are you studying with Dalia? Well, she gave you her notes.* I sounded like a high school student! Ugh, I sounded like a Millennial!

"Yes, that's true. I had to get notes from *someone*. And I didn't ask her for them, she offered."

Why should I care whether or not he studied with other people? I didn't, I thought. It was Dalia. I knew that she liked him.

"She likes you." My voice was a sullen whisper. Because she likes you. And I wasn't sure what to do about it.

I was intent on my laptop now.

All of a sudden, Tarek leaned forward and touched my hand, unwittingly sending a surge up my arm. "Dalia's just a friend."

I looked at him and dropped my shoulders. "You don't have to explain anything to me."

He smiled then, still touching my hand. "Anyway, how do you think I feel when you kiss Eric?"

"Kiss Eric?! When have I kissed Eric?"

"You kiss him hello."

"On the *cheek*!" I emphasized. I couldn't tell if he was really jealous or if this was to lighten the mood. "I kiss you and Josh hello, too. Jesus, who's keeping score? Besides, I told you that I have never thought of Eric in that way."

I knew what was going on here. We were dancing around the topic of how we really felt about each other. We were like two first-year law students who didn't really know how to address the main topic of the question on their Contracts exam. So instead, they talked about how the contract was unconscionable, or how duress was involved, when the real issue was contract formation. Was there a contract in the first place? Then I laughed at myself in my head. My comparison was so lame. If I didn't think I was a nerd before law school, I certainly was one now.

But we were doing the same thing. We tiptoed around the main issue, talking tangentially about how we felt when the real question was whether we were, or wanted to be, a couple. Well, I would be damned if I was going to tackle that question first. I wanted that, but it was the prisoner's dilemma. There were times when I thought I read Tarek really well, but other times I thought that maybe what he was saying was all talk. It sure as hell would not be the first time that a guy I liked turned out to be all talk.

The problem was that neither one of us was going to say it first. I was going to make him play another card before I did. I had played too many already.

Then my frustration boiled over. "Jesus," I blasphemed again, "how can you be so gorgeous and so freaking annoying at the same time?!"

"I could say the same about you!"

"Well, you just did!" Then I started to laugh. Tarek did too.

I looked at the time. It was almost 7 p.m.

"All right, look. We're delirious. Let's eat." I threw my pen on the table with something bordering on unnecessary force.

We stood up at the same time. Without thinking, I took his hand and squeezed it.

"Come on, see what I made for dinner," I smiled.

Tarek's eyes lit up. If he was bothered, he hid it successfully.

We ate on the sofa while watching TV, commenting about how there appeared to be a dearth of quality movies currently. Somehow, it felt like we were still friends, despite our previous conversation.

I smiled at him. "You're really good at taking my mind off of things," I told him spontaneously.

"What do you need to take your mind off of?" he asked, smiling.

"A lot." My eyes met his. Then my cell phone rang. It was my Mom.

"Do you mind if I take this?" I asked Tarek. "I haven't talked to her in a while and she's probably wondering if the Earth swallowed me or something."

"Of course not." He was smiling at my comment.

"Hey Mom," I answered, going into the kitchen to refill my water glass.

"Isabel, I haven't talked to you in so long."

By "so long," she meant more than a week.

"I know, Mom. I'm sorry I haven't called. I've been really busy."

"Is everything OK?"

"Yeah, everything's great."

"School is going OK?"

"Yes, school is fine."

"And work is going well?"

"Yes, work is going very well." That wasn't entirely true. Having to deal with the Millennials was weighing on me.

"Are you home right now?" That meant, I want to know exactly what you're doing at this moment.

"Yes." I sighed.

"I'm surprised you didn't go out tonight. After all, it's a Saturday." She meant, you shouldn't have wasted another opportunity to meet a potential mate.

"Actually, I have a friend over."

"A male friend?"

"That's right."

"The one you mentioned to me or a new one?"

"The former." I had previously mentioned to Mom that I was regularly studying with a male friend.

"Oh, cool." That meant, I'd like to grill you on him but since he's there I'll have to wait.

Then she said, "I hope your apartment is decent." That meant, I hope he's not turned off by your general slovenliness.

Oh, I don't think he's worried about that, Mom, I thought.

"Look, I'll let you go," I told Mom, "but we'll talk later."

"OK, I love you."

"Love you too, Mom."

"Be careful tonight." That meant, for God's sake use a condom, Isabel. My mother used to tell me to "use protection" until I told her that if she ever said that to me again I would never call her.

We hung up.

I sat down next to Tarek on the sofa, but put some distance between the two of us.

He looked at me then. "Why don't you get along with your Mom?"

"What makes you think I don't get along with her?"

He smirked and shook his head slightly, acknowledging that my question was a delay tactic.

"You sound frustrated with her. And also some things you've said in the past."

In the past? I thought. He and I had only known each other for two months. No, less than two months. We didn't have much of a "past."

"I do get along with her. It's—it's a little complicated."

"How so?"

I didn't want to tell him about my father's death and my relationship with my mother since then. It was too personal. Of course, Tarek might understand, since his own father had died of a brain tumor when Tarek was a teenager.

"Well," I began, "for one thing she insists on treating me like I'm ten years old."

He smiled. "I don't think that's just you. All mothers are like that." He hesitated. "When I told my mother that we were going out to dinner the other night, she told me to make sure I didn't let you pay. Like I would do that."

I smiled broadly. He had talked to his mother about me? It made me happy.

"Why do they do that?" I asked Tarek.

"I think parents, mothers mostly, can never get over the fact that you're their child, no matter how old you are."

"It's infuriating."

"I know, but—I don't think it can be any other way for them."

"I hope I'm not like that."

Tarek looked at me. "Do you want children?" he asked.

I sighed. "I don't think it's going to happen for me."

"Why not?"

"Tarek," I began, "I'm thirty-four years old and unattached. It's just—" This conversation was getting a little too deep for me and I didn't want to appear weak or sad in front of him.

"Can I get you anything else?" I asked him instead.

"No, thank you. It was really good. I can't remember the last time I had Spanish *tortilla* made by someone from Spain."

I smiled. "Would you like tea? I'm going to have some."

"Sure."

It was about 10 p.m. when he left. He had started to look sleepy and I was worried about him driving home. I was also worried because I found him incredibly hot when he looked sleepy, and was afraid that I might try something; and I doubted his ability to resist since I would probably come on very strong.

I kept telling myself that if Tarek and I slept together, I couldn't take that back. And I wasn't sure if one or both of us would regret it the next day. If *he* regretted it, I wouldn't be able to handle it. So every time I thought about ripping his clothes off, I told myself that.

I opened my front door for him.

"Hey, will you text me when you get home?"

"Sure," he smiled. "Are we still on for tomorrow?"

Oh yeah, running. "Yeah," I told him. "Let's meet at 10:30. Bring water and a change of clothes, in case you want to go to brunch afterward." I told him where we could meet.

"OK." He had smiled then, and his sleepy smile was making me melt. What if I—

Then my neighbor's door opened and John stepped out with his little Beagle.

Tarek and I were both surprised. We greeted John, and his dog came up to me, sniffing my feet. I bent down and scratched him behind his ears.

John said good night and left with his dog.

"OK, I'll see you tomorrow," I told Tarek, trying to put some finality in my voice.

"Thank you for dinner."

"Anytime." I absentmindedly reached out and touched his arm.

After he left I had the same feeling that I had had at the end of that Saturday night when we had danced together. He was wearing me down. Maybe he didn't mean to, but when I was with him I had to use my energy to resist pouring out my feelings to him. That's when I remembered that this was why I didn't like to have feelings. Feelings only made you vulnerable.

I was in bed already when I got his message.

I'm home. Looking forward to tomorrow. Good night, Isabel.

I wrote back.

Good night.

From the moment I woke up on Sunday morning, I was in a good mood.

I picked Tarek up at the King Street metro station, and we drove down to the pier, bordering the Potomac River, and parked nearby.

As soon as Tarek got into my car, I started to laugh. I laughed so hard I couldn't talk.

"What?!" he exclaimed, not understanding.

I felt bad for laughing but couldn't stop. He had pulled his hair back into a mini man-bun, tied with a rubber band.

"Dude—the man bun—I can't—I just can't!"

"Oh my God." Tarek was smiling. Thank goodness he was taking this well. "What did you expect me to do with my hair? Yours is tied back too."

"I know—I'm sorry—I just—I've never seen it like that—" I was gasping for air, then managed to spit out one complete sentence breathlessly. "Are you auditioning for a remake of Miami Vice or something?"

Tarek sighed. "If I leave it loose it will be all frizzy—"

I was still laughing, unable to get a hold of myself. My abdominal muscles were so sore. Then suddenly I had to brake hard for a red light, and the car lurched.

"Sorry," I managed to say, gulping air. "Tarek, do you mind driving?"

"Are you serious? Are you drunk?" he asked accusingly.

"No!"

"Did you start drinking after I left last night, Isabel?"

"Of course not! Seriously, could you drive right now please?"

"OK, fine." Then he sighed. "But only because you said please."

I opened my car door quickly and we changed sides. I got in the front passenger seat.

He pushed the driver seat back a little bit and looked at his mirrors. I guess they were all right because he didn't adjust them.

"Where are we going?" he asked me.

"Drive straight until you can't go anymore," I told him, stifling a giggle.

Tarek sighed again and looked at me. "I can't take you anywhere!"

"I'm sorry." I was slowly getting control of myself now. "I hadn't seen you with a man bun before. Do all the men in Miami wear their hair like that?"

"Well, there's a first time for everything." Then he paused. "I was actually thinking of cutting my hair."

My expression changed instantly. "Oh no!" I said.

"Why not?"

"Well, if you want. I mean—" Then, in a very small voice, "I like it a bit long."

"Sorry?"

"Nothing," I said.

"What was that?" He had pretended not to hear just to give me a hard time. "That you like it long?"

"I said, I like it a *bit* long," I looked away, "like you have it now. I don't mean, *right* now, I mean the length. I like the length of your hair. And I like it curly. Not that you should give a damn what I like."

He was smiling. "Oh, but I do."

I lowered my lashes automatically and smiled. I opened my mouth then but didn't know what to say.

Tarek saw me and said, "What?"

"Nothing. You've left me speechless. It's actually an incredible feat. You should be impressed with yourself. Not that you aren't already."

He smiled broadly.

King Street was the main street through Old Town Alexandria, a historic area in northern Virginia pretty close to where I lived. King Street took you all the way to the edge of the Potomac River. Once there we turned left and headed down a few blocks, then parked on the street.

Tarek remarked on how aesthetically appealing the city was.

"You haven't been here?" I asked him.

"No."

Old Town was a cool place to spend the day. It was largely residential, with the townhomes styled in old 18th century colonial architecture. There were plenty of restaurants, bookstores, and other shops. The pier was also really nice, and had a small boardwalk area. You could see across the harbor to the Maryland side. There were also boat tours that left throughout the day. Today had turned out to be gorgeous; we had been really lucky with the weather.

We parked and got out of the car. I put our water bottles and wallets in a small backpack that I carried for running. Tarek wanted to carry it for me but I wouldn't let him.

I put my sunglasses on. My theory was that wearing them regularly would slow down the appearance of crow's feet around my eyes. I felt like when I smiled I gave away my age.

"So," I began, "this path is used by runners, walkers and cyclists, so look out for bicycles. It goes to Reagan National Airport and beyond that. It's about two miles from here to the airport, so roundtrip it's about four miles. How many miles do you usually run?"

"Anywhere from three to six, it depends," Tarek told me.

"We can do more than four if you want," I said, with a bit of a challenge in my voice.

"No, that's OK."

"All right. I usually do some sprints midway through."

"Oh, I usually don't do sprints."

"Well, you can today if you want." Then I added, "only if you want."

It was a great day for a run. The views across the Potomac were amazing. I didn't know if it was because of nerves from being with Tarek that day, or adrenaline due to the same reason, but I had a ton of energy. We had both done some sprints and, afterward, I was drenched, with sweat dripping down the front of my shirt. We rested near the airport for a bit before heading back the way we had started.

"God, you're fast," Tarek said, breathing hard.

"Yeah, well, I run pretty regularly." I was breathing hard too. I wiped sweat from my brow and smiled at him.

"What?" He smiled back.

"Nothing," I said. Indeed, I didn't know why I had smiled. Maybe from the endorphins.

We walked for a little bit before finishing the run on the way back. Then we walked some more. I checked my pulse.

"So how often do you run here?" Tarek asked me. Our breathing was returning to normal.

"Depends on the weather. Usually I run on the treadmill at the gym during my lunch break. But it's good to get outside."

"And you always run by yourself?"

"Yes. Until today, apparently."

"Well, thanks for letting me tag along."

"Anytime." I smiled.

We got back to my car.

"I'm going to change my shirt," I told Tarek. "Think about what you feel like eating."

"Where?" Tarek asked.

"Where what?" I was confused.

"Where are you going to change?"

"Here." I had opened the car door. I dropped my bag on the floor and took my shirt off, pulling it over my head.

I noticed then that Tarek looked like he was about to go into apoplexy.

"Dude, relax!" I said. I was wearing a sports bra, anyway. Women worked out in them all the time. It wasn't like exposing yourself in a Victoria's Secret lacy production. "You're not going to see anything."

Tarek was averting his eyes.

"Besides," I smiled, moving my face closer to his. "You've seen my breasts before, remember? And I had less on then." I was remembering the time when I had leaned over the dining table at my apartment and unwittingly exposed the tops of my breasts. That seemed like it had happened a long time ago, but it couldn't have been more than a couple of weeks, I figured.

"Oh my God." Tarek had his hand over his face and was looking at me through his fingers.

I laughed at his discombobulation, then turned around and grabbed a clean T-shirt.

"Isabel!" I suddenly heard.

"What?" I whirled around. His tone was almost accusatory. When I saw his face, he had a look of curiosity bordering on shock. "What's that face for?" I said.

"You never told me you had a tattoo!"

I laughed. Because it was on my back, I didn't always remember it.

"Yeah well, you never asked." I paused, craning my neck to see that my tattoo was halfway visible above my shorts. "Is it a dealbreaker for you?"

"Au contraire," he smiled. "Can I see it—please?"

I sighed. "Fine." I stood there in my sports bra so that he could see the tattoo on my lower back. It was all black, a tattoo of two dragon heads in profile, one facing either direction. It was simple; that's why I liked it.

"OK?" I said.

"OK," Tarek said.

I pulled the clean T-shirt on. "Happy now?" I asked him.

"Yes," he was smiling. "When did you get it?"

"For my thirtieth birthday," I began. "I had been wanting one for a long time. So my youngest sister Ariel said she would pay for it for my birthday. I went to visit her in New York and had it done there, by someone a friend of hers goes to. He's really good. I like how it turned out."

"Do you only have the one?"

"Yes, but I'm thinking about getting another one."

"Really?"

"Yeah, but we'll see."

I wasn't sure, but it seemed to me that he was a bit turned on right now.

"Relax, I'm fully clothed again," I told him.

"If you don't mind, I'll change my shirt in the car."

"I do mind, but go ahead. My car windows aren't tinted. I can still see everything."

"You're incredible," Tarek told me.

"Tell me something I don't know." I raised my eyebrows. "No, seriously," I said then, "I won't look."

I checked my phone to distract myself until he was ready. I was thinking how modest he seemed to be. And he was reportedly Catholic. Was it possible that he was one of those people who wanted to wait until he was married?

No way, I thought. People usually didn't wait until they were almost thirty to have sex, at least not by choice.

But he *was* kind of modest. So if I came onto him, would he turn me down? Would he want to wait for some reason?

That thought made me think even more so that holding off was the right thing to do for now.

Oh God, this was going to be so difficult.

We went to brunch at a place nearby that I had been to before with Lara and Patrick. Old Town was populated with people who were brunching after running or playing tennis or some other sport. It was also very dog-friendly, and there were tons of people out walking with their doggies.

We were waiting for our food.

"I like this place," Tarek said. "Old Town is really cool."

"You haven't seen the pier yet," I told him. "I'll show you after lunch—I mean, if you have time."

He smiled. "Sure."

A moment of silence hung between us.

Tarek broke it. "So you hang out with your sister here?"

I shrugged. "Usually, or I just hang out by myself. I mean, Lara's usually really busy so—actually, last time I was eating here I was with her."

"So when can I meet your sister?" Tarek asked.

I looked at him sideways, not understanding.

"You want to meet my sister?"

"Well," he seemed to be gathering his thoughts, thinking about how to word what he was going to say. "You talk about her all the time—"

"Tarek, you can meet my sister when I meet yours."

He smiled. "She's in Miami."

"She's never going to come visit you?" I drank my water, unsure where this conversation was headed.

"Actually, she wants to."

"That would be fun. When would she come?" I remembered that she was about twenty-five years old and that meant that she was almost ten years younger than me.

"She's in grad school right now, and she wants to come for her spring break, which is the same week as ours."

"So what's she like?" I asked, curious.

"Well, you've seen her photo."

"Yeah, she's gorgeous."

He chuckled. "In all honesty, she's a lot like you."

"You mean bitter and mad at the world?" I said with a hint of sarcasm.

"No, I mean independent and strong-willed. She's quite stubborn." He winked at me.

"I have no idea why you think that I'm stubborn," I said, hand to chest in fake surprise.

"Oh, I'm sure you don't." Then Tarek became a bit more serious. "Zaida and I fought a lot when we were younger, but now we're really close."

"Well, you guys are close in age too."

Tarek chuckled. "There were times when she made me so angry. When I was home from college, sometimes we would go out with our friends, like in a big group. My mother always told me never to come home without my sister. I would always have to wait for her. We would go out to some club and I would be waiting for her to drive her home." Tarek shook his head, remembering. "It made me mad because she would take forever. She's very social. She would go around saying goodbye to all her friends. And sometimes I would be waiting for her, only to find out that some friend of hers had driven her home."

"And you were waiting for her but she was already home?" I was incredulous.

"Exactly." Tarek crossed his arms.

"Oh my God." I rolled my eyes. "My sister Lara is kind of like that. I remember going out with her and wanting to go home and she would go around and talk to all of her friends for a couple of minutes. I would be so impatient."

"You? I never thought that you were impatient," Tarek said sarcastically.

"Whatever." I smiled.

Our food arrived and I tried to control myself. I was really hungry and wanted to cram it in my mouth. Instead, I chewed slowly and with my mouth closed.

I was on my third cup of coffee when I remembered what I had been meaning to ask Tarek for a couple of days. I figured that this was a good time, since I was about to pull a real coup and needed him to be distracted.

"Oh, hey, I have a question for you."

"Sure. Go ahead." His expression was open and friendly.

"It's accounting-related."

He laughed. "OK. Do you want me to do your taxes for you?"

"Noooo," I said. "I do my own taxes, thank you. It's about charge-offs." I explained to him the translation project I had been working on for my day job, and what I understood about charge-offs.

"OK, so accounts receivable are an asset for a company; it represents money that the company expects to collect," he explained.

"I got that," I said, nodding.

He went on. "So when it becomes clear that an account receivable represents a bad debt, an account that the company will not be able to collect, the company moves it to be an expense on the income statement. You know what an income statement is, right?"

"Yes, I'm not a moron."

He smirked but didn't respond to my comment.

"OK, so at that point the bad debt is charged off and it becomes an expense that can be written down—"

"So then the company can take a tax deduction on it, right?"

"Yes, that's right. The company writes off the uncollectible amount."

"So at what point does the company decide to write off the bad debt?"

He smiled. "You can ask different accountants and get different answers."

"OK, I get it. That's how I understood it." Then I remembered my manners. "And thank you."

"Anytime. You can ask me anything." Then he hedged a bit. "I may not always know the answer, though."

"Wow," I smiled.

"What?"

"That must be difficult for you to admit that you don't always know everything." I winked.

"Well, look who's talking," he retorted.

I smiled broadly then because I saw that our waiter was bringing the check.

"What's so funny?" Tarek asked. He seemed a bit suspicious.

"I'll tell you later."

As soon as our waiter brought our check I held out my hand for it and took it, thanking him.

"Oh no, Isabel. I'm paying."

"Go ahead," I told him. I would wait until he had figured it out.

He instinctively reached for his wallet, then had a look of shock on his face.

I had my running bag on my lap and took out his wallet, which he had given to me to hold before we started our run. I held it out to taunt him, but near my face so that he couldn't reach out and grab it.

I shook my head. "Epic fail, dude. Epic fail."

"I can't believe you did that!" he exclaimed

"*I* didn't do anything," I countered, my hand to my chest. Then I laughed. "I'm buying you lunch, so now you have to do what I want."

"And what is that?" His eyes narrowed.

"Come to the pier with me and I'll show you around."

"OK, that's innocent enough."

I wondered if he would acquiesce if I ordered him to take me to his apartment and, well, you know. But I didn't dare say that, even in jest.

The rest of the day passed by quickly. We walked around the pier, where there were several boats around. Then we walked along King Street, doing a little window-shopping. At some point we stopped and got croissants.

"Are you still hungry?" Tarek had asked me, unbelieving.

"Yes," I said adamantly. "Why?

"My God—"

"Tarek, the last guy who made a comment about how much I ate, I kicked his ass."

"Really?"

"Well, not literally. Figuratively." Then I told Tarek about when my brother-in-law, Patrick, had commented about how much *all* the Vilanova women ate, not just me. Indeed, the Vilanova appetite was legendary. I had given Patrick a solid tongue-lashing.

Tarek smiled. "Oh, so you verbally kicked his—" he paused, apparently unable to say the word "ass."

"Something like that." I smiled.

It was about 4 p.m. by the time we got back to my car. I had promised to drive him home. But it was a selfish act, too. This way I could spend a little more time with him. We both sank into the seats, exhausted from the day. I put on some music, then had a thought.

"So what kind of music do you like to listen to?" I asked Tarek.

"Pretty much everything."

"Well, I know you like merengue, so—" I put on some Elvis Crespo.

Suavemente, besame, quiero sentir tus labios esta noche otra vez . . .

I was thinking about that Saturday night that we had gone out with Eric and Josh. The mere thought of holding Tarek that close to me again was making me crazy.

Then, as if he had read my mind, he said, "We should go dancing again sometime."

"Sure." I looked at him sideways. "I mean, we'll see. I'm getting a little worried about exams."

"Already? There's plenty of time."

"Tarek, the semester is halfway over."

"Yeah, well—" he began, his voice growing quieter. He was looking out the window and suddenly he sighed.

"What's that for?" I asked him.

"Nothing." I couldn't see his face, so I couldn't tell what he was thinking.

A little later, I pulled my car in front of his apartment building. We looked at each other. Neither of us appeared to be in a hurry.

"Tarek, I had an awesome time today. Thanks for coming with me."

"Thank you for inviting me." He smiled and his eyes twinkled. I also noticed for the first time that he had a few creases around his eyes when he smiled.

"Do you want to come up?" he asked then.

"Yes," I said automatically, then mentally kicked myself.

He paused, like maybe he was waiting for me to say something more. "OK, there may be parking over on that street." He inclined his head to show me where I could park.

"No, you asked me if I wanted to come up. I do, but I'm not going to." I smiled nervously and involuntarily lowered my lashes, looking down.

I couldn't believe I had said that. If he understood my innuendo I was going to be beyond embarrassed.

"Why won't you then?" he asked.

I finally got the courage to look up, and noticed that his smile was suggestive. At least, that was how I read it.

"I need to shower. *Estoy hecha un asco.*"

"Oh, I don't care about that." He was still smiling.

"I do, though." I paused for a second. "Thanks for the invite. I'll see you tomorrow."

I was still trying not to laugh about his hair, which was still pulled back. Then I couldn't help giggling.

"What are you laughing at now?"

"Nothing."

"Isabel, are you still laughing about my hair?"

"Yes, I mean, *no*. I mean—I'm sorry."

Tarek sighed.

"I have the urge to take that rubber band out of your hair." As I said that, I tried to reach to pull it out, but Tarek must have anticipated it because he grabbed my hand.

"You're incredible. Why are you so goofy today, anyway?"

"I don't know." The truth was that I was starting to get this way when I hung around him.

"Well, it's good to see you laugh anyway, even if it's at me."

"Thanks. You're a good friend." Then I noticed that I was still holding his hand. Or was he still holding mine? I quickly let go and put both my hands on the steering wheel.

"I'll see you tomorrow, Tarek," I said again.

"OK, have a good evening."

"You too."

I drove away and exhaled a long breath. It was the best day that I had had for a long time. All my days with him were beginning to be like that.

Something was going to have to happen soon or I would go nuts.

Uncharacteristically, I was walking to campus with a huge smile on my face. The guys at work had all noticed my good mood.

"Why are you so happy today, Isabel?" my coworker Abdul had asked me before I made up some excuse to leave quickly.

"She probably got laid over the weekend," someone else had said.

Classy, I had thought, and likely enough to file a harassment complaint.

Dude, if I *had* gotten laid this weekend, I would be floating. Then the thought of doing that with Tarek made me shudder.

Get yourself under control! I thought.

Tarek had texted me while I was on the metro, telling me that he might be late to class. Why, I didn't know. Because I was running a bit late too, I went upstairs to class as soon as I got to campus, plopping down into my seat. I took out a protein bar and started munching.

Eric arrived shortly after I did and was eating a sandwich.

Josh and Dinesh got there and took out their own snacks. I stole some almonds from Dinesh. Josh was eating an apple.

God, this is like the cafeteria, I thought, laughing to myself.

"Where's Tarek?" Josh asked.

"He's going to be late," I answered absentmindedly, as I reviewed my notes on my laptop.

"Why?" Eric asked.

"Dude, I don't know. I'm not the boss of him."

"I thought you were the boss of everybody," Dinesh said then, laughing.

"I wish! If I were, things would run a hell of a lot more smoothly, I'll tell you *that*."

"He's not usually late," Josh said then. "I mean, he's certainly never later than *I* am."

I didn't answer right away, as I was still reviewing my notes, trying to block out the annoying chatter.

"Whatever," I finally said, without looking up from my computer screen. Then I was thinking about the day before, and I smiled. "Maybe he's sore. I'd be surprised if he could walk after what we did yesterday."

As soon as the last word left my mouth, I wished I could take it all back. I hadn't been paying attention. Maybe they hadn't heard.

But I wasn't that lucky. Josh and Dinesh were doubling over with laughter. Eric almost choked on his sandwich. In fact, the sound he made seemed so dire that I turned around to see if he needed the Heimlich.

Once I saw that Eric was all right, my embarrassment set in. "That's not what I meant, you guys. Get your minds out of the gutter!"

"After what you *did* yesterday? *Your* mind is in the gutter! We don't want to know about your sex life!" Dinesh managed to get out before gasping for air again.

He had been too loud. People had turned around and were looking at me now. I figured the best course of action would be to ignore it. If they saw me worked up, it would be like air to feed their fire.

I leaned my elbow on the desk in front of me and rested my head in my hand, covering my eyes. I tried to block everything out. Then suddenly there was a hand lightly on my left shoulder. I looked through my fingers and saw Tarek.

"What's going on? Are you OK?" His eyebrows were drawn together.

I shook my head and smiled weakly.

"Isabel told us—" Dinesh began in between gulps of air.

No! I thought. Oh God, no! I was trying to appear like I didn't care, but I was mortified.

"—that you wouldn't be able to walk today after what you guys did yesterday," Josh managed to finish.

"You know what I meant," I said to Tarek. He smiled at me.

"Tell us what you guys did yesterday," Eric said then.

Tarek was opening his laptop. "A gentleman never reveals those things."

"Oh, come *on!*" I said to him. He was ganging up on me with the guys. I couldn't believe it.

I slinked down into my seat and looked at my laptop screen.

"Just ignore them," Tarek told me.

"Easy for you to say. You're not the object of the joke."

"Well, I kind of am."

Then for the first time I noticed that he was wearing a suit.

"Hey, what's the occasion?" I asked.

"I had an interview today for a possible internship next semester."

"That's great. You didn't tell me," I said a bit accusingly.

"I was going to but I forgot."

"Where?"

"At the Federal Reserve Board."

The others were still chuckling but we ignored them.

"When do you find out about it?" I asked.

"I'm not sure. And something else—"

I looked at him expectantly. "What? Tell me."

Class was starting. He looked at me and smiled, almost in a conspiratorial way. I didn't get it.

I raised my hands, palms up, in a gesture of impatience.

The professor was already lecturing so Tarek lowered his voice. "The DC firm made me an offer for a summer associateship today."

It took about three seconds, then I smiled. I bit my lip to avoid it, but the smile became huge, and I felt my eyes crinkling up. I couldn't help looking into his eyes at that point. They had an emotion that I couldn't quite read, but I could tell that he was glad.

I made myself look ahead; otherwise I was afraid I would kiss him right there.

SEVENTH WEEK: **TUESDAY**

I was walking to campus, glad that I had worn a jacket. The wind had picked up and it was downright chilly. It was mid-October, and Halloween was in a couple of weeks.

Oh my God. The semester was halfway over.

I was a little more pensive than usual today, constantly lost in my thoughts and finding it a bit difficult to concentrate. I had been telling myself that at some point I would have to have what Lara called "the talk" with Tarek.

Let me rephrase. I didn't *have* to do anything. That was basically my life's motto. However, the more time I spent with Tarek, the more I wanted to tell him how I felt. Over the past few days, I had been trying to convince myself to talk to him. But, as usual, I was inventing a bunch of excuses.

It hadn't been a good time the week he went to New York because I didn't want to bring it up when he had an important interview. Then it wasn't a good time because maybe, just maybe, he liked Dalia and I would look like a fool. In a couple of weeks it wouldn't be a good time because we would be studying for exams.

And next week we would have to register for our spring classes. I still hadn't made up my mind what I was taking. I wanted to ask Tarek what he was taking, but I didn't want to make it seem like I wanted to take the same classes as he did, even though that was precisely what I wanted.

Wait, how old was I again?

I arrived at school early today, and saw Josh inside the main entrance. He was chatting with Alyssa. I gave her a knowing smile and she glared at me, giving me a hard look.

Tarek and I are right, I thought then. There is something more to her.

I greeted Josh and then, because I had been in a fairly good mood recently, inclined my head at Alyssa, acknowledging her presence without saying anything. She made no motion in return, at least none that I noticed.

"Let's sit down," I told Josh. "We have some time before class."

We walked to the lounge area and saw Tarek, joining him at his table. I was a little perturbed when Alyssa sat down with us.

"Hey," I told Tarek as I sat next to him.

"Hey, Isabel." He smiled.

As I sat down I noticed that there was a table set up in the hall, across from us. It wasn't unusual for various law-school groups to do this in order to sell stuff for fundraising events or publicize other lame things. Today there was apparently a blood drive.

"Ugh," I said aloud. Everyone was walking around with the little Red Cross stickers, announcing that they had committed to donating blood. They were announcing their self-sacrifice to the entire world. Look at me! I may be a vacuous, superficial law school student, but gosh darn it, I'm a saint because I donated blood!

I couldn't help smirking.

"What?" Tarek asked me.

I looked at him and then motioned toward the table with my head. "Don't you love it? People giving a little bit of blood, eating some cookies and drinking some juice, then they go around with this haughty attitude like they've saved the world, like they're better than we are?"

Tarek chuckled. "Don't get me started. The same people throw some money at someone and feel better about themselves, when they should really be asking themselves how to give people the tools to improve their lives, to be self-sufficient—"

"Capitalism does that. It's equal-opportunity."

"That's exactly my point," Tarek agreed.

"So you guys aren't going to give blood then?" Melanie asked as she sat down. Eric was with her. She was smiling. It hadn't been a serious question. She and I had had this discussion before.

"I'll *sell* my blood," Tarek said then. I looked at him in surprise, but not for the reasons one would normally think.

"What?" Josh asked then. He was laughing, and I knew why. In fact, Melanie and Eric were chuckling too.

"It's simple supply and demand," Tarek said. "I should have the legal right to sell my own blood. Remember that Torts case—"

"*Moore*," I stated the name of the case. "The Supreme Court of California decided that case."

"Right," Tarek said. "The Court decided that people don't have legal ownership of their cells—"

"But's that wrong," I added.

"It *is* wrong," Tarek said.

"The plaintiff had leukemia," I summarized, "and his doctors used his cells to commercialize a cell line, and he couldn't share in the profits—"

"How can you remember all these cases?" Eric asked me incredulously.

"Because they're interesting," I told him, shrugging my shoulders.

Tarek continued. "So if the Red Cross, or hospitals, need blood so badly, then why don't they buy it?"

Everyone was still laughing. I was giggling with my hand covering my mouth.

"Why is that so funny?" Tarek was confused.

I looked at him. "They're laughing because they hear this every time there's a blood drive—from me."

"Yeah, that's what Isabel always says," Josh said then.

"It makes sense," I explained. "You can sell your bone marrow, and men can sell sperm; you can sell your plasma—"

"Exactly!" Tarek backed me up.

"Well, donating bone marrow is very painful," Josh said.

"Irrelevant." I waived his comment away with my hand. "Anyway, the criteria for whether or not you have to pay for something is the amount of pain involved? That makes no sense. If my type O blood is needed so badly, then economics dictate that I can get paid for that."

Alyssa piped up then. "You have type O blood? You're a universal donor! You *have* to donate!"

"Excuse me." I looked her full in the face. "I don't *have* to do anything. And I'm not going to donate my blood because it's fashionable to do so, or because I'm pressured to do so."

Tarek crossed his arms, looking at Alyssa. "We're free-market capitalists." We're apparently the only ones at this law school, I thought then.

"Oh God," Alyssa scoffed. "You two are perfect for each other. No wonder you're a couple."

The table became silent all of a sudden. No one said anything for a full five seconds. That was unheard of, especially when Josh, Eric, Melanie and I were together.

Tarek didn't say anything during those five seconds. And I was figuring out what to do. I concluded that if I let it go and didn't say anything, then everyone would assume that we were. And I wasn't sure if Tarek would be all right with that. I figured the only thing to do at that point was to tell the truth.

"We're not a couple," I said, looking at Alyssa.

Then I saw confusion on her face, and was trying to reconcile it with our conversation the other day, when she hadn't said Saul's name in front of Tarek. Was that it? Had she thought then that Tarek and I were dating? But that still didn't explain why she hadn't screwed me, did it?

"Well, you should be," Melanie said. I closed my eyes for a second. I should have known that she wouldn't be able to keep from saying anything.

To their credit, Eric and Josh didn't say anything, probably because they knew I really liked Tarek. My eyes met Josh's and he gave me a friendly smile.

I was finally able to think again, and decided to ignore the entire exchange. "Alyssa," I said, looking at her. I was curious to ask her about her career plans, given her conversation with the career counselor that I had overheard the other day. But I had to ask her in a way in which she wouldn't know that I had eavesdropped.

Well, I hadn't really eavesdropped. I mean, the office door had been open and all—

"Where are you going to end up interning next semester?" I asked her. At first, she didn't know that I had asked *her* the question. So I continued looking at her.

"What do you mean?" She looked cautious, as if she wasn't sure why I was asking her that question.

"The question is clear on its face," I said, with a hint of a smile.

When she didn't respond to my comment, I continued. "Everyone is interning somewhere, it seems. What will you be doing?"

"I'm not sure yet," she said dismissively. Oooh, I'm on to something, I thought.

"What kind of law are you interested in practicing?" I asked her then. I caught Josh looking at me out of the corner of my eye, wondering why I was asking her these questions, and why I was engaging her in conversation at all.

"I'm not sure yet."

"Aren't you graduating next year?" I pressed.

"Yeah, so?" She shrugged easily, but her rapid blinking gave away that she was bothered.

"Well, shouldn't you know what you want to do by now?"

Finally she became annoyed. "Why the hell do you care?" She got up quickly.

"Oh, I *don't*," I retorted, crossing my arms.

"I'm going to class," she said as she left hurriedly.

I watched her leave, then turned to Melanie. "Isn't she in one of your classes?" I asked.

"We had Legal Writing together," Melanie answered. "What's with all your questions? Are you mad—?" Her eyes darted in Tarek's direction for a second. No doubt she thinks I'm pissed off with Alyssa for saying that he and I were a couple. Uncharacteristically, I wasn't angry about that.

"No, but—" I looked around the table, and decided that I would grill Melanie on this one-on-one. No need to air my theories in front of everyone. "It's nothing."

"Dude," Eric said then, "are you on something, Isabel?"

I half-smiled at him. "Just caffeine."

On the metro on the way home, Tarek and I were talking about Alyssa.

"What's she hiding?" I asked out loud, as much to myself as to him.

"I don't know, but you shouldn't worry about it," he said.

"I'm not, I'm just—"

"You're nosy." He was smiling.

"*Curious.* By the way, look who's talking."

"What do you mean?" he asked.

"Remember the first day we studied together?"

"Yes, and?"

"You were full of questions." Then I tried mimicking his voice as best I could, which was difficult. "Where are you from? How are your grades? Where were you born? Etc., etc."

Tarek laughed. "Oh my God, *that* is how my voice sounds to you?!"

"*Yes,*" I said, even though it wasn't. Then I was laughing too.

"Hey, you two lovebirds, quiet down!"

We both looked at Josh. I don't know why exactly, but his comment didn't bother me the way it would have in the past. I guess it didn't bother

Tarek either, since he didn't say anything.

Josh and Dinesh were a little way away from us chatting, no doubt, about patent stuff.

"Freaking patent people," I said to Tarek, loud enough for Josh and Dinesh to hear. "They have better job prospects than we do."

It was true. Josh and Dinesh were patent agents at different law firms. Dinesh's firm was paying for him to go to law school, and he had an almost guaranteed patent attorney position when he graduated. Josh worked for a smaller firm, which wasn't paying for his law school tuition, but he at least had a (practically) guaranteed attorney position there after he graduated.

All in all, the patent law industry did not seem to have been as hard hit as other law-related sectors, especially when compared to the corporate practices of most firms. Josh and Dinesh also both had doctorates in hard science areas, which was a big help for them as far as job-seeking in the patent world. I was a bit jealous, I would admit, especially since Dinesh didn't have to pay for his tuition. But I couldn't fault him for it. Who wouldn't take that opportunity? On the other hand, he had signed an agreement with his firm to continue working there for several years after he passed the bar since they had paid his tuition. At least I didn't have that obligation.

But I would have six figures of debt when I graduated, I thought, sighing.

"What are you thinking about?" Tarek asked me then.

I looked at him.

"You were totally zoned out."

"Law-school debt," I decided to answer honestly.

"Are you serious?" He seemed surprised.

"Yes." I looked at him. "Aren't you worried about it?"

"I try not to worry."

"Well, you have a summer associateship, which will no doubt lead to a full-time job after graduation." I started thinking, a dangerous trend. If he did stay in DC after graduation, then I felt less bad about staying at my current job long-term, as long as it meant I could see Tarek regularly.

Wait, I stopped myself. What was I thinking? I was assuming he would still want to see me after graduation.

That got me thinking about Tarek's DC offer.

"Hey, have you accepted the DC offer?" I asked him, trying to appear like it was an afterthought. But the fact that he hadn't yet told me that he had accepted it made me think that he hadn't.

"Not officially, no." He was trying to figure out what to say exactly, I could tell. "They gave me some time, in case the New York firm makes me an offer."

My face began to fall, but I pasted a smile on it to hide my chagrin. "So New York's your first choice. That makes sense with your finance background. That's great."

Tarek chuckled. "Isabel, you're a horrible liar."

"On the contrary, I'm a great liar."

Tarek sighed a long sigh. "I haven't decided what I'm going to do yet, assuming I even get an offer from the New York firm, which I probably won't."

The next stop was Pentagon City, and Tarek left. "I'll see you tomorrow," he told me. Then he smiled, and his eyes lit up, and I thought how unfair it was of him to smile at me like that.

The train doors closed and I was left staring at them. Josh was talking to me, but I didn't hear him.

I wonder what he thinks about me, I thought. I mean, I wonder what he *really* thinks.

SEVENTH WEEK: **WEDNESDAY**

I was rushing to campus like always, but was actually making good time today for my 3:50 class. As I walked into the law school building, I was struck by a strange sight.

I saw Sorority Girl, uh, I mean Alyssa, talking to Saul. They were standing right inside the entrance.

Fortunately, I hadn't seen Saul for a while. Unfortunately, I was seeing him now.

Saul was good-looking. He was a little taller than Tarek, with shorter, dark hair and kind of a lean build. He had high cheekbones and piercing eyes.

Looking at him now, talking to Alyssa, brought back memories that I did not care to recall at the moment. It wasn't that they were particularly bad memories in the abstract, for what they were. Saul was one more guy I had hooked up with. But after what I was experiencing with Tarek, I felt ashamed because Tarek knew Saul. Logically, it shouldn't matter, especially since it had happened over a year ago, but it did.

And even if I did tell Tarek about what had happened, what would I say? Uh, I need to tell you that I hooked up with this guy that you know. How would I begin to talk about that? Was I required to tell him about every guy I had ever hooked up with? If so, then he was required to tell me about any girls he had been with, right? Did I care about that?

Not really. I mean, I was curious but I didn't think it mattered in the end. And we were only friends, anyway. Well, we were friends, but it was different than being friends with Josh and Eric. We were friends who were mutually attracted to each other. But I didn't have any kind of claim on him.

I also didn't like what I saw for another reason. Saul looked like he was coming on to Alyssa. The way he was looking at her, with his eyes bright and his mouth curved into a half-smile, was the way he had looked at me right before we had started hooking up.

But why should I care about that?

I was tired of avoiding Saul, I decided then.

I went right up to them. "Hey," I said to Alyssa.

She looked at me a bit strangely, then said hi back.

"Hi, Isabel," Saul said then, looking at me.

"Hi," I glared at him.

I looked back at Alyssa. "I need to talk to you."

"I need to go anyway," Saul said then. He spoke with a slight accent. "See you in class, Alyssa."

When he left, I turned to her. But she spoke first.

"If you're going to laugh at me, or make fun of me, then don't even open your mouth."

I stopped with my mouth open. She was spunky. I had to respect that.

Then I found my voice. "Tell me you're not sleeping with him, or considering sleeping with him."

Her eyes widened. "Why would *you* care?"

"He can be a bit obsessive, Alyssa."

"I guess you would know." Astonishingly, she didn't say it in a mean way. Then she looked me up and down. Women always sized each other up like that. I can't tell you how many times I had been walking down the street and some woman looked at me, from head to toe, whether judgmental or envious or both, I did not know. I think it was this town.

Women were so hard on each other, and I realized then that I had been like that with Alyssa. I had talked to Josh and Eric about how skinny she was, with practically no hips. Why had I felt the need to remark on her physical appearance?

"So do you like him?" I asked her point-blank.

"We're just friends. We've had some classes together."

I had the feeling she was curious about my relationship with Saul, and what exactly had happened.

"Do you want to ask me about him?"

"No, it's OK." She shook her head with the slightest of movements.

"I won't tell anyone, Alyssa." I decided to try logic. "I mean—you have some information that could really screw me over. So I have no incentive to do that to *you.*"

She smiled at me, understanding.

"OK, then."

I checked my phone to see the time. "Let's walk. I have some time before class."

We walked outside the main door, back the way I had come so that the guys wouldn't see us, and out into what the students called the quad.

"Hold on," I told her, taking out my phone. I sent Tarek a text message.

I'll meet you in class.

That way he wouldn't wait downstairs for me.

I briefly told Alyssa about Saul. "It was a hook-up for me, Alyssa. I won't lie, he's sexy and all, but I wasn't interested in him intellectually. And, in case you're wondering, he's not interested in a long-term relationship."

"If he had been, would you have gone out with him?"

"No," I said automatically. "Look, do what you want. But he kept pursuing me for a long time afterward. It took weeks for him to stop calling and texting and stuff. You should know that."

She nodded, pensive.

I changed the subject.

"So—you thought Tarek and I were a couple, huh?"

"Isabel, everyone thinks so." Alyssa was looking at me like I was crazy.

"Who's everyone?"

"*Everyone*," she emphasized. Her next question surprised me. "So why aren't you?"

I looked at her, and realized that it was a serious question. I opened my mouth, then sighed. "It's—complicated."

"Well, it doesn't seem that complicated to *me.*"

"Let me ask you something," I said then. What the hell. We were actually having a decent conversation. "Why didn't you screw me over the other night?"

"What do you mean?" She looked confused.

"You were talking about me liking dark men, and you came this close," I held my thumb and first finger together, "to mentioning Saul in front of Tarek, but you didn't. I didn't stop you. I was too shocked."

She didn't say anything, and looked down for a second.

"So why didn't you out me?" I pressed her, wondering.

"It would have been cruel to do that to someone, even to you."

I smiled. *Even to me.* She was starting to sound like my mother.

"What do you mean exactly?"

"I figured you like Tarek as much as you do, you wouldn't have told him about Saul, who he happens to know. When a girl really likes someone, she prefers to minimize her past indiscretions."

Minimize her past indiscretions? Who the hell *was* she? I had never heard her use language like that before.

"What makes you think I like him?" I was serious.

She smiled and laughed a low laugh. "Isabel, you don't *like* him. You're crazy about him. It's written all over your face when you're with him."

I was floored. If it was that obvious to her, then it was that obvious to everyone. "So you think he knows?" I didn't bother to deny it, figuring it was a waste of energy and time.

"I don't know. Men are dense. It wouldn't surprise me if he had no idea."

This girl knew more about men than I thought.

She continued. "I will tell you he feels the same way about you."

I stared at her, my brows furrowing. "How would you know that?"

"Same reason. It's written all over his face, in his eyes."

"I don't know." I wasn't convinced.

"How long have you known Josh and Eric?" Her tone was like a big sister now. It intrigued me.

"Since I started school, since 2008." I didn't get the question.

"Do they bring you coffee regularly?"

"What? No."

"Do they make a point of studying with you every weekend?"

"No, but they're not nazis about outlining like I am." I didn't bother to question how she knew this. Josh had told her. Once again, I was reminded that he loved to gossip.

"You think Tarek is?"

"Yeah, I guess."

She smiled, not without kindness. "Oh, Isabel—" she left it hanging.

She may be right. Hadn't he basically said that studying was a pretext to get to know me the night that we had gone out to dinner and dancing?

I checked the time. "I have to go."

"Well, it was nice talking with you." I couldn't tell whether she was being ironic.

I turned to leave then stopped. "Look—"

"I won't say anything, I promise."

I didn't know if I could believe her, but it was too late. The cat was out of the proverbial bag.

"See you later." I started to walk away.

"Isabel," Alyssa called.

I turned around and faced her.

She shook her head. "Time waits for no man—or woman." She grinned a sisterly grin. "Remember that."

She suddenly looked much older. In that moment I doubted everything that I had ever thought I knew about her.

I nodded, pondering. "Thanks."

She was still grinning. "Sure."

On my way upstairs to class, I was pensive. *Time waits for no man?* That was something *I* would say.

Whatever. I had other concerns. Like what I was going to do about Tarek.

I walked into International Law class about two minutes before class started. Then I saw him sitting there, looking over his textbook, his black curls hanging in front of his face. God, he was gorgeous.

I sat down in my chair.

"Hey," I looked at him, managing a smile.

He looked up. "Hey there. What's going on?"

"Nothing."

He gave me my coffee and I thanked him.

"What are you thinking about?" he asked me.

"What do you mean?"

"You have this thoughtful expression on your face."

I smiled. It was getting more and more difficult to hide my feelings around him.

I made something up. "I was wondering how many bottles of mousse you go through in a week to get your hair to look so perfect."

"Oh, please. I couldn't do anything with it today. It's all over the place."

"Well, it looks really good," I told him.

"Thank you," he smiled.

Class started and I tried to pay attention.

Today had been kind of crappy so far. I had received an email from another firm that they would not be offering me a callback interview. Honestly, I had no idea why I was surprised. The interview season was wrapping up, and pretty much everyone who was getting callbacks had done them already, and some people had even gotten their offers. If I hadn't heard anything by now, then that meant I wasn't getting any. And to add insult to injury, the other firms I hadn't heard from yet hadn't even said anything one way or the other. That was just rude.

I was rushing to campus as usual, trying to make my afternoon class. As I approached the law school building, I saw Tarek just outside, talking to Sameer.

My heart stopped. I could only see Tarek's face, and couldn't see Sameer's. Tarek looked pissed off, but under control, as usual.

I had to walk right past them; I couldn't avoid it. Tarek's eyes met mine, and I stopped and stood next to him. I was suddenly sure they were talking about me.

"Hey," I said to Tarek.

"Hi, Isabel." His eyes were pensive.

I looked at Sameer but, other than that, didn't acknowledge him. I wanted to punch the smirk right off his face.

"You can get going. This conversation doesn't concern you," Sameer told me.

"Don't talk to her like that," Tarek snapped.

My stomach churned as I thought that maybe Sameer had told him about my past with Saul. How was I going to explain that?

As I was organizing my thoughts on the subject, Tarek turned to me. "Come on, Isabel, he and I are done."

We left Sameer there and went into the law school building.

I didn't know where to start. "Is that the first time you've talked to him since—?"

"Yes."

"Are you angry?"

"Yes."

"OK, I'm sorry." I turned to walk in the other direction. I felt like crying.

"Wait." Tarek's hand was on my arm. "Isabel, I'm not angry with *you*."

"I know, I—it seems like you want to be left alone, so—"

"No, that's not true." We were looking at each other.

"What did you say to him?" I asked quietly.

"I told him not to talk to you again. I hope you don't mind that."

"I don't mind." I shook my head.

Both our classes were pretty uneventful that evening. I was glad for it since I had had enough drama in my life recently.

Tarek and I hadn't talked that much the entire evening. I was worried about what Sameer had told him. Then, when we were walking to Property class, I couldn't stand it anymore. I stopped Tarek in mid-conversation with my hand up. He looked surprised.

"Tell me what he told you about me."

"What? Sameer?"

"Yes. I can't shake the feeling that he told you some shit about me. You have to understand, Tarek—he doesn't know me. All he knows is what other people say about me—"

"Isabel, wait." Tarek was gathering his thoughts. "What would he tell me that I don't already know?" His tone was telling me not to worry.

"Nothing," I sighed, feeling a bit dumb. "But he could make shit up about me."

"Honestly, Isabel, I wouldn't believe him anyway."

"So what did he say to you?"

Tarek sighed. "I saw him and told him he had nerve to talk to you like he did. He doesn't understand why I hang out with you."

Why *do* you hang out with me? I thought. Tell me!

"Look, Isabel, forget about him. Please."

"OK," I smiled weakly.

"Are we on for Saturday?" he asked me then, smiling.

"Sure."

"We can meet at my place if you want."

I nodded.

I was subdued on the way home. Tarek and I were waiting at the metro station with Josh, Eric, and Dinesh. I was thinking again about how to bring up the subject with Tarek, about how I felt about him. I hit roadblocks every time. I was trying to think of a low-risk way in which I could find out how *he* felt about *me*, without me having to tell him how I felt about him. That way, if he didn't want to be with me like that, I wouldn't have revealed any information and it would be no hard feelings.

But I couldn't think of a foolproof way to do it. No matter how I considered it, it was the prisoner's dilemma all over again.

"Isabel." Tarek's voice was firm.

I looked at him, shaken out of my thoughts. "What?"

"I was asking you a question and you were out of it."

"I was thinking."

"What's on your mind?"

I answered without thinking, still a little lost in my thoughts. "You."

He raised his eyebrows, and his eyes were alive.

"I mean—" I stammered, trying to think about how to correct this, "I was thinking about studying with you, on Saturday. What time do you want me? I mean—what time do you want me to come over—to study—only to study—"

He smiled, apparently amused by my discombobulation. "Come over anytime in the afternoon and we can have dinner later."

"OK," I said shyly. "Shy" was not a word that I had ever previously associated with myself.

"Oh, and I've been meaning to ask you something," Tarek said then.

My eyes shot up. Was this it? Was he going to ask me out on a "date?" I couldn't read his expression.

He continued, looking away for a brief second. "What classes are we taking next semester?"

"We?" I asked, slightly amused, my eyebrows raising.

"Well, I thought—that since we study really well together, we could—"

I smiled, waited a few moments, then felt bad at leaving him struggling without an answer from me. I waved a hand. "What about Corporations? It's at 6 p.m. on Mondays and Tuesdays."

"Sure, I wanted to take that class."

All right, one down. I would try for two. "And Constitutional Law II fits my schedule but it's at night too, Wednesdays at 6 p.m. and then every other Friday."

"Sure."

Two down, I thought. Wow.

"That gives me seven credits but I need three more," I told him. "And, honestly, I'm not sure about the last class."

"Well," Tarek began, then hesitated for a second. "Would you be interested in taking a Money Laundering class?"

"Oh, I see, so we could learn how to do that properly."

"Exactly." He winked at me and I felt my pulse race.

"When is that class?"

"Thursdays and every other Friday at 6 p.m. Not the same Fridays as Con Law. And it's three credits."

"All right," I agreed. "Sounds like a winner."

Our train arrived then and we got on, chatting with the others. But my good mood quickly deteriorated right before Tarek left.

"Isabel," he began. The train was pulling in to Pentagon City.

"Yes?"

He didn't pull any punches. "I got an offer from the New York firm today."

My face fell. I couldn't hide it, or else I refused to.

"That's great," I lied. "I'm really happy for you." I didn't even try to put on a fake smile.

The train doors opened and I took a step back, allowing people to pass me to exit. Tarek left and I didn't look at him.

I felt hopeless.

I got home that night and threw all my stuff on the floor.

"What the fuck *was* that?!" I yelled at nobody. Let me get this straight. He tells me that he got the New York offer right before he left the train, because he didn't want a big scene. He didn't want me to scream and curse and shit. Why else would he wait to tell me? God forbid he upset the high-strung, fiery Latin woman!

In fact, why would he tell me at all? He could've accepted the offer and told me then. "It's been fun, Isabel, but I'm going to New York, to the big time. Thanks for your outlines and stuff."

I picked up a pillow off the sofa and lobbed it across the room, smack against the opposite wall. I was pissed off beyond all recognition.

Stupid, stupid girl! Why would such a gorgeous, intelligent guy hang around you?! To get laid! And when he didn't get laid, he was done! Of course!

I was too angry to sleep. So I nuked some leftovers and sat on the sofa, taking deep breaths. I turned on the TV to find some mindless drivel, which, depressingly, wasn't that difficult.

So the hell what? I thought. I wanted to date him but it's a moot point now. Screw him, and every goddam man in this town.

I was successfully ignoring my feelings about him for the moment, but pretty soon I wouldn't be able to.

My phone blipped. I almost didn't hear it, but I had the TV on mute and was thinking in silence. I grabbed it from my purse, hoping for it to be Lara.

But it was Tarek.

Can you talk?

Yes, I *can*, but I won't, I thought.

I ignored the message.

Last weekend, after spending so much time with him, I had been asking myself what I was waiting for, and why I felt like I had to wait for some perfect moment to kiss him. I had begun thinking that I would kiss him this weekend.

But now I was glad that it hadn't happened, because he was going to New York and he would forget about me. Maybe he had been interested in me at one point, but was tired of waiting. I couldn't blame him. It made me want to cry.

Twenty minutes later I had closed my eyes, with my head on the sofa, when my phone rang. It was Tarek again.

Well, he can stew, I thought. I turned my phone off and went to bed, falling asleep only after my anger subsided.

SEVENTH WEEK: **FRIDAY**

I was in a crappy mood all day, and felt only marginally better after weight-lifting during my lunch break. I didn't talk to anyone, not even Peter.

During the day I decided to go to the shooting range that night. I hadn't been in a while and needed to practice. I would take my 9-millimeter, my revolver and maybe my AR-15. There was practically no one at the range on Friday nights. Everyone would be out having a good time. Except me. I didn't have a good time.

As I walked into my apartment at 6:15, thinking about what to have for dinner, my phone rang. It was in the bottom of my purse and I was so frustrated after hunting for it that I almost dumped the entire contents of my purse on the floor. Then, at about the fifth ring, I found it and answered it hurriedly.

"Hello?" My tone was somewhere between pissed off and downright postal.

"Isabel?" It was Tarek.

"Yesss?" I prolonged the word and then sighed.

"Are you OK?"

"Why?"

"Why what?"

I sighed again, as much to calm myself as out of frustration at my pre-dicament. I said slowly, "Why do you want to know if I'm OK?"

"Because you're not answering my texts or my calls."

"So? I'm not your girlfriend. You don't have the right to know where I am."

"Yeah, well, you make that painfully obvious," he said, and I couldn't tell if he was joking or not.

"Yes, Tarek, I'm fine."

His next question surprised me.

"What are you doing tonight?"

"Why?" I asked again.

"Do you want to do something?"

Yes, and it involves the two of us naked.

"I have plans," I said instead. "I'm going to the shooting range tonight."

"Can I come?" Tarek asked, a bit animatedly.

Oh that's right, I thought. We had talked about going at some point.

"No," I said.

"Why not?"

"Because I'm pissed off!" I had trouble keeping control.

"Why?"

"Because you're going to New York!" I was trying to force myself to calm down, but it wasn't working.

"I don't know if I am or not yet." His voice was calm.

"Well, the way you're talking you are! Besides, you should go. New York is a great place for a single guy like you."

"What does *that* mean?" He was remaining calm, or trying to. It was difficult to tell over the phone.

"Take it at face value. There's no hidden meaning there." I was pissed off at the fact that he had waited until the last minute to tell me on the metro, I supposed so that I wouldn't have a fit.

"Tell me why you're *really* pissed off, Isabel."

"I'm pissed off ALL the time! Haven't you fucking figured that out by now?!"

"Tell me *why*, though." He was so calm, he was making me angrier.

"I'm pissed off at the human condition, at my own life. What the fuck else?!"

"So would it make you happy if I turned down the New York offer?"

"Nothing makes me happy, Tarek! Haven't you noticed! I'm not supposed to be happy! That's how this works out."

"You mean you don't *let* yourself be happy, Isabel."

"Screw you," I said. But my voice came out really small. "You want to know why I'm pissed off?" I asked gently.

"Yes."

"Because I'm playing all my cards, and you've only played like one."

"What do you mean?"

"If you think I'm going to put myself on the line, then you can—forget it!" I was going to curse but reined myself in. "Figure it out for yourself, Tarek. You think you have everything all figured out, well, figure out what I said." I paused, took a deep breath and calmed down. "I have to go."

"Isabel." Tarek's voice was soft. It was also friendly, which I didn't understand. I was being such a jerk to him. "I'll ask you again. Is there anything you want to tell me?"

I hesitated, holding my breath like my life depended on it. I could do this.

"No, I've said everything."

Liar! I thought. Liar, liar, liar, liar!

"Well, there's something I want to tell *you*."

"Tell me," I said, calmed down. What would it be? That he didn't want to hang out with me anymore? That I was too high-maintenance?

"Look, come over tomorrow at 4. We'll outline, then I'll make dinner."

"What, like a date?" I blurted out, without thinking, almost accusatorily.

"No, not—not unless you want it to be."

"OK, well, I don't know." I was taken aback. I had expected him to be angry. "I mean—I'll come over but—I don't know if I want it to be a—a—" I couldn't say it.

"OK then, it won't be." I couldn't tell over the phone whether or not he was disappointed.

But something else had intrigued me. "So you cook?"

"I have been known to." I could tell that he was smiling.

"Well, that's what you said when I asked you whether you danced." If he cooked as well as he danced, I was in trouble.

Tarek was chuckling. "Well, you'll have to see."

"OK," I said. "Thank you."

"Of course. I'll see you tomorrow."

"OK, see you tomorrow."

"Good night, Isabel."

I hung up, trying to figure out what had just happened. I had been such a jackass. How could he have been so calm?

I didn't have anything ready to eat, so I ordered a pizza for dinner and scarfed it down. It was about 8:30 and I was packing up my firearms, still planning to go to the range. Ever since hanging up the phone, under a blanket of uncharacteristic calm, I had been thinking about my conversation with Tarek. What had it all meant?

Maybe he had played another card. It had kind of sounded like it. And he had been—oh my God. I was such a moron.

I stopped what I was doing and stood there for a moment. I didn't feel like going to the range anymore. I felt like—

I packed up my firearms and put them away safely. Then I washed my face, brushed my teeth and changed my shirt. I had put on a T-shirt for the range, but now put on something a little more feminine, along with foundation and lipstick.

I couldn't believe I was doing this.

I got in my car and took off. When I parked near Tarek's apartment building, I had second thoughts. It wasn't like me to do something like this but I was tired of being afraid. I was tired of all the open-endedness between us.

I opened my car door and got out in one motion. The chilly air hit me at once, making me suck in my breath. All right, let's do this.

I walked across the street to his building and toward the main entrance. There wasn't anyone around. I guess at 9 p.m. people were already out or had decided to stay in. Of course, there was no guarantee that he was here either.

As I grabbed the main doors, they opened and someone stepped out. I stepped back to avoid colliding into them, then half-turned sideways to slink through the doors.

Well, this was going to be a surprise for him, since he hadn't had to buzz me in. This was either going to be my greatest decision ever, or my worst mistake.

In front of Tarek's door, I took a deep breath and exhaled slowly. Before I could think about it, I reached out my fist and knocked.

Maybe I should leave, I thought.

All of a sudden, the door opened in one movement, and Tarek was staring into my eyes.

"Isabel." His tone was surprised. Oh my God, he looked happy to see me.

"Hey," I said. "I, uh—I came to see you." I paused, putting my hands in my jacket pockets nervously. "But if it's not a good time—"

"No, no," he said, touching my elbow and leading me inside. "Come in."

I stood there right inside his door like an idiot, with him waiting for me to say something.

"Tarek, I'm here because—" I looked down, then gathered my courage and raised my eyes to his. "I wanted to apologize."

"For what?"

I was still looking at him. My God, did he really not know? Did he really think that I had nothing to apologize for? Maybe he was merely humoring me. But his eyes were questioning.

I still had my hands in my pockets. "I was such a jackass to you on the phone and—you were—you were so nice to me. You were so nice." I shook my head, incredulous. "You're always so nice to me. Even when I don't deserve it. And I don't—I don't deserve it."

"That's not true," he insisted.

I sucked in my breath sharply. "But I'm getting away from what I really wanted to tell you."

"Tell me," he said without hesitation.

I realized I was holding my breath. I exhaled as I painfully said, "I can't stop thinking about you."

Tarek's eyes widened. I guessed he had not been expecting this.

There was no going back now. "I'm crazy about you," I breathed. "And if you don't feel the same way, we should stop spending time together, because I can't do it anymore. It would feel awful to spend time with you, if you don't—" I choked on the words.

My pulse was racing, my entire body on fire.

But apparently Tarek was more impatient than I was, if that were even possible, because the next few moments shocked the crap out of me.

His eyes met mine, and then I saw the intensity that, up until now, he had been holding back. His lips were parted, and his breathing had quickened.

He had that look that told me that he was about to throw down.

I had no time to react, because Tarek took two strides and had me against the door, his hands at my waist and his tongue down my throat. Whatever small bit of resistance I had left fell away.

My jacket was on the floor before I even realized what was happening.

Tarek's hair was in my face, and the musky scent of his hair gel together with his man smell assaulted my senses, driving me crazy.

"Stay tonight," he breathed into my ear.

It was a plea, not a command. He knew better than to give me orders.

My throat was dry but I managed to choke out a whisper, "Yes."

I tore his shirt up and over his head, running my hands all over his chest. The sight of my light skin against his dark chest made me crazy. I put my arms around him, lowering my hands and grabbing his firm ass. I pulled him against me, and noticed that he was already hard.

I moaned against his neck, and tried to reach for his belt, but he brushed my hands away so that he could take my shirt off, revealing my pink bra underneath.

"Ohhhh, Isabel," he said softly, then kissed me as he reached behind me and unclasped my bra. It fell to the floor, along with the rest of my inhibitions.

Tarek stole a glance at my breasts and ran his hands over them. I tilted my head back against the door, enjoying that immensely.

"Is that OK?" he breathed against my neck. "Do you like that?"

I turned my head to look at him, smiling. "Tarek, there is nothing you could do that I would not like."

We kissed again, then I thrust my hand in his hair and brought his head down to my breasts. He ran his tongue over one, then dragged his mouth across my chest to put my other nipple in his mouth, sucking gently as I held him there.

I let escape a "Holy fuck—"

Tarek pulled away from the door and grabbed my hand, pulling me to his bedroom. We left a trail of clothing from the front door. He turned the bedroom light on.

"Turn the light off," I told him between kisses.

"No, I want to see you."

I didn't care. I sat on the edge of his bed and leaned back as he slipped off my black thong.

Suddenly, we were completely naked. As soon as he got onto the bed with me, I pushed him down and sat on top of him, maneuvering him inside me. I moaned as I thrust downward to meet him.

He was looking at me, his eyes wide and lips parted. I loved the fact that he was totally turned on by watching me on top of him.

I leaned down and kissed him, smiling as I did so.

Then he held my waist and rolled over, so that I ended up beneath him. I should have known he wouldn't let me be on top the entire time.

I was panting and sweating a little. Tarek's hands were all over me, stroking my breasts, my hips and my face. I looked at him and smiled, and he smiled back.

Then he leaned toward me and kissed me, next moving his mouth to my ear. He held me down by my upper arms. That and the feel of my breasts against his hard chest made me insane.

"You drive me crazy," I breathed into his hair.

"Is that right?" he teased.

"God, you have no idea," I whispered, barely able to get the words out. He was moving more quickly, but gently. He said into my ear, "I want you to come so bad."

I smiled. "Don't worry," I said into his neck, "I promise you'll get your wish."

The sound of his laugh against my cheek made me tingle all over. "Hold on," I told him.

He relaxed his grip on my arms.

"Stay like that," I said. Then I grabbed his hips and grinded his pelvis against mine. I opened my legs a little wider and moaned softly with the immediate increase in pleasure. Then I rotated his hips in a circular motion right over me.

I opened my eyes and looked right at Tarek. "This is how I can come with you on top," I said.

He grinned broadly and put his hands in my hair. From the sounds I made, I was sure that he could tell I was about to let loose.

As my orgasms came in waves, Tarek kissed my neck. I held him tightly against me with my right arm, and reached out and gripped the sheets with my left.

"Oh, God!" I cried out, implicitly thanking him for giving thirty-something women the gift of multiple orgasms.

I reached this, like, crescendo of spasms, where I arched my back and thrust my pelvis upward, enjoying the sensation. This was followed afterward by several smaller ones.

As he lay on top of me, both of us fully satisfied, and kissing softly, I thought how incredible it was to have this connection with him.

Tarek rolled over and pulled me against him, with his arms around me. I lay my head on his chest.

Then he was chuckling.

"What's so funny?" I asked, startled.

"At first, I thought you came over here to kick my ass."

I smiled. "I hadn't decided yet. It was either that or jump you."

"I think you made the right decision," he retorted.

"I'm not sure yet," I teased, kissing his chest. "I'll tell you tomorrow."

He laughed and kissed my forehead. My adrenaline began to subside, and my eyelids felt heavy.

The thing was, Alyssa had been totally right. I was completely falling for Tarek. I didn't just *like* him. And I knew in my heart that I couldn't go back, I couldn't stop the descent, even if I wanted to.

There was no looking back now.

After what seemed like no time at all, I woke up. You know the state you're in between sleeping and waking. You're not quite awake and, sometimes, if you dreamed the night before, you're not quite sure if the dream was real or not. When I was younger I used to dream that my Dad was still alive, and then would wake up and realize, sadly, that it wasn't the case.

Fortunately, this morning was the opposite. I woke up slowly, aware that it was light outside. Then I was vaguely aware that I was lying in bed. But then, before opening my eyes, I realized that the bed didn't smell like my bed. It smelled muskier, a little exotic. Was I still dreaming?

Then I was aware that I was naked. Why would I be naked in my own bed? I never slept naked. Then I started to remember the night before, and earlier this morning, and began to slowly open my eyes. Wait, I thought, this isn't my room.

I sat up suddenly and looked around. OH—MY—GOD. Apparently, last night and this morning really happened! I looked in the bed, but Tarek wasn't there. I put my face in my hands, giggling.

I smelled coffee and realized that I was absolutely starving. And sore.

With the sheets covering my chest and still sitting in the bed, I started to look around for my clothes. Then Tarek appeared in the doorway, and my heart suddenly seemed to expand. He was wearing sweatpants and a white T-shirt. God, he looked incredible in anything.

What was the current protocol for the morning after? I hadn't done this since Santi, and the men between him and Tarek, well, I had never stayed the night with them. I would play it by ear. I looked at Tarek and smiled. "Hi."

"Good morning," he said in his deep voice. I shivered.

He saw me shiver. "Here." He handed me an oversized shirt, then sat down next to me on the bed.

"Thanks," I said, all giggly like an idiot. I pulled the T-shirt over my head and through my arms.

"Are you OK?" he asked.

"More than OK." I smiled. He kissed me.

"Are *you* OK?" I asked him.

His expression changed. "Isabel, I'm always OK when I'm with you."

I put my face against his and my arms around him, nuzzling his neck. He kissed me again, then pulled away.

"Come on," he smiled, his eyes alive and playful, "I made you coffee."

My brain suddenly kicked in. "Wait, you don't have coffee here."

He pursed his lips, then said, "Maybe I do, for a certain someone."

I grinned from ear to ear. "Thank you."

"No problem," he said slowly, his eyes lingering on my face.

I rolled my eyes, still grinning. "And please tell me you have something to eat here."

"For you, anything."

We ate breakfast and I tried not to shovel food in my mouth like an animal, since I was so hungry.

I was surprised how comfortable we were. We sat at his dining table and couldn't keep our hands off of each other. The thought occurred to me that I would miss him when I wasn't with him. But I quickly pushed that thought from my head. I didn't want to get ahead of myself.

Then I reached over and brushed his unruly hair from his face.

"I know, it's frizzy in the morning," he said, smiling.

"I love it," I said. "And I see now why you need all those hair products."

He laughed. "You think I'm bad? You should see what my sister has to do to her hair."

Then something occurred to me. "Are you going to Miami for Thanksgiving?"

"I'm not sure yet," he said. "In fact, I should start thinking about that. What are *you* going to do?"

"I'll probably go to my Mom's house. That's what I usually do. I don't know what my sisters are doing, though. If they don't come over, then I'll go to Mom's on the Thursday night and I'll work Friday."

"You're going to work the day after Thanksgiving?"

"I usually do. It's really quiet and I can get a lot of stuff done."
He paused for a moment. "Well, if I stay here then you could come over that day."

I smiled. "I could do that." After a moment, I stood up. "I'm going to get more coffee if that's all right."

"Of course. I'll get it for you." He took my cup and went to the kitchen.

I couldn't stop myself from giggling.

"Hey, one thing," I said.

Tarek looked at me from the kitchen. "What's that?" He was smiling and his eyes lit up.

"I totally hold you responsible for what happened last night—and this morning." My tone was serious but I was suppressing a smile.

"Me?" he asked in mock surprise. "What did *I* do? If I remember correctly, *you* came over *here*."

He brought me my coffee and I thanked him. Then he sat down at the table with me again.

"Excuse me," I defended myself. "*You* called *me* last night. You obviously wanted me to come over here and bang you. I didn't have to be a mind reader to figure that out."

Tarek's expression became more serious. "So you came over here because you thought I wanted that?"

"No," I answered automatically. "I came over here because—" My brows furrowed as I considered how to explain. "I didn't intend to sleep with you if that's what you mean. My purpose in coming over here was to tell you—how I felt about you." I ran a hand through my thick, messy hair. "I had no idea how you would react to that."

Tarek smiled deviously. "Riiight. Then you jumped me anyway."

My eyes widened in shock. "What?! *You* jumped *me*, dude! You pinned me against that door," I said, pointing.

Tarek stood up, pretending to be in disagreement by fake huffing. "Well, do you blame me? You come over here, looking all gorgeous—"

"I do blame you!" I was serious now, and he read my expression.

"For kissing you?!"

"No! That part was great! And—afterward—was great too!"

"Wait, what do you blame me for, then?"

"For taking so long!"

There was silence as it dawned on him.

"Dude, you have a hard time reading women," I told him, smiling.

"Really?" he asked sarcastically, crossing his arms. "*I* have a hard time reading women?"

"Yes." I nodded.

"Isabel, you wouldn't know if a man was interested in you to save your life!"

"Well, maybe men aren't direct enough." I crossed my arms in defiance.

"Was I direct enough last night?"

With my chin up, I retorted, "Well, I'm not sure. I may need extra convincing."

Tarek leaned down toward me, his face about an inch from mine. "What do I have to do to convince you, then?" he whispered as he drew his mouth against my cheek, then up to my ear.

I shuddered. "That'll do it, I think," I breathed, standing up and pulling him against me.

His face was against my neck and his hands under my T-shirt, then he was dragging me back to his bedroom.

A little later that day, I was back in my apartment throwing clothes into a duffel bag. Tarek had asked me to stay over again tonight, and I needed to get a few things from my place.

We had also agreed to try and study a little that weekend, although I had serious doubts about our ability to concentrate.

I was preparing to take a shower when my phone blipped with a message from Tarek.

Everything OK? I miss you.

I smiled to myself, then called him.

"Hey," he answered.

"Hi. So—can I tell you something?"

"Anything."

"I had this crazy dream last night."

"You did?" he said with mock interest.

"Yes. You won't believe it. I dreamed that I went over to your place—"

"Doesn't sound like you."

"Then I dreamed that we had sex!"

"Oh my God, that *is* crazy." He was chuckling.

"Yeah, I mean. I'm sure that would never happen in real life."

"Are you *really* sure?"

"Oh, you would never have the guts to like, back me up against your apartment door or anything, there's no way."

"You don't think so?"

"Well, I don't know. If you do have the guts, then you can show me tonight."

"Maybe I *will*." Then we both laughed.

"I can't wait to see you," he said softly.

"I'll be over in a little while."

"Whenever you want."

"Well, I should shower first."

"Oh, that's a nice image."

"Shut *up*!" I said, blushing. "I'll let you know when I'm on my way."

"OK, see you soon."

"OK, bye." We hung up. My heart was swelling. This could either be a very good thing or a very bad thing. I will wasn't sure what I was getting myself into.

A little while later, I drove to Tarek's place. I found a parking space a few blocks away from his apartment building, and lugged my backpack and purse along with me.

Once in the vestibule area, I pressed the button for his apartment.

"Hello?" he said through the intercom.

"Hey, it's me."

"OK, hold on."

There was a buzz and I pushed open the door.

In the elevator, I realized that I was a little nervous. But not as nervous as last night, thank goodness.

As I approached his apartment door, it was ajar and I heard his voice from inside. When he opened the door he was on his cell phone. I walked inside, and he held the phone away from his mouth for a moment.

"Hi, Isabel. I'm sorry, it's my Mom."

"I can wait downstairs," I told him.

"No, no," he said, motioning for me to come inside.

I entered and put my bag and purse on the floor. I was struck by the delicious smell of spices. Oh, he was cooking! My God, that smells good, I thought.

I took my sweater off. Then, to have something to do, I took out my

Property book and sat on the sofa. I looked up at Tarek then and caught him looking at me. He winked. I smiled.

He was chatting rapidly in Arabic and pacing in the kitchen. His jaw was set and he pursed his lips. I wondered what was going on but told myself that it was none of my business. Instead, I concentrated on my textbook.

After a few minutes, he was wrapping up the conversation.

"Well, I have to go. I have someone over, so—" he said in English.

Then his mother must have said something else, and then he answered in Arabic. He smiled and hung up.

He turned to me then. "I'm sorry, Isabel. She just called me and I hadn't talked to her in a while."

"That's totally fine. You don't have to apologize to me for talking to your mother. I'm sure she misses you."

"Yeah, she does."

He sat down next to me on the sofa, very close, not like other times when there was at least a foot of space between us. I put my textbook on the sofa on my other side.

"So how often do you talk to her?" I asked him.

"Usually at least once a week. How often do you talk to *your* Mom?"

"About once a week, but it depends. Sometimes we email instead of chatting on the phone. But she worries about me since I live by myself." I rolled my eyes, thinking about my usual conversations with my Mom. "If she doesn't hear from me for a while, she starts calling Lara."

His face was only inches from mine. He leaned toward me and kissed me, gently at first, then more passionately, his lips parting as he searched for my tongue. I felt the now-familiar heat throughout my body.

After a minute or so we pulled away.

"I meant to do that earlier, like when you walked through the door," he told me.

"Well, I'm not leaving anytime soon, so—"

He smiled broadly.

I hesitated for a second. "I'm going to get a glass of water, is that OK?"

"I'll get it for you." Tarek went into the kitchen and got two glasses of water, handing me mine.

"So what are you cooking?" I asked him. "Because it's making me so hungry." I walked over to the counter and looked in the dishes. I was always nosy like that about food. My mother laughed at me because whenever I walked into her house, I automatically went to the stove or the oven to look at what she was cooking. My mother was an excellent cook.

He grinned. "I have chicken, and I have tabbouleh."

"Oh my God." I might have to marry him, I thought, chuckling.

"What's so funny?"

"Nothing." I was leaning with my back against the counter and he was a couple of feet away from me. "I was thinking that my mother always laughs at me because I always want to know what she's cooking." Well, that was a half-truth.

He smiled.

"Tell me something," I said then.

"Sure."

I hesitated for a second. "You sounded a little tense on the phone. Is everything OK?"

He raised his eyebrows, then sighed a long sigh.

"More or less," he answered.

"Tarek, if you don't want to tell me, I'm not going to make you."

He smiled at me. "It's kind of a long story."

"I have time," I said in response, taking a sip of water.

He put his glass on the counter and came over to me, putting his hands at my waist.

"I don't want you to worry about it."

"OK, I won't but you do realize that if you don't tell me, I will worry more than if you *do* tell me."

He laughed lightly. "That's right. You'll think the worst since you're a pessimist."

"Exactly." I put my arms around his neck and kissed him once, then hugged him to me. It seemed to me that, if we were going to do this, then we should tell each other things. There was a lot that I didn't remember, but I did remember that my parents' relationship had been solid, and one of the reasons why was that they talked to each other about both the good and bad things, and that they unloaded their concerns on each other when they had to.

I was looking at him and could see in his eyes when he made the decision to tell me.

"OK, so—" he began, "my mother has two older brothers. They both live in Miami, and they run their own business."

He took a step back. I crossed my arms, listening.

"We're all very close. They helped us after my father died. When I decided to go to law school, they said they would help pay for it. At first, I said no, that I would get loans. But after looking at the tuition and everything, and seeing how much I would have to borrow for three years, the agreement was that I would take out loans for the tuition and they would help pay for living expenses."

"So when you went to school in Miami you had your own place?"

"Yes, because I wanted to live by myself to be able to study. My mother and my sister have hectic lifestyles. My mother works nights often and my sister goes out a lot. And when I'm home they ask me to do stuff, which is fine, but—"

I smiled. "I totally understand. When I go home my mother asks me to take her shopping and grade exams for her."

"She's a teacher?" Tarek asked, curious.

"She teaches Spanish at the local university. But—go on. Sorry for the digression."

"That's OK. You know I like hearing about you."

I smiled and felt myself blushing. "But we were talking about *you*, so—"

He grinned. "So, anyway—at the time they only agreed to help me with that, there was no other agreement. Then I transferred here, mostly because I wanted to be at a better-ranked school in DC or New York, but also because, honestly, I wanted to be away from my family for a little while." He hesitated. "I love them. It's just that—when I live close by them, I get sucked into the family drama and gossip and I don't need that all the time."

I laughed.

"What's so funny?" Tarek asked me.

"That sounds exactly like when I lived in Barcelona, and my aunt called me to complain about my other aunt, and my grandmother called me to complain about my cousins, etc., etc." I paused. "I'm sensing a lot of cross-cultural similarities here."

"I guess that's true." He smiled.

"So are they still helping you financially?" I asked, to get the conversation back on track.

"I took out loans to pay for tuition which, as you know, is about $25,000 a year. But my uncles are paying for most of the rent on this place and the utility bills."

"OK." So that solved the mystery of how he could afford this place.

When he didn't continue right away, I asked, "And are you not comfortable with that?"

"The thing is, Isabel, my uncles are making it clearer that they expect me to go back to Miami after law school and work for them, or at least help them on a part-time basis or something. And I don't want to do that."

"What's the nature of their business?"

"Like, import/export. Actually, they wanted me to work for them after I did the CPA exam. But I didn't."

"I see."

"They keep mentioning it to my mother. That's what we were talking about right now. How I owe them and everything."

"I'm sorry, Tarek."

"It's OK. Honestly, I would rather be independent and I should not have agreed to their help. It was a mistake on my part."

"Well, it's hard to turn down money. I can understand that."

There was a pause.

"So what have *you* done, Isabel? Are you getting loans or—?"

I sighed. "Yes, I'm borrowing money for tuition, through student loans, but, like you said, that's still going to be around $100,000 when I finish school." I could kick myself, thinking about how I could have gone to the state school close by for about one-third of that cost.

"Well, I think you made a really good decision to work full-time and go to school at night. I'm regretting leaving my job to go to law school full-time."

"Yes, but—that also means that I don't have time to do internships and other things, like summer associateships and journal. It's a trade-off."

Tarek changed the subject somewhat. "So have you heard from any of the other firms you interviewed with?"

I shook my head. "It's all a bust. No callbacks."

"I'm sorry."

"It's all right," I shrugged. "I guess it was meant to be that way. Frankly, I'm not sure my boss would have let me take the summer off anyway." Then I had a thought. "So if you don't want your uncles to have a say in what you do after school, could you tell them not to help you anymore, not to send you money?"

"That's what I was talking to my mother about now. She understands but she also told me that they would not like that. They would probably be somewhat *offended*." He over-articulated "offended," as if he loathed the term.

"And you'd have to take out more money in loans."

"Exactly. I'm also thinking about looking for a cheaper apartment when the lease expires."

"When does it expire?" I asked him.

"July 1."

"I'm sorry. It's a difficult situation to be in." It was also sounding more and more like my family. When I had moved into my apartment in Barcelona, my grandparents and my uncles had insisted on coming to paint the entire place. I had protested and they had gotten pissed off. But in the end they had done the painting. Later, I had complained about it to my mother.

"It's OK." He smiled. "Thanks for listening."

"Anytime. You know that."

He took a step forward and ran a hand down my arm. "Thank you."

"OK," I said then, taking control of the situation, "the sooner we study Property, the sooner we can—do other things."

"Like what?" he asked with mock confusion.

"Like have dinner," I smiled.

I won't lie. We did study Property for a little while, but there was a lot of kissing involved.

"She's *smart*," I said, emphasizing the point with my fork. I was telling Tarek about Alyssa.

We had studied Property for a while, and it was around 7 p.m. We had decided to have dinner and were in the kitchen getting the food ready.

"Wait," he stopped me. "Are you saying that she *hides* the fact that she's smart?"

"I think she does," I nodded pensively. Then I told Tarek about the conversation I had had with her the other day. I left out the part where we had talked about Saul.

"She's very observant. I had been thinking that she was a total ditz, but she's not. I mean, she knew I liked you."

"Wait, so you *like* me?" He was smiling at me knowingly.

"Oh, please Tarek, obviously only as a friend."

"Oh, whatever."

I smiled, blushing.

"By the way, I can totally tell when you're blushing," he said, his eyes twinkling.

"Yes, I know! My face turns totally red and it feels hot. I know!"

He stood beside me and put his arm around my waist. "I'm kidding," he said in my ear.

"I know," I told him, raising my shoulder to my ear. "That tickles!"

"Oh, you're ticklish?"

"Yes!"

"Well, that's good to know."

"Anyway, we were talking about Alyssa." I tried to focus so that I wouldn't jump him right here. But I couldn't help turning my face and kissing him quickly.

"That's right, I'm sorry," he apologized.

"Why do you think she would hide the fact that she's smart?"

"Well, she's young and impressionable. Maybe she thinks that's not what men want."

"It's a sad day if that's the case." I pursed my lips. "I think there's more to her. I also think it's interesting that she doesn't seem to have any female friends. She only hangs around guys."

"*You* only hang around guys." Tarek smiled.

"And Melanie, and my sisters," I corrected.

He reconsidered. "Well, you *mostly* hang around guys."

"That's true." I paused. "You know why that is, right?"

He seemed pensive for a second. "Not really, no."

"Women can be really hard on each other, critical, especially over-achieving, hyper-competitive Millennial types in law school."

"That certainly seems to be the case," Tarek agreed.

"Melanie and I were actually drawn to each other as friends because we were different. We're older and we're in different places in our lives. We also both work full-time. Law school isn't the end-all of our existence."

"You *are* competitive, though, Isabel."

"Oh, I'm not denying that. I mean, I refuse to help people who don't help *me*, or whose only goal is to use me. Anyway, like *you're* not competitive."

"I wasn't being critical when I said that, you know?"

I looked at him.

He continued. "Because you're also generous to the people you care about." He hesitated. "You help Eric with Crim Law all the time, and you share your notes with him and Josh and Dinesh."

I shrugged. "Of course, they're my friends."

Tarek smiled. "Exactly."

I smiled then, too. "Hey, I have to tell you something." I leaned toward his ear and put my hand on his chest. "I—am—*starving*."

He laughed. "OK, I got it. Would you like any wine?"

Now I laughed, a deep-throated laugh. My sides hurt.

"What's so funny?" Tarek was surprised.

"Dude, how many times have I been here and you've never offered me wine! That can only mean one thing!"

"What does it mean?"

"That you want me drunk!"

"I do *not*!"

"Yes, I'll have some wine. Whatever you have open."

"Oh," Tarek raised his eyebrows, "so you *want* to get drunk?"

I laughed again. "Just one glass." I rolled my eyes. "Oh my God."

After dinner, we were sitting on his sofa with the television on. I was pleasantly full.

"Tarek, that was really good. Thank you."

"Of course. Would you like some more wine?" he asked, smiling.

"A little bit. I don't want to fall asleep."

I had leaned back against the cushions, my legs crossed and my right hand leaning lazily against Tarek's chest. The television was on and the lights were strategically low.

As he poured more wine into my glass, I told him, "I don't have to be drunk to sleep with you, you know? I think we've established that."

"Oh, I'm sure it helps, though," he said.

I laughed, then sat up and put my wine glass on the coffee table. Then he put his arm around my shoulders and I leaned into him.

He pulled me to him and kissed me. Then every cell in my entire body became alert.

I ran my tongue along his lower lip, and suddenly his tongue was in my mouth and mine was in his. Then my hand was in his hair, wound around his curls, and both his arms were around me. I hooked one leg around him and it was like when we were dancing that one night, and there was no space between our bodies. Except that this time there was no one else around.

It went on like that for a little while, making me incredibly hot. Tarek ran his hand along my side. Then I took his hand and ran it across my breast, on top of my clothes.

He kissed my neck and was touching my breast with the back of his hand, over the nipple, which became instantly hard. Then I pulled him even closer to me and wrapped my arms around his chest, laying my head on his shoulder and nuzzling his neck.

My shirt had become untucked in the back and Tarek put his hand underneath, massaging my back a little bit.

"Oh my God," I said softly.

"Isabel, are you OK?" he asked me.

"Hm-mm," I murmured.

"You are the sexiest woman I have ever seen," he told me.

I laughed lightly, enjoying the compliment.

He leaned back against the sofa with his arms around me and I put my head against his chest. A few moments passed.

"Let's go to bed," Tarek whispered then in my ear.

I kissed his neck and breathed, "OK."

I was walking to campus with a huge smile on my face. The entire weekend had felt like a dream.

The day before I had driven to Lara's house and had lunch out with her. When I told her what I wanted to talk about, she made Patrick stay home.

"It would be TMI for him, anyway," she had told me.

I felt bad but not bad enough to insist that he come with us.

I told Lara everything.

"Oh my God, I can't believe you did that!" she had exclaimed, her mouth full of risotto. We had gone out to some posh Italian place.

"Do what?" I had asked her. What part was she talking about?

"Go over to his apartment like that, to tell him how you felt about him!" She paused, chewing. "I can't believe that you did that! That's so unlike you."

I sighed. "I know—" My voice trailed off, as I made the belated realization. "It *is* unlike me."

"You are crazy about him!"

"Yeah, I am."

"We all told you that he liked you! You didn't believe us!"

"I'm a pessimist," I shrugged, as if that explained everything about me.

"Yeah, but come on! You couldn't read the signs?" She had put her fork down. "Oooo, Isabel has a boyfriend," she teased.

"Do I really?"

"What do you mean?" Her brows had furrowed.

"Well, at what point do you start referring to a guy as your boyfriend?" She had been pensive for a moment. "I guess it depends. I mean, it certainly sounds like that's what's going on." She smiled a bit deviously. "Sounds like you haven't had the talk yet."

I had rolled my eyes and sighed. "I knew you would bring this up." The talk. The 'where are we headed? what are we?' "talk."

"I'm not having that yet. It's too soon," I had said. "I don't *need* to have it. I'm happy with how things are for the moment."

Lara had been happy for me, positive as always. That's why I needed to be around her.

I was happy too. But the pessimist in me was always waiting for the other shoe to drop. If this didn't work out, then Tarek and I would have to face each other at school. And next semester we would have all of the same classes again. But I quickly pushed that thought from my mind, determined not to derail this before it even started.

Now, on Monday, walking up the stairs to the law school building, I got suddenly nervous. How should I behave when I saw Tarek? What should I say?

Oh my God! I thought. I should've asked Lara all this yesterday, but I forgot. Would he kiss me in front of everyone?!

My mouth became dry all of a sudden. *Relax*, I told myself. But that was easier said than done.

I walked into the building, passing the elevator and the staircase, into the lounge area. Then I saw him, all gorgeous and well-groomed wearing a black V-neck sweater.

I walked toward the table where he was sitting with a bit of trepidation, thinking about how to do this. I didn't walk as surreptitiously as he did; he saw me before I sat down.

"Well, hello," he said as I sat down next to him, giving me a smile.

I could feel myself blushing and it was worse than ever because now I knew that he could tell when I was blushing.

I couldn't look at him at first. I put my hand to my forehead and ran it nervously through my hair, ending up with my hand at my chin.

Then I looked at him.

"Hi," I said.

He put his arm around my shoulders and leaned over. I was deathly afraid that he was going to kiss me and I would be completely mortified because everyone would see.

But he said into my ear, "I won't kiss you here if you don't want me to."

I sighed. "I don't want everyone to know my business." I placed the back of my hand against his chest. "I mean, everyone will find out eventually because this place is like high school and gossip is the principal commodity." He chuckled at that. "But there's no reason for us to broadcast it. I mean—"

"Isabel, you don't have to explain. I understand."

"If someone were to ask me about it, I wouldn't lie."

"And if someone asks *me* about it—?" Tarek began.

"Then don't lie. I mean, say whatever you want but you don't have to lie for me." I paused. "Why? Has anyone said anything to you?"

"Not recently."

"So someone said something to you a while ago?"

"Well, Sameer thinks we're—together like that. He's thought that for a while."

"I don't care what he thinks."

"Isabel, don't worry about him."

"The truth is," I said then, "I had already forgotten about him."

"Really?"

"Yeah." Our faces were still close together. I inhaled. "Oh my God, you smell so good," I breathed.

Then there was a huge noise. We both practically jumped out of our chairs.

Eric had dropped his textbooks on our table. He looked stressed.

I had automatically sat up straight, looking ahead. I felt like Eric had caught us doing something we weren't supposed to be doing. Tarek took his time removing his arm from around my shoulders.

If Eric had seen us or noticed our posture, he didn't say anything. Josh was with him, and he was much more observant; he stole an amused look at me. I rolled my eyes.

"Sorry, are we interrupting something?" Josh asked.

"No," I said automatically. I couldn't help sneaking a look sideways at Tarek, who smiled at me.

Eric sat down with a heavy sigh. He lay his head on the table. Josh sat down too.

Tarek looked at me questioningly. I sighed. I thought I knew what this was about.

I turned to Tarek. "Eric gets like this once a semester. It's his *modus operandi*. He goofs off the first half, then midway through the semester, he starts to freak out that he hasn't been serious enough and that he hasn't done enough reading."

"I see." Tarek was smiling.

"Actually, it's to his credit," I said then. "Most people goof off the entire semester and don't freak out like this until the week before the exam."

"But I haven't done shit, Isabel!" Eric looked up at me. "I haven't done any of the reading!"

"You always say that! *Relax*. You know I'll give you my outlines." Then something occurred to me. "Well, I'll have to check with him," I motioned to Tarek, "since we're doing our outlines together."

"It's fine," Tarek said then, with a look that told me I was crazy for asking his permission.

"Isabel, your outlines are like ninety pages long! That won't help me!" Eric sounded desperate, but I wasn't worried. We went through this every semester.

"Eric, I'm in the same boat as you," Josh said then.

"Your grades don't have to be that great, because you already have work experience and a Ph.D.," Eric said.

"Well, thanks," Josh said sarcastically.

"Josh's grades are fine, and yours are fine, and you will do fine," I told Eric. "We'll send you what we have of our outlines so far and you'll have plenty of time to go over them before exams."

Eric smiled weakly. "OK, thanks."

Jesus, it's like having a kid, I thought.

Eric changed the subject then. He looked at me and Tarek. "So what did you guys do this weekend?"

I froze, then raised my eyes to meet Eric's. His question was innocuous. I didn't see any ulterior motives in his eyes. He was asking for the sake of asking, or to get his mind off of studying. But I didn't know how to answer.

"Just did some outlining," Tarek said, shrugging.

And we had sex, like, five or six times, I thought, tallying up in my head. But other than that, it was pretty uneventful.

"I saw my sister yesterday," I said, then looked down.

Then I looked up and saw Josh's face. He was looking at me intently, smirking, then looked quickly at Tarek and back at me, obviously reading between the lines.

"It's time for class, guys," I said then. "Get up, Eric. Walk it off. You'll be fine."

He sighed a long sigh. Typical Brazilian, totally dramatic. "If you say so," he told me.

When we got to class, Dinesh was there.

I had thought that class that evening was going to be uneventful, but I was wrong.

"How was your weekend?" Dinesh asked me.

"Oh my God, why is everyone so interested in my weekend all of a sudden?" I was freaking out a little.

"Well, I'm sorry." Dinesh was laughing, with his hands up in the air. "It was just a question."

"It was fine. I studied. I saw my sister yesterday."

"Alicia said that she saw you out on Friday night," Dinesh told me.

"Since when the hell does she care about my life?" I said with annoyance. "Dude, she doesn't even know who I am!" When could Alicia have seen me? I only drove to Tarek's that night.

Alicia had started law school with us. She was a slight, dark-haired girl who dressed to show off her body. She was only nice to people when she wanted something from them. I knew who she was, but hadn't thought that she knew who I was.

"Everyone knows who you are, Isabel," Eric said then.

"That's not true," I countered.

"Actually, it is true, I'm afraid," Tarek said.

"Oh, really?" I looked at him.

"Yes, whenever I talk about you, people always know who you are."

I smiled at him. There was no way I could be mad at him today. I made a point of remembering to ask him later what exactly he talked about when he talked to people about me.

"She said she saw you driving through Arlington," Dinesh said. Why he couldn't shut up, I had no idea.

"Isabel, if you were in Arlington on Friday night, you could've told me!" Eric said. He lived in Arlington. "Who were you with?"

I couldn't see any way out of this now. They would be like scavenger dogs on fresh meat until they got the answer out of me.

"With him," I motioned to Tarek while still typing on my laptop, trying to make it appear as if it weren't a big deal.

"Are you serious?" Eric said.

I heard Dinesh snicker next to me and gave him a look of death. I was wondering what else Alicia had told Dinesh. If she had said something else, Dinesh wasn't mentioning it.

"Yeah, so what? I told you that we were studying."

"You were studying on Friday night?"

"No," Tarek said.

"Yes," I said at the same time he did. I glared at him, spreading my hands in a way that asked, What the hell?

Josh, Eric, and Dinesh all erupted in laughter.

"We weren't studying on *Friday*," Tarek explained. I guess he thought that he was helping me, but I felt like this was getting out of control. "We studied on Saturday and we had dinner on Friday."

Great. Another lie I would have to keep track of.

"So how come you left that part out when I asked you what you did this past weekend?" Eric asked me.

"Because it's not a big deal. So the hell what? I have dinner with Josh occasionally."

"You haven't had dinner with me all semester," Josh said.

"Well, you haven't asked me to," I said.

"Oh, so now you have to wait for an invitation to have dinner with me?" Josh was smiling. I could tell that he wasn't really upset, and that he was totally enjoying making me uncomfortable.

"You guys," Tarek said then, looking at all three of them in turn. He was trying to be serious, but there was humor in his eyes. "This entire conversation is juvenile. Just—stop."

There was silence for a few seconds and I dared to hope that was the end of it. But then Eric said very quietly, "Spoken like a man who got some action this weekend." Then Josh and Dinesh were laughing but, thankfully, I didn't think that anyone else had heard that.

"I'm not engaging in this conversation anymore," I said in my best pissed-off voice. But when I looked at my laptop screen again, I was trying hard to suppress a smile.

So much for keeping all this on the down-low.

Thankfully, everyone was relatively quiet for the rest of the night, even at the break. I thought that Eric was still stressed about studying. Oh well, he was so young, he didn't know what stress *was*.

We were on the metro and Eric left at Rosslyn. Tarek and I were standing close together, chatting. Josh and Dinesh weren't bothering us for the moment.

"Do you have plans during the week?" Tarek asked me.

"No, I mean, other than work and class."

"Well," he began, with some hesitation, "would you like to have dinner sometime?"

"Sure, um—Thursday would be best, since I can get to work late on Friday.

Talking about Friday reminded me of something.

"Oh, that reminds me, I wanted to ask you something." I stepped closer to him so that nobody else would hear our conversation. Our faces were practically touching, and it was making me hot. Then I couldn't resist and took his hand loosely in mine. I didn't care that Josh and Dinesh were here. They would know sooner or later anyway.

"If you're free Friday, you could come to the range with me."

"Really?"

"Yeah. But I have to be honest with you. I'm a little nervous about taking you. Will you promise to listen to me?"

"When have I not listened to you?" Tarek asked, with a bit of a devious grin.

I sighed. "Will you promise to listen?"

"Of course."

"OK, when was the last time you shot?"

"A few years ago."

"What did you shoot?"

"Um, rifle."

"OK, what caliber?" I asked.

"I'm not sure. The bullets were really small, I think."

"And it had no kick—I mean, it was easy to handle?"

"Yes."

"OK, .22 caliber probably. Have you ever shot handguns?"

"Yes."

"OK, what kind?" I asked

"I'm not sure. It was with my father."

"OK, so we'll do handguns on Friday."

"Are we going to rent them?" he asked

"No, I'll bring my own."

"How many do you have?"

"Enough for us both to shoot." I looked at him and winked.

The train was arriving at Pentagon City. Tarek and I were leaning into each other. He said in my ear, "I'm not inviting you over only because you have to work tomorrow, but you know that you can come over anytime, right?"

"OK," I said softly.

"Seriously, Isabel, any time you want."

There was something implicit in that statement, but I couldn't quite figure it out. It was like something simmering just below the surface of his words. My intellectual capabilities were clouded at the moment, anyway. With Tarek here, and the law of diminishing returns setting in after working all day and then being in class, I had difficulty thinking straight.

The train was stopping. Tarek squeezed my hand.

"Come here," I said to him. He turned his face more toward mine and I kissed him full on the lips. When he left the train, he was smiling broadly.

When the train was moving again, I heard Josh say, "Isabel."

I exhaled slowly, ready for the teasing that was to come.

"What?" I turned and looked at Josh, as nonchalantly as I could, as if his addressing me were a mere annoyance.

"Is there something that you want to tell us?"

"If there were, don't you think I would have told you already?" Then I softened a bit. Josh and Dinesh were my friends. We had bonded the first year of law school, complaining about people and classes and our dismal employment prospects, and sharing notes.

I moved over to where they were. "Look, guys, you know this is all new territory for me. I don't want people to know my business."

"I'm sorry," Dinesh said. "I shouldn't have said anything in class. I really didn't know. I was only asking about your weekend, honestly."

"I know, it's OK." Then I remembered. "So what did Alicia say about me?"

"She said that she saw you in Arlington. That's it."

I believed him but wondered if that was really all she knew.

"Yeah, well, like I said before, we went out on Friday night."

Dinesh gave me a look as if I were his little sister.

I smirked and shook my head. I didn't see the need to elaborate.

"So you're going out with him?" Josh asked.

I still didn't know how to answer that question.

"I guess." I shrugged.

"What do you mean you guess?" Dinesh asked.

"I haven't like, really gone out with anyone in a long time, so I don't know how to answer that."

"Do you want me to talk to him?" Josh asked.

I was tempted to have him do just that. "No, dude, thanks, but I'm thirty-four years old. I should be able to handle this, more or less."

"Well, it looks like you resolved the prisoner's dilemma in your favor," Josh told me, grinning.

I smiled. "I'm not sure yet. I think the jury's still out on that."

I was still a pessimist, after all.

I got to campus at around 3:30, enjoying the refreshing, cool air.

I had an unofficial agreement with my boss, Martin, that I could skip out early on Wednesdays and Thursdays, when I had a 3:50 class, and make up the time either during the week or from home. Sometimes Martin let me work from home on Wednesdays and Thursdays. It depended on what was going on at work those days. Some days I had swarms of people waiting at my desk to ask me questions.

Why do they want my opinion? I thought, if they usually don't like what I tell them?

Peter had said, "Maybe they're fishing around for the answers they want, or maybe they know that they'll do a good job if they listen to what you have to say."

I preferred the latter possibility, but wasn't sure which was really the case.

The week was going by in a blur. Tuesday had been a repeat of Monday, but the guys had pretty much left Tarek and me alone.

Eric had cornered me at the break during Crim Pro and had asked me point-blank what was going on. That was his style, direct and to the point. That's the American in him, I had thought.

"Don't ask me," I had told him, "I'm still figuring it out."

"I don't want you to get hurt," he had told me.

I had softened when he had said that. He was my friend, like a little brother to me.

"I'll be OK," I had said, smiling and touching his arm.

At the moment, I was actually less worried about "getting hurt," as he put it, and more worried about how to do this, I mean, how to be someone's other half, if that was indeed what was going on.

When I walked into the law school building, I found Tarek in the lounge area, sitting on one of the sofas in the back. I went over and sat next to him, dropping my bag on the floor and taking off my jacket.

"Hey," I said, leaning toward him.

He put his arm around my shoulders and said into my ear, "Isabel, you don't want me to kiss you here but you wear *that*?"

I chuckled, amused at his discomfort. I was wearing an emerald green shirt that wrapped around my torso, showing a bit of cleavage. I caught him looking at my chest.

"Don't look there!" I whispered.

"I can't help it!"

I touched his chest with the back of my hand, right over his nipple. I had done that on purpose.

I rubbed his chest with my hand and said softly, "Maybe I wouldn't mind if you kissed me now."

"*Really*?"

"Well, you'll have to do it to find out for sure." Then I touched his face and we leaned toward each other. I could feel heat rising in my body and my breathing rate increased. I didn't care if anyone else saw.

His lips had barely touched mine when I heard someone clearing his throat, very close to us.

I suddenly noticed that someone was standing right in front of us. I automatically pulled away and looked up. When I saw who it was, I looked down.

Sameer was standing there, with a smug grin on his face. Damn him, what was he smiling about?

I didn't address him right away. My face felt flushed and I was embarrassed.

"Hey," Tarek said to him. "Do you want something?"

Sameer looked at Tarek and then back at me. "She's a little old for you, isn't she?" he said to Tarek.

I rolled my eyes. That's the best you've got? I thought. Then I realized that he was likely speaking in English for my benefit, so that I would know what he said. *Jackass*.

"Don't talk about her like that," Tarek snapped. "If that's all you came over here to say, then you can leave," he said icily.

Sameer crossed his arms. "I don't believe you don't care."

I guessed that Tarek thought that that comment was still about my age, but I knew that Sameer was talking about Saul. His comment suggested that he had believed me when I had lied to him, telling him that I had told Tarek about that. I supposed that that was a good thing, although it still didn't absolve me of the need to tell Tarek at some point.

"Isabel, let's go," Tarek said then. We both stood up and grabbed our stuff.

We were leaving when Sameer said something to Tarek, this time in Arabic. Tarek said something back, looking at Sameer directly in the face. Tarek was pissed off, but under control. If Sameer was telling him about Saul, I didn't know what I was going to do. I looked around for a quick exit and saw no way out.

When Tarek rejoined me, he didn't seem angry with me.

"Are you OK?" I asked him.

"Yes," he said and gave me a warm smile. We were OK, I thought, exhaling. "Don't worry about him."

We walked upstairs to class. Then a thought popped into my head.

"Do I really look that much older than you?" I hadn't thought so, but was beginning to feel self-conscious after Sameer's remark.

Tarek sighed. "No, Isabel. He knows how old you are."

"How does he know how old I am?"

"I told him once, when—when we were still on speaking terms."

"Why would you tell him that?" I was confused.

"He asked me once, or he brought it up or something. I don't remember exactly." He looked at me then, half-smiling. "I talked about you all the time."

I blushed and looked down as we walked.

International Law class went by fairly smoothly. Interestingly, Zara made a point of greeting me when I walked in. Usually she was too shy.

"Hi," I had told her, smiling. She had looked like she was going to say something else, but remained silent. She must think I'm—how had Tarek said that Sameer had said it?—rough around the edges.

Later, when we were walking to Property class, I could hear Eric's voice from the hallway. Damn, he's vocal tonight, I thought.

"Oh, by the way," I said, turning to Tarek as we were about to enter the classroom. We were walking very close together, and he was holding my textbook for me.

"Yes?" he said, smiling.

"You owe me."

"What do I owe you?" He sounded surprised.

"You know," I whispered. "A kiss, because we were interrupted before."

"Oh, yes, you're right."

"Of course. I'm always right."

"And modest, you're very modest," Tarek said.

I shrugged one shoulder. "That too."

When we got to our row, Melanie was there. We smiled at each other.

"Isabel, what's going on?" she asked casually.

"Nothing, same old, you know," I told her.

I caught Josh's look then. His smile and his eyes were saying, Really? There's *nothing* going on?

"Can we go to dinner sometime?" Melanie asked me. "I feel like I haven't seen you in such a long time."

I turned around in my seat to look at her. "I know, I'm sorry," I told her. "Anytime. We can do dinner on a weekend if you want. Let me know when you're free."

"OK, let me check my calendar and I'll let you know." Melanie's social calendar was always packed. Mine was almost always open, except for lately. I smiled at the thought.

"Great." It was true; we hadn't really talked in awhile. I missed having Melanie in all of my classes.

I turned back around to face forward and, at that moment, Tarek leaned toward me, his face right next to mine.

"Hey, one thing," he said.

"Dude, why are you all up in my curtilage?" I said playfully, turning my face to look at him.

And that was my grand mistake, because when I did that, he kissed me full on the lips, in front of God and everyone. And the worst thing was, I couldn't pull away. Before I could even think about acting, I was kissing him back.

"Oh my God!" I heard Melanie's exclamation from right behind me.

Then I pulled away, startled and embarrassed.

"They've been like this all week," Dinesh told Melanie, as if it were old news. Then he was laughing, like always.

"Dude!" I said, glaring at him. My face was flushed.

"I ask you what's going on and you tell me nothing!" Melanie raised her voice, incredulous.

"I can't believe you did that!" I said to Tarek, but I couldn't look at him.

"God, get a room!" I heard Eric's voice behind me.

I couldn't handle it anymore. I sank down in my chair as far as I could go, and then put my open Property book over my face so that it was completely covered.

"Isabel, we are definitely going to talk later!" Melanie was saying.

I exhaled a long breath. Yes, *Mom*, I thought. Then the professor started lecturing and I managed to calm down enough to remove the book from my face, even though Dinesh was still chuckling.

After class, I tried to leave quickly but Melanie wasn't having it.

"Wait, wait, wait right there!" she told me, as if she were my mother about to lay me out for arriving home too late.

I looked at Tarek. "Dude, you just got me in so much trouble."

"I'm sorry." He furrowed his brows to give a look of contrition. Well, now I guess everyone knew my business.

Melanie left class with us and started to pepper me with questions, but I put her off, telling her that we would talk later, and that I wasn't ready to discuss it in front of everyone.

"OK, look, I'm sorry. I won't ask again," she said.

"Thank you. We'll talk later, OK?"

We all ended up congregating in the hallway of the lounge area, right in front of the main law school entrance.

Melanie was done asking about me and Tarek but apparently she wasn't done embarrassing me.

"I told you he was your type," she said to me.

"When was that?" Tarek asked, amused.

"The first day I saw you in class," Melanie told him. "I thought, that guy has Isabel Vilanova written all over him."

"Oh my God," I said. "Could you honestly embarrass me any more tonight?"

"I'm sure I could try," Melanie laughed. Then she left to run to the metro, after giving me a hug. Now we were waiting for Josh, who was, as always, talking to some girl.

Then I noticed that he was talking to Alyssa.

"Hey, we're waiting for you over here," I called to him.

"Oh, I was waiting for *you*," he said with a knowing smile. Eric was with him.

I rolled my eyes.

We went over to Josh and Eric. Alyssa met my eyes and smiled. But it wasn't a cruel smile. In the past, those were the only kind of smiles we usually exchanged with each other.

"I saw you took my advice," she said. I thought that there was a bit of warmth in her voice.

"About what?" I asked.

"I think you know." Her eyes were bright and her smile was genuine.

In that moment, she reminded me of my younger sister Ariel. Not because of the way she looked physically, but because of the way she held herself, and the expression on her face. Alyssa appeared to be more self-confident than I had ever seen her. I smiled back.

"It's like you said," I told her. "Time waits for no man."

Her smile grew broader.

EIGHTH WEEK: **FRIDAY**

The rest of the week went by in a flash. On Thursday, I had dinner with Tarek at his apartment. We ordered food and talked for a while. I couldn't lie to Lara when we talked the next day. There had also been some physical activity.

Tonight we were going to the shooting range. I was a little nervous about taking him but we would take it slow.

I was also excited as I walked in my apartment door. I changed quickly, putting on jeans and a T-shirt with a sweatshirt. It was chilly outside and the range didn't have heat, so it would be cold inside too.

I prepared my bag, with a couple of pairs of safety glasses and earplugs. I also had a couple pairs of the electronic "ear muffs" to cancel the noise at the range.

I took out three firearms and put them, unloaded, in my carrying case. I left the case and my bag with the rest of the stuff in my bedroom.

I ordered pizza, because I had nothing prepared in the fridge and we had decided to eat in, then sat down on my sofa to wait.

I sighed. It was a weird feeling not to have anything to do except wait. I wasn't used to it. In fact, I wasn't sure what to do with myself after law school. There would be the bar to study for, but after that, how else was I going to occupy my time? I guess I would need to find a part-time job.

I still wasn't having much luck with interviews. I had had a couple of offers for unpaid internships with government agencies during the spring semester, but couldn't justify taking them and foregoing a salary. Tarek and I thought differently about that. His recommendation was that I could do an internship two or three days a week, and work only two or three days a week, and that way I would have a partial salary. But I still wasn't totally convinced that Martin would let me work only part-time for a couple of months. Tarek thought that I should at least ask him, and I was still debating it. The thing was, I had heard that most government agencies were not hiring entry-level attorneys, so I figured that logically these unpaid internships would not lead to full-time attorney jobs, which is what I wanted. So then why do them? It was true that they would be good experience and would allow me to make networking contacts.

I was still pondering what to do when my doorbell rang.

I opened the door for Tarek.

"I'm disappointed," I said, with a look of mock sadness.

"Oh?" Tarek raised an eyebrow.

"I thought you were the pizza delivery guy."

"I'm sorry." He gave me a wry smile.

"Come here," I said, pulling him inside and closing the door.

"Your neighbor let me in downstairs," he told me.

"I know, they let anyone in off the street." I kissed him, leaning against his body, and he put his arms around me.

"Oh, your face is cold!" I said.

"I know, I'm sorry. It's cold outside."

"I'll make tea."

The pizza arrived shortly after that and, as we ate, I explained to him all the rules at the shooting range. They were numerous, and all designed for safety.

"Never load a gun until you're ready to use it. And never put your finger on the trigger until you're ready to shoot, OK?"

"Got it," he said.

"And always keep the gun pointed in a safe direction, i.e., away from people, animals, etc., even if you know that it's not loaded."

"OK," he nodded.

"I'll show you how to check if they're loaded or not. One of the ones I have has a safety switch. I'll show it to you when we're there."

"How long are we going to be there?"

"An hour, hour and a half maybe. They're open until ten, so—" I shrugged. "And it'll be empty tonight."

When we were ready to go, I went to my bedroom to get all my stuff.

"OK, can you carry this bag?" I said to Tarek, handing him my small duffel bag with the earplugs and other stuff.

"Sure."

"And I'll carry this case." I knelt down to pick up the case.

"Nice visual of your tattoo," Tarek said seductively.

My shirt must have come untucked.

I stood up quickly. "Dude, I need you to focus tonight. No distractions. Promise me you can do that."

"I promise."

"OK, then let's go shoot."

As I had suspected, there were very few people at the range. It was always like this on Friday nights. Most "normal" people were out partying, or maybe relaxing at home watching television after a long week. That was the reason I almost always went on Fridays.

There were three gentlemen behind the counter. I handed my card to the youngest one. I had known him for a while from my visits to the range. He was of medium height, kind of stocky, with shoulder-length dark hair.

"Hey, Isabel," he said. "I haven't seen you here in a while."

I smiled. "Yeah, I've been busy. I'll need to get a guest pass for him, please," I said as I motioned to Tarek.

"Oh, is this your boyfriend?" the guy behind the counter asked, looking at Tarek and then back at me, as he handed me the visitor pass. He seemed overly curious.

I smiled, then handed Tarek the card to fill out as I shrugged and said, "Whatever."

He looked kind of embarrassed, not having expected that answer. "Sorry," he said, "I've never seen you with anybody before."

"Yeah, I get that a lot," Tarek said, smiling.

I rolled my eyes. "Fill that out, please," I said to him.

He completed the guest card.

As we picked up our stuff and walked away, he turned toward me, with his face close to mine. From his half-smile, I knew exactly what he was going to say.

"You're cute when you blush."

I had been right. I sighed.

"Tarek, tonight we're all business. I can't have you all wigged out on me in there."

"All what?"

"All—I can't have you joking around or anything. Listen to me and do what I tell you."

"Yes, Ma'am," he nodded.

Then we both smiled.

The range was pretty small, and you could smell the lead dust every-where. It was cold, as I had expected. We had on sweaters and jackets and caps.

When we were at our lane, I opened my case and contemplated my three handguns.

"OK," I said, "I haven't taught anyone to shoot in a while, but I am an NRA-certified instructor so—"

"You are?"

"Yeah, I figure if the attorney thing doesn't work out, I can always do that on the side."

Tarek smiled. "Sounds like a plan."

"So you've shot before, right?" I asked him, half-yelling over the noise of the range.

"Yes, I've shot a 9-millimeter before," he said, looking at the one that I had brought.

"Oh, OK, so we can start with that one."

"Are these all the guns you have?" he asked me.

I smiled. "They're all the *handguns* that I have."

"I see." He paused. "What are you afraid of?"

I looked at him. "Nothing," I said firmly. "Look," I said then, "do you remember how to load this?"

"I think so."

"OK, I'm going to go over everything anyway."

I showed him how to load the 9-millimeter, where the safety switch was, and how to hold it. Then I ejected the magazine. I would load it again right before I fired.

"OK, this is a semiautomatic, so that means that you load it and pull the back slide on top of the barrel. That loads the bullet into the firing cham-ber." I demonstrated. "Now you can fire the entire clip, OK?"

"Got it."

"If your arms get tired from holding it up, bring your arms into your chest like this," I said, demonstrating by bending my elbows and drawing them to my sides. "Above all, take your time, there's no rush."

I put the target sheet that I had purchased up on the rail and hit the button to send it way back.

"Is thirty yards OK?" I asked Tarek.

"Sure."

"OK, I'm going to shoot a clip first. If the gun doesn't fire when you pull the trigger, keep it pointing down range and count to thirty. That's what you're supposed to do," I explained. "Once in a while when you pull the trigger, the bullet doesn't eject completely from the chamber and it doesn't fire."

"OK."

I loaded the 9-millimeter.

"All right, stand back."

He complied.

I pointed the firearm down range and aimed. After years of practice, my hands were pretty steady. I always took my time. When I was here at the range, ready to fire, there was nothing else in the world except for me, my firearm and the target. It required total concentration, such that it cleared the mind. I put everything else out of my mind, law school, my father, my mother, work, my problems, everything.

I fired once, twice, three times. The third time, a shell casing fell on my head, but I hardly noticed. I fired the rest of the bullets and then brought the gun down, carefully ejecting the magazine.

Then I looked at the target and nodded. "Not bad," I said out loud.

"Not bad?" Tarek said then. "You've got one hole in the center of the target. It doesn't get any better than that. That's pretty impressive."

I looked at him. "Well, I've been doing this for twenty years."

"Really?"

"Tarek, my father had three girls." I smiled. By that I meant that I supposed that I had been his son surrogate. "Your turn."

I was glad to see that he took his time loading and firing. I didn't want him to be impatient. I checked and corrected his posture.

"OK, you're good," I told him. "Whenever you're ready."

His aim was better than I had been expecting. He must have remembered enough from the last time he shot.

Then I heard the familiar click.

"You're empty," I said, putting my hand on his arm. "You can't really see it from your angle, but the back part of the barrel is all the way back, see?" I moved his hands downward.

"OK."

"How does it feel?" I asked him.

"Good." He smiled at me.

"Is it too much kick? Could you handle something with more recoil?"

"Oh, yeah."

"OK, let's shoot this one a little more. Then we'll try my revolver."

We each shot the 9-millimeter a couple more times. Then I put it away and took out the revolver.

"Now, the trigger on this gun is really heavy. This gun is meant for personal protection. It's meant to be carried loaded in like a purse or something. So the safety mechanism is the heavy trigger pull. It's pretty much impossible for this gun to fire accidentally."

"Do you carry this with you?" Tarek asked me.

"Not always. I have a concealed carry permit, so I can. But the District doesn't recognize Virginia concealed carry permits, so I can't carry it there." I paused, thinking. "I've never carried when I've been hanging out with you, if that's what you're wondering about."

"I'm assuming you would tell me if you did."

"I would." I winked at him.

I showed him how to load the revolver. "You hold it the same way as the 9-millimeter." I looked at him. "You got this?"

He looked at me and nodded.

"OK, I'll shoot first."

The grip on this gun was smaller. The trigger was so heavy that my hands were always sore after shooting it.

When I was done I studied the target and nodded. "That's all right." Most of my shots had been around dead center, with one outlier a little to the right of center.

"Wow," Tarek said, looking at me.

"I haven't shot this one in a while, that's why the random bullet off-center," I explained. "Your turn. First, load it."

He loaded it properly. It was easier to load than the 9-millimeter. "So is this what they call a .38 special?" he asked me.

"Well, .38 special refers to the type of bullet." I picked one up. "See, here it's stamped .38 special on the bottom."

"I see."

"OK, listen. Like I said, the trigger is really heavy, so be patient. Your hand will be sore from shooting this." I hesitated. "Got it?"

"*Sí, Señora.*"

"*Señorita,*" I corrected. "Jesus."

"Oh, sorry."

"Just concentrate."

He took his time, shot once and then shook his right hand. "Oh my God!"

"I told you, Tarek! The trigger's super heavy."

"But you made it look so easy!"

"Because I've been shooting that gun for years!" Then I became serious. "Are you OK? You don't have to shoot the rest of the bullets."

He looked at me and smiled. "I'm all right."

"Dude, don't go all macho on me now."

"I'm not. Don't worry."

When he was done, I took the gun from him and he shook out his right hand. I looked at the target, then at Tarek.

"You've never shot a revolver before, right?" I asked him.

"No," he shook his head.

"Well, it's not bad for your first time," I said, and couldn't help smiling.

He smiled back at me a little suggestively.

We shot the 9-millimeter again and then called it a day. It was about 9:45 and the range would be closing soon.

"That's a wrap," I said.

We loaded everything in my car and headed back to my apartment.

"So what do you think?" I asked Tarek when we were in the car.

"You're a good teacher," he told me.

"Thanks. I try. You did pretty well." I paused. "You were holding out on me."

"What do you mean?"

"You made it sound like you didn't know how to shoot at all."

"I haven't been shooting that much. The last time was with my father."

What else was he holding out on? I thought, stealing a look at him.

He caught me looking. "What?" he said, smiling.

I suddenly felt a surge of emotion for him. Maybe I felt that way because he had mentioned his father. I wasn't sure. "Nothing," I smiled back.

Nice time to go all googly, I thought then.

When we were back inside my apartment, I put the kettle on.

"Can you watch the kettle?" I asked Tarek. "I'm going to clean the guns."

"Sure."

I cleaned them in the bathroom, since it was certainly more hygienic than cleaning them in the kitchen.

"Do you clean them every time you shoot them?" Tarek was standing in the doorway between the bathroom and my bedroom.

"Not every time."

I finished and washed my hands, then put my firearms back in my safe.

"So where are the rest of your firearms?" Tarek asked me. He was still standing in the door frame.

"In the closet, locked up."

"So you have what—rifles?"

I looked at him and smiled. "Maybe. Or maybe I have a grenade launcher."

He laughed. "That would be something."

We walked into the kitchen together. I went over and put my hands over my mug of tea, watching the steam rise and warming up a little. Tarek came to stand next to me.

"Thanks for coming with me," I told him.

"Well, thanks for taking me."

"You know I like spending time with you."

He smiled and leaned over and kissed me. I kissed him back and leaned into him, snaking my arms around his neck.

Then I remembered something.

"Oh! We'll have to shower. I mean—not like together! I mean, you have to shower when you get home. But—because of the lead residue, it's on your clothes and everything."

Tarek smiled. "You're cute when you're discombobulated."

"Oh, I wish I had never taught you that word."

He laughed. "Too late." Then he touched my face. "I should've known you had guns and a tattoo the first time I saw you."

"Really?"

"Yes, when I first saw you, you walked into the law school building as if you owned the place."

I chuckled. "I feel like I *do* own the place, with the amount of tuition I'm paying." But something was nagging at me. "Wait, that wasn't the first time you saw me. It was in class, the first day of class."

Tarek sighed and looked down. I thought he looked a bit nervous, like I had discovered something that he hadn't wanted me to know. We still had our arms around each other. When he looked back up at me, I saw the hint of some emotion in his eyes but wasn't sure what it was.

"Are you all right? Did I say something?" I said, concerned.

"No, no," he said quickly. "That wasn't the first time I saw you, Isabel."

I looked at him questioningly.

He continued. "The first time I saw you was earlier in the day, when you walked into the law school building."

"Are you serious?"

"Yes."

"And?" I prompted.

He sighed. "You were wearing this dark suit and green blouse. You looked incredible."

"Go on." I couldn't help smiling.

"Nothing. I just—" now *he* was discombobulated. "I was—kind of hoping that you had the same class as I did. And when I walked into Crim Pro, I—I looked for you."

"You did?" I said with genuine surprise.

"And then I saw you, and sat next to you."

"You are such a liar." I couldn't believe it.

"No, it's true. When I first saw you downstairs, I was with Sameer and Zara, and they both noticed me, um—"

"Checking me out?" I offered.

"Yes," he admitted. "So you could ask *them*."

"You're incredible."

He smiled and I kissed him.

A few minutes later, we were drinking our tea on the sofa, when he asked me a question that surprised me.

"So—the first day of class, how come you let me have Josh's seat?"

"How do you know that I gave you his seat?" I crossed my arms.

"He told me."

I sighed. I was going to have to staple Josh's mouth shut. "OK. First, what has Josh told you about me?" I was a little bit worried about that, but figured that Josh was savvy enough not to have slipped and mentioned anything about any of my past indiscretions.

"Not much, Isabel."

"Well, I know that you asked him if I had recently been dating anyone."

"He told you that?" Tarek was surprised.

"Yes, because I specifically asked him what he had told you about me.

And I also threatened him." I paused, smiling. "And I guess now I know why you were so interested."

Tarek looked away and sighed, but couldn't help grinning.

I put my lips against his ear. "Don't worry. If you only knew what I wanted to do to you when I first saw you—"

"*Really?*" He breathed the next words into my ear, "Well you could show me."

My whole body shuddered. Then he chuckled. I guess he figured that my shudder hadn't been because I was cold.

"Oh my God, you are so bad," I said, rising from the sofa.

"I'm going to shower," I announced, turning away from him. Then I cocked my head around to look at him, raising my eyebrows in a direct challenge. "Are you coming?"

I woke up very slowly on Saturday morning. I had dreamed about my father. I hardly ever dreamed about him. In fact, I couldn't remember the last time. When I was fully awake, I struggled to remember what the dream had been about.

In the dream, I remembered that he and I had been chatting in Spanish. I remembered his Castilian accent and the way his s's sounded like z's and he pronounced the c's and z's as a "th" sound.

I was trying to remember what we had talked about. In my dream, he had looked like he did right before he had passed away, young. Well, he had been in his forties at the time, and I considered that young. In a couple more years, I would be staring forty right in the face.

What was he telling me? I thought. I tried to remember.

Deberías hablar con tu madre más a menudo, he had said.

Yes, I know I should talk to her more often, I thought then. But it's too painful. Talking to me makes her remember. I don't want her to remember.

No tengas miedo.

"About what?" I had asked him. "What should I not be afraid of? What?!"

But then I had woken up, slightly unsettled.

What did he mean? I wasn't afraid of anything.

That's not true, I thought almost immediately.

I closed my eyes and opened them again. It was all moot. My father wasn't around. I missed him every day. And this had only been a dream.

I wanted to stay in bed and avoid the chilly air. I pulled the covers up and almost completely over my head. Then Tarek was pulling me against his chest.

Things had been going really well between us, but it had also only been one week. The pessimist in me thought, Give him time. Sooner or later he'll come to realize that I'm too high-maintenance.

Interestingly enough, Tarek already knew a lot about me. In fact, he knew more about me than Josh or Eric did. And it was scary how quickly that had happened. I did the math. We had known each other for two months. I had known Josh and Eric for almost two-and-a-half years.

Well, I knew stuff about him too, but I always wanted to know more.

"What time is it?" Tarek asked me, stroking my shoulder.

"Too early to get up," I whined. "I need to sleep in. I can't sleep in during the week like some people."

Tarek chuckled. "Yeah, I'm usually up late, so I do tend to sleep in."

"*Millennial.*" I emphasized the word, teasing him. "Of course, you don't have a job to go to," I said, smiling. Then I became more serious. "Is that by choice or—?"

"My staying up late?" he asked to clarify.

"Yes. Do you have trouble sleeping?

"Sometimes. I mean, usually I sleep OK. But after class at night, sometimes your mind's been working all day and—"

"It's difficult to turn it off and sleep."

"Right," he said.

"I get that." It happened to me all the time. "So, what do you do when you can't sleep?" I asked him.

"Watch TV, listen to music, or maybe try to read for class. That usually puts me to sleep fairly quickly."

Then he asked me, "What do *you* do?"

"What do I do about what?"

He rolled his eyes. As usual, I was stalling and he knew it.

"What do you do when you can't sleep?"

"I think about things," I shrugged.

"What do you think about?"

"You, mostly." I was immediately embarrassed and he smiled, kissing my forehead. "But I don't know why because thinking about you doesn't help me sleep. In fact, it has the opposite effect."

Then he kissed me full on the lips to shut me up, his hands all over my body.

*   *   *

Later that day, I was preparing to go to Tarek's place. I had told him to go ahead of me so that I could pack things to take with me, and study without distractions for a little while.

It was a little difficult to concentrate, but I finished most of the reading I had wanted to do.

In the afternoon I decided to take the metro. It was a gamble, I realized, and not just because there was going to be weekend track work. I wasn't sure how late I was going to be back home tonight, or if I was going to be back home at all.

I was wearing dark jeans and one of my sexiest tops, a dark burgundy form-fitting top with fitted sleeves and a square neck. When I wore it to work, I always got stares.

Tarek must have liked it too because he stared at me when he saw me in it.

I couldn't help smiling. "What are you staring at?" I asked him.

"Nothing," he said in a way that told me that I knew perfectly well what he was staring at.

He looked incredible. In fact, I had never seen him look so sexy. The funny thing was, he was wearing a shirt that I had seen before. So it wasn't like I was seeing him in it for the first time.

I dropped my backpack on the floor and kissed him. It was all I could do not to tear his clothes off. His hair was all curly and his goatee was neatly trimmed.

"I see you kept the goatee that you were growing out. It looks really good." It was a little fuller, and crept up around his jawline. It was damn sexy.

"Do you like it?" he asked, smiling.

"Yes, very much." That was an understatement.

"Isabel," he began, as I put my textbooks on his coffee table.

"Yeah," I said, opening up my laptop.

"I wanted to know if you wanted to go out to dinner tonight."

"Sure," I smiled. "But I'm wearing jeans. Is that OK?"

"Yeah, of course. You look great." He paused. "You always look great."

I blushed. "You're blind." I sat down on the sofa, and Tarek sat next to me.

"So what are we doing today?" he asked me.

"Whatever you want." I looked at him, and involuntarily raked my eyes over his body. He caught me.

I turned my head away, smiling in embarrassment. "Sorry. I couldn't help it."

"Isabel, come here," he said.

I put my Property book on the table and leaned into him, with my head against his chest. I was totally hot right now. I took a deep breath and sighed.

"Are you OK?" Tarek asked me.

I decided to explain myself. "Tarek, I'm using all my reserves right now not to jump you right here."

He laughed.

"It's true!" I told him.

Then I couldn't stand it anymore and tilted my face upward and kissed his neck, then his jaw and then his mouth.

We actually did manage to study for a little while.

"So how long is your outline for Crim Pro going to be?" Tarek asked me. We were sitting at his dining table.

I sighed. "I'm not sure. It depends how much time I have to spend on it." My outline for Crim Pro was the most developed of all my classes.

"But you typically don't do, like, multiple outlines for the same class?" he asked.

The first semester of law school, the professors taught us to start outlining with one detailed outline, then to shorten the outline until we had about twenty-five pages, and then to shorten it again to one basic one to two page outline with all the main points and significant cases from class. In an open-book exam, students would bring all of their outlines.

But I had a different system. I would make my outlines as detailed as possible, but didn't have time to make multiple outlines, and few students that I knew did. So I ended up using my detailed outlines during the exams. Sometimes my outlines were so long that I tabbed them to be able to flip to pages quickly to find a particular subject.

"No, I don't have time for that," I told Tarek. "And I also don't have time to make super-detailed outlines for all of my classes. So I'll usually make one really detailed outline for my favorite class, which is Crim Pro this semester, and for the other classes my outlines will be less detailed." I paused, about to make a confession. "In fact, I started my outlines for most of last semester's classes literally a week before the exams.

"Really?"

"Yes, I just summarized the main cases and main points from the lectures, and still managed to do well in those classes."

"Wow."

"But I figure, if I *uber* prepare for one class and manage to get an A plus, then that balances out the mediocre grades in the other classes."

Tarek smiled. "By 'mediocre,' you mean A minuses?"

"You got it."

"You're very calculating."

I had to be. I was competing for jobs with students who were almost ten years younger than me.

I smiled back. "Like you didn't know that already. I'm *always* calculating, except—" I stopped, realizing what I was about to say.

But Tarek never missed details like that. "Except what?"

I sighed, then looked at him. "Except for my relationship with you. Nothing about that is calculating."

His grin broadened. "Is that right?"

"Yes." I thought that he seemed to be waiting for more of an explanation from me.

When I didn't give one, he said, "How is it, then?"

I didn't say anything at first. Then I looked outside the window of his apartment. It was a cold day, and the sky had been clear and blue. Now, however, the sun had set a while ago and it was dark. All I could see were lights from the adjoining buildings.

"It's very—emotionally—emotionally charged for me." Then I looked at him again. "That's why I say that it's, like, a new type of endeavor for me. It's not logical."

"What's not logical about it?" He was looking into my eyes. His eyes were sparkling and alive.

"Well, I'm—five years older than you are."

"So?" he shrugged.

"And—I can't think of anything else." I laughed then. "But that's because you're here, and when I'm with you, sometimes I can't think."

He chuckled, and I touched his face, brushing back his curls. He took my hand in his and kissed it.

Then I remembered something I had wanted to ask him.

"Hey, have you heard about the interview for the internship with the Federal Reserve?"

He looked at me intently, raising one eyebrow, as if he were chiding me for changing the subject.

But he answered me anyway. "No, not yet."

"You will. There's still plenty of time." I wanted to ask him about whether he had decided to take the New York or DC offer for next summer, but I didn't dare. I still felt like it wasn't really my business. Instead I continued talking about studying.

"We should also work on our exam language, but there's still time for that," I said. Tarek still had hold of my right hand on the table.

"You mean, like, practice exams?" he said.

"No, I mean writing language explaining concepts that will likely be on the exam, and then taking that language to use for the exam. For example, for our International Law class," I continued, "you write up what the arguments are for and against corporate criminal liability under the Alien Tort Statute, because that's something that we've discussed in class. You take that language to the exam with you, and if you get a question on it, you already have it written out and you copy it, and one question is entirely done without you having to think about it."

"Oh, that's a really good idea." He seemed impressed.

"I know," I said, with an attitude that conveyed, What else would you have expected of me?

"So these are your secrets, huh?" he asked, slightly amused.

"Yes, because I don't have as much time as the day students, and I'm competing with them. Anyway, the exam language isn't a secret. People know about it. Most are too lazy to do it. They're too busy drinking and having sex, which reminds me—" I smiled at my lame attempt at a segue. "When do you want to go to dinner, you know, so that we can have sex afterward?"

He laughed. "Whenever you want."

"I'm ready anytime." I rose from the chair and stretched, then bent down and kissed him. "And by the way," I said to him, "I'm spending the night tonight so—what you were thinking about earlier, there's plenty of time for that later. So don't get annoyed that I changed the subject."

"How do you know what I was thinking about?"

"Well, it's what all men think about when they think about having a woman in their bedroom."

"You mean the fact that they hope their bedroom is clean and straightened out?"

I laughed, then said sarcastically, "Yes, that is exactly what I'm talking about."

We took the metro downtown. Luckily, this time I didn't see anyone that I knew. Not that I knew many people, but Washington, DC wasn't that big of a town. And since last time we had run into my coworker Miguel, I was a little nervous.

When we were on the metro, talking, with me leaning against Tarek and his arm around me, I suddenly realized that I was comfortable. I was comfortable with how we were. Part of me felt that I shouldn't be, that I should be on my guard. But I wasn't listening to that part. I liked him too much.

We went to a restaurant near Dupont Circle. I hadn't been in that area for a long time.

When I told Tarek that, he asked me, "So where do you usually go when you go out?"

"I told you before, I don't go out that much, except when I occasionally go dancing with Josh and Eric, like the other night." That night that we had gone out dancing seemed like ages ago.

"You almost kissed me that night," Tarek said, looking at me as if to gauge my reaction.

"I almost did a lot of things that night," I said without thinking, popping a small bit of bread in my mouth.

He didn't miss a beat, as usual. "What else did you almost do that night?"

I chewed, thinking. I didn't want to talk with my mouth full. After I swallowed I said, "Oh, I think you know," raising an eyebrow.

Tarek smiled knowingly. I felt myself blushing.

"What would you have done if I *had* kissed you that night?" I took a sip of wine.

"You're asking me," Tarek began incredulously, "what a man would have done if a beautiful woman had kissed him late at night?"

"No, I'm not asking what the average man would have done. I'm asking what *you* would have done."

He lowered his voice, leaning his elbows on the table. "I would have kissed you back."

Then I lowered my voice, to make sure that nobody heard me. "And what would you have done if I had dragged you into my bedroom?"

"Is that the other thing you almost did?"

I sighed. I saw no point in denying it. "Yes."

"I would have complied," he said, looking down.

"You have would *complied*?" I laughed. The wine was making me feel warm inside. "What do you think, that I would've given you military orders?!" My voice was a loud whisper.

"Isn't that how it would have been?" he said, with mock earnestness.

"Well, if that's how you would have wanted it, then yes."

"Is that how *you* would have wanted it?"

"I didn't say that," I said quickly.

"I know you didn't, but I'm asking."

"No," I said immediately, then qualified. "Not—ideally." I shrugged. "But I'm open-minded."

Tarek paused, his eyes intent, like he was trying to figure something out.

"How then?"

"How what?" I asked.

He rolled his eyes. I was going to make him say it.

"How would you have wanted it—ideally?" he finally asked.

"Wanted what?" I smiled, drinking from my wine glass.

"Isabel, humor me, please," he said with mild frustration.

"OK, but only because you said please." I paused, exhaling. I had no idea what to say. "It's a loaded question, you know?"

"You don't have to be specific." I saw passion in his expression then. The thought of sleeping with him later was making me crazy.

"Anyway, you know already," I shrugged.

His look was questioning. "Is there anything else I should know?"

I hesitated. "For me it's really about who it's with, rather than—the specifics."

He nodded, still intent. "You still haven't told me one thing."

"What's that?" I asked, my brows furrowing in uncertainty.

"Why you didn't do it."

"Do what?" I wasn't sure what he meant.

"Why you didn't kiss me that night and—do what else you said." He looked away quickly then looked back at me. "Why didn't you? I—I was hoping you would."

His shyness endeared him to me even more.

"Tarek, that answer is easy." When I didn't continue, he looked at me expectantly, elbows on the table, arms crossed.

I sighed and figured I would bring this conversation full circle. "I didn't want it to be only a one-night thing." And then, looking at him, feeling the color rise in my face, the words tumbled out of my mouth. "Because I liked you too much." I looked down.

"And now?" he asked me, smiling.

"Oh, now I don't like you at all," I said, smirking. "*Obviously.*"

He laughed.

We walked to the metro with our arms around each other.

On the metro, I checked my phone.

"Ugh," I sighed.

"What's the matter?" Tarek asked me.

"I have a missed call from my mother," I said with a bit of annoyance. Then I felt guilty for being annoyed with her.

"I'm going to text my sister," I said then, "to tell her that if she talks to my mother to let her know I'm OK. Because otherwise she'll freak if she can't get in touch with me for a couple of days."

I texted Lara.

> Have a missed call from Mom. If you talk to her tell her I'm OK. Am out with Tarek right now.

"Didn't you say that she lives close by?"

"More or less; she lives about an hour from here."

"When was the last time you saw her?"

"About two months ago. The fact is—I really should see her more often." I didn't always feel like I was a good daughter. "But I'm spending all my time with you on the weekends."

I thought about Tarek meeting my mother, but the idea of it made me tremble with dread.

"Plus, she embarasses the shit out of me."

Tarek smiled. "Isabel, everyone's parents embarrass them."

"She's very direct." Then I started thinking out loud. "She's an interesting person, though. She's kind of like me but—nicer." We both smiled. "Sometimes I think that we butt heads so often because we're similar. Lara is better able to deal with her than I am." My mother had been through a lot. I couldn't deny that. "Anyway," I said quickly, to close the subject, "we'll talk about that later."

"OK." He smiled.

When we got back to his apartment, we made tea.

Then I brought something up that I had been meaning to mention. I was aware that it might kill the mood, but it was important that I say something.

"Tarek," I began.

He looked at me.

I sighed. There was no nice way to phrase this. "I feel bad that you always pay for me when we go out." Tonight had been no exception.

"I told you before, Isabel. I don't like letting you pay."

We were standing in the kitchen, waiting for the kettle to boil.

"I know, and I love that about you." Then I freaked out a little, because I had used the word "love" and hadn't intended to. To cover that up, I kept talking. "But it makes me feel bad because—because I'm working and you're not."

He half-smiled. If he was upset that I had brought this up, he didn't appear to be.

"Look, I appreciate you saying that, but I don't mind."

"I know you don't mind, but—let me pay once in a while. Besides—if I buy you dinner then you have to do what I tell you," I added playfully.

"Oh, really?" he raised one eyebrow.

"Well, isn't that how it works?" I said with a bit of sarcasm.

"You know I'll do what you want regardless."

I sucked in air quickly. "Oooo, good answer." I smiled.

"It's an honest answer." His gaze was intense again.

I was leaning against the counter. I took his hand and pulled him over to me. I put my arms around his waist and leaned my head against his chest, listening to his heartbeat.

The kettle boiled then, derailing the moment. We got out mugs and sat on the sofa.

"Do you want the lights off?" Tarek asked me.

I giggled and looked away.

"What?" he said, amused.

"Dude, don't ask *me*. It's *your* house. Turn the lights off if you want."

"But do you *want* me to turn the lights off?" He was smiling now. My discombobulation was amusing to him, as always.

I couldn't answer that question because it was really a proxy for another question, which I refused to answer directly.

But I would say *something*. "All I'll say is, if you want to turn the lights off, then I don't have a problem with that." There, that was a compromise. I was starting to blush furiously, so turning the lights off seemed like a good idea at this point.

"OK, I'll leave them, like, really low. Is that OK?"

"Whatever you want." I was still giggling. Then I turned the television on to distract myself, but turned the volume way down. I couldn't even tell you what was on the television at this point.

In the end, the only light was coming from the hallway on the other side of the living room, and the television.

Tarek sat next to me and I kicked off my heels and rested my legs over his knees. He put his arm around me and I lay my head against his shoulder. Once again, I was very comfortable there.

"You're so funny," I told him.

"Why?"

"You know why."

At that moment I stopped thinking. I put my hand against his chest and found myself unbuttoning the buttons on his shirt. Then I placed my hand inside his shirt to touch his bare chest, but he was wearing a T-shirt underneath. I leaned into him and kissed his neck, moving up to his jaw and then his mouth. He kissed me back, with his hand in my hair, and then our tongues were in each other's mouths. I shivered.

I crawled on top of him, sitting on his lap, with my legs bent on either side of him, and continued unbuttoning his shirt.

Then I looked at him. "Do you mind?" I smiled nervously.

"No, of course not," he whispered.

"Seriously, you can tell me to stop anytime," I said.

"Isabel, you must be crazy if you think I want you to stop." Then he kissed me again.

I finally took his shirt off and lifted his T-shirt a little, running my hands over his chest. I noticed, not for the first time, how more muscular he was than I had previously thought. I was going to have to revise my former opinion of him as "scrawny."

He was rubbing my upper arms and then took my shirt off. He put his hands on my bare waist and, for a moment, I thought that I wasn't going to last any longer.

The kissing was becoming more and more intense and then he was kissing my neck and my shoulder.

"Isabel," he said into my ear.

"Tell me," I whispered.

"Nothing; just saying your name."

"I like it when you say my name." My voice was somewhere between a soft moan and a whisper.

"Is that so?"

"Yes, that is very much so."

He reached around my back to unhook my bra, still kissing my neck. Everywhere his lips touched my skin, I felt like a minor electric shock.

He took my bra off and dropped it on the sofa next to us.

I pulled his T-shirt over his head and got rid of it. Then he pulled me against him and I put both my hands in his hair.

He kissed my neck, my collarbone and then worked his mouth to my breasts. He kissed them tenderly. My nipples had been hard for a while already. He ran his tongue over my left nipple, very slowly, and I shuddered once. I could feel the heat continuing to rise in my body. At this rate, I was not going to last very long.

"Oh my God, I love that," I whispered.

He dragged his mouth across my chest to my other breast and proceeded to do the same there. I hugged him close to my chest, then realized that I was digging my nails into his back. I forced my hands to relax a little.

He was holding me tightly around the waist, then he flipped me over, laying me on my back on the sofa. He ended up leaning over me. I grabbed his face with both hands and brought his mouth down on mine.

Then he was whispering in my ear.

"Isabel, what do you want to do?"

"Oh my God, whatever you want," I said breathlessly.

He looked at me and smiled. "That's not very specific."

It was meant to be unspecific. "I know, I—I'm serious, though."

He kissed me, then ran his hand very carefully from my face to my breast, then to my stomach. My abdominals instinctively tightened.

Then, still kissing me, his hand was at my waist, then unbuckling my belt. He pulled my jeans off; then I sat up.

"Take your pants off," I ordered, making it a command.

"Anything Your Majesty says," he answered, taking off his belt.

"Oh my God, that is so hot that you call me that," I breathed, pulling him to me so that I could kiss him.

He was on top of me in no time, and with the feel of his chest against mine, I lasted no time at all.

We ended up in a sweaty heap. My hair was matted against my face as Tarek kissed my neck. I held him to me, tracing his backbone with a finger.

"Come on, it's late," he told me between kisses. "Let's go to bed."

"OK," I acquiesced.

Tarek gave me one of his T-shirts to wear. It was a bit small for me, and stretched over my breasts.

"Oh my God, you look great in my clothes," he told me, raking his eyes over me.

"What are you talking about?!" I said accusingly, like he was half-crazy. "They're too tight on me!"

"No, they're not. They're perfect." He smiled suggestively.

"Whatever," I said, shaking my head.

In bed, I started chuckling.

"What's so funny?" Tarek asked me.

We had our arms around each other, and my head was against his chest and he was stroking my hair.

"If someone had told me two months ago that we would end up like this, I wouldn't have believed it."

"Like what?" he asked, but I could hear the smile in his voice.

"You know, studying together every weekend," I said, as if there couldn't be any other answer.

He laughed. "Really?"

"Oh yeah. I mean, if someone had told me two months ago that we would end up in bed together, I would have believed *that*." That was actually a true statement. The part I would not have believed would have been if someone had told me two months ago that I would be falling for him now.

"Oh, of course," Tarek said sarcastically.

I kissed his chest, breathing him in. Then I tried to stifle a huge yawn, but didn't do a very good job.

"You're sleepy," Tarek told me.

"And you're observant," I said.

"Oh, my God." He laughed.

"I'm sorry, you set yourself up for that," I said.

"And here I was thinking that now you would be nicer to me."

"I *was* nice to you tonight."

"Well, that's true. I can't argue with that," he said.

"And I can be nice to you tomorrow, too," I said shyly.

He hugged me close. "Good night, Isabel."

I laughed.

"What now?"

"In the past, you told me that via text message," I said, giggling.

"That's true. Would you prefer that I text you good night now?"

"No, I like hearing you say it." I was getting giddy with sleep. I put my hand under his shirt and rubbed his back.

There was a pause then. "OK, good night then," he said. His voice was suddenly full of emotion. He kissed my forehead.

"Good night, babe," I told him. I took a deep breath and fell asleep right away.

I woke up but at first wasn't sure why. I could see through the blinds of the bedroom that the sky was turning grayish, with the very first rays of the early morning poking through the clouds. It was too early to be awake.

I was on my side, with Tarek's arms around me from behind. I squeezed his hand and snuggled against him. I couldn't tell if he was awake or not.

Then I realized why I had woken up. I had to pee.

I slowly extricated myself from his arms and he stirred slightly. I turned around and kissed him very lightly, on the outside of his mouth.

I went to the bathroom. I didn't want to have morning breath so I looked around and found mouthwash and used that. Thank God, I thought. I also smiled looking at all of the hair products on the counter. He had more than I did. Then I caught a glance of myself in the mirror. My hair was tousled and my eyes were sleepy but I looked relaxed.

Of course I'm relaxed, I thought, laughing to myself. That thought led to me thinking about Tarek's incredible body. And, of course, that led to me getting turned on.

When I went back to the bed, he was half-awake.

"Hey," he said, taking me into his arms.

"Good morning," I told him, "but it's still really early."

"You're not a morning person?" he asked me.

"I am, but—it's still really early for a Sunday."

I leaned into him and hooked one leg around him, pressing him against me.

I kissed him deliberately on the mouth. Then he was kissing me back and I parted my lips. Then it became an all-out makeout session. His hand went under my shirt and over my breasts, and then on my back.

We ended up with him on top of me.

"I don't remember my clothes coming off," I joked.

"Don't you?" Tarek breathed as he kissed my neck.

"Come here," I told him, pulling his hips closer to me.

"Isabel, you are sooo impatient."

I bit his earlobe lightly. "And you are such a tease," I said, tracing my lips from his ear across his cheek, over his goatee and to his mouth, kissing him. Then he held me tightly, and the feel of my breasts crushed against him was putting me on fire. He kissed my neck again and ran a hand very gently along the outside of my breast. I shuddered, then whispered into his ear.

"Please, Tarek, for the love of all that is holy, please don't make me wait any longer."

"Listen to you, talking about holiness on a Sunday."

"*Jackass*—" I tried to get him on his back but he held me down, which made me even crazier.

He made me wait about sixty more seconds. After that, all I could think about was how incredible this connection was. And right at my crescendo, I wrapped my legs around him to hold him there, then bit his shoulder with enough force to make him cry out.

Afterward, I lay there for several minutes, catching my breath. When I could think again, I leaned over him and said, "Let me see your shoulder."

Tarek was inspecting it. "I can't believe you bit me!"

"Really? You can't believe that? Don't you *know* me?" I couldn't help laughing.

Tarek smiled at me. "Woman, you almost drew blood!"

I loved hearing him call me *woman*. I said matter-of-factly, "That was for making me wait, babe."

Half an hour later, we were still lying in bed, talking.

"Oh, my God," I said aloud. Something had just occurred to me.

"What's wrong?" Tarek asked, concern in his voice.

"I just had sex with a guy in his twenties. Jesus."

He chuckled. "Well, I just had sex with a woman in her thirties, so we're even."

I laughed softly. "Well, there's a first time for everything, so—" I buried my face in his chest.

"Well, in a few months I won't be in my twenties anymore," Tarek said then.

"It doesn't bother you, does it?" I asked him.

"Does what bother me?"

"Turning thirty," I clarified. "It's just a number, you know?"

"Oh, it doesn't bother me." Then he asked me, "What did you do for your thirtieth birthday?"

"I went to New York to see Ariel," I said, "and I got a tattoo." I chuckled.

"Oh, I almost forgot that you had it," Tarek said then.

"That's because—you couldn't see it from—your angle." I laughed out loud.

"Come on, let me see it," he said.

"You've seen it already," I weakly protested.

"It was only for a second. Now that you're naked I can get a better look."

I leaned up, picked up a pillow and lightly hit him in the face.

"That's for thinking about me naked," I said.

Then he half-tackled me in a bear hug and I ended up underneath him.

"I'm afraid," he said, "that from now on it's going to be impossible for me not to think about you naked." He smiled suggestively.

"Well, I guess I can't prevent that," I said with some attitude.

"No, you can't," he said, then he kissed me full on the lips, and we kissed for a while.

Then I rolled over on my stomach and pulled down the sheet low enough to expose my tattoo.

"There," I said, "are you happy now?"

"Yes, thank you," he said, running his hand down my back.

Then he exhaled quickly and lay on his back. "Isabel, that is a serious turn-on."

"What?"

"Your tattoo."

I was still lying on my stomach, and Tarek turned on his side to face me. His demeanor had shifted and I sensed a change in subject was coming.

"Seriously, you should've told me sooner how you felt," he said.

"You mean how I felt about you?"

"Yes," he said, touching my shoulder.

"I was afraid," I shrugged.

"Of what?"

"That you didn't feel the same way."

"Isabel," Tarek began slowly, "just so you know, that's impossible."

I smiled. "I'm a pessimist."

"So what made you tell me?"

I hesitated. I hadn't been expecting this question. "I don't know," I answered honestly. "I was tired of tiptoeing around it. It felt awful to be with you and not tell you."

"I know that feeling." Tarek's voice was almost a whisper. Our eyes locked and we both smiled.

I laughed lightly, then rolled over and he put his arms around me from behind. He took my hand and I reached my other hand around my head to run it through his curls.

"One thing," Tarek whispered into my ear.

"Tell me," I said.

His arms tightened around me.

"I—" he paused and it made me wonder. Then he sighed. It was a slight movement and I wouldn't have noticed except that his chest was against my back and I could feel it. "I'm really glad that you told me."

I smiled to myself. "I am too."

I squeezed his hand and we both fell asleep like that.

We were at Tarek's apartment studying or, more aptly, trying to study.

Tarek was preparing tea.

"I still can't believe you *bit* me," he said from the kitchen.

I looked up from my Property book. "Dude, you only have yourself to blame."

"*What*?!" He turned around to stare at me. "What did *I* do?"

"What did *you* do? You kept talking about sex last night at dinner."

"I did *not*!" he protested.

I narrowed my eyes at him. Then I said in my best French-Arabic accent, which was more French than Arabic, "Oh, Isabel, if you would have wanted to that night I would have complied. Military orders? Well, if that's how you would have wanted it—" My eyes widened at him. "You made me so *hot*. Don't tell me that wasn't intentional."

Tarek laughed out loud. "First, I do *not* sound like that."

"Don't cloud the issue. You said that last night."

He crossed his arms. "I neither confirm nor deny that."

"So don't blame *me* for jumping you last night—and this morning."

"But I *do* blame you," he said deliberately, his brown eyes huge and smoky.

I sighed and shook my head. I opened my mouth, thinking of a retort but failing. "I am—without blame in all of this."

"Whatever," he said. "First, you come over here looking all gorgeous."

I crossed my arms and rolled my eyes.

"Even now, you look so hot in my clothes." He drew his eyes over me, and his look was so intense that I felt that they would burn right through me. I felt myself blushing.

"Tarek, I'm a mess. I'm not wearing any makeup, and I haven't even brushed my hair—" I was starting to feel self-conscious.

"Doesn't matter." That look on his face was still there.

"Dude, you're blind."

"And you're impossible."

"Well, you're improbable!"

Tarek laughed. "That's the best you've got? I'm *improbable?*"

"Yes!"

"What does that even mean, Isabel?"

"Improbable. It means doubtful, unlikely, not probable—"

"Oh my God." He shook his head in mild frustration. "I know what the word means, Isabel. What did *you* mean when you said it?"

"That *you're* improbable. That it's highly unlikely that someone as gorgeous and sexy as you would be interested in dating me. That it's unlikely that we would have so much in common. That it's—" I was going to say that it was unlikely that I would fall for you, but stopped myself. He didn't seem to notice.

"Oh, so we're dating?" His eyes sparkled and he raised his eyebrows.

Damn, I must have been more discombobulated than I had thought to let *that* slip. He had me. I blushed and smiled nervously, looking down. All of a sudden I couldn't think of anything to say.

Then I found my voice. "Tarek, I'm not doing this with you unless we're dating. I'm not going to do the casual thing with you."

I must have looked on edge or something, because he immediately came over and sat next to me on the sofa.

"Isabel," his tone was urgent, "I'm sorry. I didn't mean to put you on the spot. I—I want to know—"

When he didn't continue speaking I sighed, deflating a little. It was a sigh of semi-resignation. I had ended up playing another card. I did a quick mental calculation and realized that I only had like one or two left, then would show my entire hand. Little did I know, I wouldn't play my most important card until a couple of weeks from now.

"Tarek, I'm not going to continue to sleep with you unless this is going somewhere." I wanted to obliterate any misplaced assumptions.

He stood up, pulled me to my feet and put his arms around me. I held onto him like I was afraid to let go. He put his lips against my ear and his goatee was tickling me. "What I want is—" he hesitated. "I want you to be with me. I mean, I want you to *only* be with me—"

I laughed softly.

"Is that amusing?" he asked me.

"No, it makes me—happy."

"Hey," I said then, looking at him. "Before starting to do this with you, I hadn't spent the night at a man's house in like twelve years. Just saying." That was my way of telling him that I wanted that, too.

He grinned and kissed me.

The truth was that I had wanted him to be mine since practically the day we met.

I was walking to the law school campus, elated. I was going to have to try hard to concentrate on the lecture tonight. Thankfully, I only had one class. I was also going to have to control myself around the guys, lest I turn into the butt of their jokes again.

I had slept at Tarek's place again last night. We had spent Sunday afternoon walking around downtown and going out to eat. Afterward, I had had to read a couple of hours for class. It had been difficult to concentrate, but I had managed.

Then, in the early evening, I had been sitting on the sofa, nerding out and reading my Crim Pro textbook.

"So here's the thing," I had said aloud, still looking at the book, "when a police officer asks you if he can do something, such as 'Do you mind if I check the trunk of your car?', that means that he needs your permission, because if he didn't, he would go right ahead and look, he wouldn't ask." I looked up. "That's what people don't understand—"

I had caught Tarek looking at me with a fierce expression.

"What?" I had asked him.

His expression relaxed.

"I wanted to know if you wanted to stay over again tonight," he began, then added hastily, "but I know you have to work tomorrow."

"OK," I had replied, smiling. "Are you sure you'll be able to stand me for another night?" My tone had been in jest but the question was a serious one.

"I think you'd be surprised at what I can stand," he had answered.

We hadn't studied for the rest of the night. Instead, we had made dinner and relaxed on the couch, before attacking each other. The sex had been urgent but also very tender, as if we were done with the transition of our relationship.

The next morning, Tarek had prepared coffee and I had scarfed down a bowl of cereal before leaving for work. I had kissed him for a long time with my arms around him, thinking about what we had done the previous night.

"Isabel, you can't kiss me like that and then leave," he had said.

"I'm sorry," I had said, then reconsidered. "Well, no, I'm not really sorry. I'll see you in class."

I had been so giggly at work today that almost everyone had asked me what was wrong. Even Peter had asked me if I was hungover.

"No," I had told him, "*es que—*" and all of a sudden I had the realization. I found it so funny that I started laughing.

Peter looked at me like I had begun to lose it. In all actuality, I thought, I lost it a long time ago.

I finally calmed down enough to speak. Whispering, I told Peter, "*Es que tengo novio.*"

That had been my realization. Countless acerbic exchanges, several study sessions, a few dinners out, one semi-declaration, a night at the shooting range, and—how many times had we slept together?—I had a boyfriend.

Jesus. I had a boyfriend.

"What?!" he had exclaimed. We had stepped out of the office to grab coffee in the afternoon, and, like a gossipy old Spanish woman, Peter had made me tell him everything. It actually felt good to talk about it.

"*Nena, porque no me habías dicho nada?!*"

"I didn't tell you because I wasn't sure where it was going to go," I had told him. "I wasn't sure how he felt about me."

Peter was happy for me. I guess anyone in this town would be happy for a woman in her mid-thirties who had finally been saved from the torment of singlehood. That wasn't actually how I felt; being single isn't "bad." If you find someone who is a good partner for you, then that's fantastic. But if you don't, then you shouldn't settle for someone who isn't. I told Peter as much that day.

He had also told me that everyone at work had asked him what was "going on" with me, that I wasn't my usual jackass self.

Yeah, it's amazing what regular sex does for someone, I had thought.

Now, walking to campus, I smiled broadly as I thought about that conversation with Peter. Peter was only a few years older than me, but we were in very different places in our relationships.

Relationships, I thought. It was kind of a scary word to me. But I wouldn't think about that right now.

After going to the gym at lunchtime, I had moussed my hair and taken time with my makeup. I wanted to look extra good; and shaded my eyes with dark shadow and eyeliner.

Walking into the law school building, I found Tarek where I usually found him, in the lounge area, in one of the booths in the back. I excitedly noticed that he was by himself.

We didn't stand on ceremony this time. He smiled as he saw me approach and I sat down next to him and buried my face in his neck, not caring who saw us.

We put our arms around each other and he tilted his face and kissed me on the lips, once, twice, three times.

"How are you doing?" I asked him.

He smiled. "Better now that I see you," he answered.

That made me blush.

"I have something to tell you," he said then.

I looked into his eyes, but I was nervous, wondering what the news was. His arm was around my shoulders and he put his lips against my ear.

"I took the summer offer in DC," he said.

I closed my eyes for a second. "That's awesome," I told him, concealing my exuberance.

"I thought you'd be happy," he said.

But I immediately felt bad, because this subject had been the source of our argument just over a week ago. I hoped he hadn't made this decision only because of me. I mean, I hoped he had but I hoped that he hadn't at the same time.

He continued. "I was talking to my friend who lives up in New York. I don't think I want that lifestyle right now. I mean—DC has great connections."

"That makes sense," I told him, smiling. I kissed him furiously on his cheek and then on his mouth. Then we were both laughing softly.

"We can celebrate tonight," I said.

"Oh, I intend to," Tarek said suggestively.

Then he put his hand against my face and kissed me very slowly. Suddenly, like an explosion, I heard a huge *whump!* and Tarek and I both jumped.

It was Eric, and this time he totally knew what he was interrupting.

He had dropped his textbooks on the table, purposely making a loud noise. I glared at him, pissed off.

"You did that on purpose, you jackass!" I said.

"Sorry if I don't want to watch you two make out," Eric retorted, with some attitude.

"Then go sit somewhere else," I said as I motioned my hand to the other tables.

"Calm down," Tarek said to both of us, looking at Eric first and then me. Then he looked at Eric again, "And don't get her riled up."

"Oh, I think everyone knows who gets her riled up around here, and it's not me," Eric said, raising one eyebrow. He was still standing up.

"That was unnecessary," Tarek told him, shaking his head.

Eric liked to rile me up; that was characteristic of him. But I couldn't tell if these were his usual antics or if he was really pissed off about something.

I decided to ask him. "Dude, what's wrong with you?" I said, raising and lowering my shoulders.

"Well, I thought you'd be nicer, Isabel, since now you're getting laid regularly."

"Come on, Eric!" Tarek was annoyed. "Just sit down—or leave, if you want."

Eric looked at me then. "Are you going to let your boyfriend talk to me like that?" No doubt he had used the term "boyfriend" to see if it bothered me.

"Yes, I am," I said decisively. "Now do what he says." Then I added with more than a little irritation, "*¿Qué te pasa?*"

Eric glared at me. Then Josh appeared.

"Thank God you're here," Tarek said to him. "It's like dealing with two children." He motioned to me and Eric.

Josh smiled. "Welcome to my world," he said.

I didn't know what Eric's problem was, but I was going to try to find out.

Josh and I were chatting about the cases for class that night when Alicia came over to our table.

I didn't like Alicia, which wasn't unusual since I didn't really like anybody at the law school. I liked Alicia even less than I liked Alyssa. Let me rephrase. I liked Alicia even less than I had liked Alyssa at the beginning. I liked Alyssa more now.

Alicia thought very highly of herself. She thought she was gorgeous and brilliant when she was really only decent-looking and mediocre. She was petite, about 5'3" or so with slight features, although not as petite as Alyssa. Alicia had long, straight dark hair; it was almost black. I wasn't sure if she dyed her hair or not. I had never paid attention before.

The thing about Alicia was that she only talked to you if she wanted something. I didn't trust her. I hadn't really dealt directly with her, but I had heard rumors, mostly from Melanie, and I had overheard things that Alyssa had said about her. I had also heard stuff from Josh and Eric. In fact, now that I was thinking about this, I remembered that Saul had also said things about her, how she had been more than willing to screw him, and how she was so fake.

That was a memory that I did not want to have. Alicia and I had screwed the same guy, except that I had screwed him out of sheer loneliness and the desire for some kind of physical connection and she had screwed him because—well, maybe she had screwed him for the same reasons. Who knew? As far as I knew, she and Saul weren't a couple. It would be easier for me if they were, because then maybe he wouldn't ogle me whenever he saw me. Although, maybe he would tell Alicia about him and me. Oh hell, maybe he had told her about us anyway.

There was next to nothing that I could do about that. However, it worried me that so many people knew that I had slept with Saul. That meant that, at any moment, someone could slip and say something in front of Tarek. Tarek should hear that from me, but I was too petrified to tell him.

I decided to put all of that out of my mind and study Alicia, because it was odd that she had approached us.

She must have known that I was on to her, because, although she occasionally glanced my way, she avoided eye contact altogether. She was talking to Eric and Josh about their classes. Evidently, she had a class with Eric, which I hadn't known.

I didn't get it at first. Then it dawned on me.

Eric was pissed off, and Alicia was here.

There was something going on. Something that I had missed, that if maybe I had paid closer attention, I would have understood. But Tarek had been taking up all my thoughts for the past two months, and I had not been my usual observant self.

Never mind, I thought. I would figure this out.

When we were in class, I was still pondering the previous few scenes. I sent a message to Josh.

Hey, what's up with Eric? He's totally pissed off tonight.

When Josh answered me, I could almost hear the frustration in his words.

I don't know. He's been snappy with me today.

Then I wrote back.

Do you think he's stressed about exams? Tarek and I sent him our outlines. He should be fine.

I don't know, Josh answered.

I was puzzled. Eric usually wore his emotions on his sleeve. At the same time, I felt that maybe I had been neglecting him recently. The truth was that I hadn't been spending much time with any of my friends recently, but Eric sometimes needed hand-holding. He was younger than the rest of us and more impressionable.

Afterward, at the metro station on the way home that night, I spoke to Eric before his train arrived.

"Hey, what's wrong?" I asked him. The two of us were a little set apart from the others.

"Nothing," he said adamantly.

"Eric, I know that's not true," I shook my head. Then I sighed. I couldn't force him to tell me if he didn't want to.

"Well, if you want to talk, you have my number," I finally said.

Then I had an idea.

"Hey, why don't we all go out for a drink on Thursday after class?"

He shrugged. "OK," he said as if he didn't care one way or the other. But I saw his eyes light up a little bit.

On the metro, I said goodbye to Josh and Dinesh right before I left at Pentagon City with Tarek.

"Oh, so you're sleeping at his place tonight?" Dinesh asked me, laughing.

"Where I sleep is none of your damn business," I said, glaring at him.

"What would your mother think?" Dinesh said jokingly.

Josh laughed, likely because he knew my mother, an Argentine Catholic, and knew that she likely would be less than thrilled.

"Where I sleep is none of my mother's business either," I said as I exited the train with Tarek. Jesus. I was six years away from being forty years old! At this point, no one should have a damn thing to say about where I slept.

But Josh got a parting shot before the doors closed.

"Hey, Tarek, I hope your kitchen is stocked, with the amounts of food that she eats!"

I gave Josh my middle finger through the metro doors and my last sight of he and Dinesh was of them laughing.

"Goddammit!" I cursed under my breath.

Tarek was laughing. "They know you really well."

"Oh, don't start with me!"

"Are you angry?" he asked me as we left the metro station, incredulous.

"Yes!"

"Isabel, they were only joking."

"Not about that. Why did Josh have to mention my mother?"

"So?"

"With what I have planned to do with you tonight, I really don't want to be thinking of my mother right now!"

Tarek laughed again. "Relax. There's plenty of time to de-stress before we—you know." We exchanged a look and his eyes were smoldering.

Now I was pensive, thinking about Eric. I told Tarek as much.

"I don't know what's wrong with him. He's usually not a jerk like he was tonight."

Tarek sighed. I got the feeling that he was thinking about something. "Would Josh know what's going on?"

"I asked him already," I said. "He doesn't know." I turned to face Tarek then. "I told Eric we could all go out for a drink on Thursday after class, if that's OK with you."

"Sure."

We were at his apartment door. When we went inside, Tarek took my coat and then hung it with his in the small closet by the front door.

"Isabel, I think I know what's going on with Eric."

I looked at him, confused. "What?"

"I told you before that I think he's crazy about you."

I rolled my eyes. "That's not true."

"I think that now that he knows that we're together, he's upset about it."

"Tarek," I began, a million thoughts fluttering around my head, "he's known that I've liked you for a long time. And, as far as I've seen, he has no problem with it." I proceeded to tell him about my encounter with Sameer, in front of Josh and Eric, and that they had both stood up for me. I still left off the part where Sameer had mentioned Saul.

"Look." Tarek stepped toward me, putting his hands at my waist, "I have no doubt that he cares about you. Whether that's as a friend or as more than that, I'm really not sure. It's just my opinion."

"Well, I'm not with Eric, am I?"

He smiled and nodded, acknowledging my statement. Then his smile turned a little devious, and his eyes sparkled.

"So how long have you liked me then?" he asked me.

I averted my eyes from his face. "I don't see how that's relevant."

"You're right. It's probably not." Then he kissed me gingerly on the lips. "It's getting late and you have to work tomorrow. Let's get dinner."

I couldn't argue with that.

The week had passed by in a blur.

Nothing of any great significance had happened since my exchange with Eric last Monday evening. He was still in a fairly crappy mood. He tried to hide it, but I could tell. So could Josh, who kept giving me frustrated looks, rolling his eyes, and then glancing in Eric's general direction.

I worried that maybe Eric was getting caught up in the law-school drama. Unlike Josh and me, Eric didn't have a full-time job, so he had time to be more social, which was also more likely to lead to drama. Josh and I tried to avoid it mostly, but I had to admit that I wasn't doing a great job of that, and that was mostly because of my own doing.

I had arrived at work that morning later than I had wanted to. Consequently, I was now rushing to campus in time for the 3:50 class.

As I rushed into the main doors, I saw Tarek waiting inside for me.

"Sorry I'm late." I kissed him quickly. Indeed, I had hopped on the metro to get here as the doors were closing.

"So," he began as we walked upstairs to class, "did she give you a hard time this morning?" His smile was one of amusement.

I chuckled and shook my head. He was referring to his next-door neighbor. I hadn't remembered seeing her before this morning. I had run into her as I left Tarek's apartment to go to work. She was tall and thin, with straight blond hair, and I guessed that she was about my age.

She had looked at me briefly and had smiled, a knowing smile, as if inwardly she were laughing about something. I wouldn't understand until several days later what the smile had meant.

We had awkwardly walked to the elevator together. Once we were in the elevator, she had looked at me.

"So," she had begun slowly, "are you Tarek's—girlfriend?"

I had suppressed a smile. I guessed she assumed that a random hookup wouldn't have ended up with a woman staying over on a weekday night. "Yes." Then I remembered my manners. "I'm Isabel."

"I'm Amber," she had introduced herself. "I've seen you once or twice," she had explained, "but never in the morning."

Wow, I had thought. That was ballsy. I had grinned at her, and said, "Well, there's a first time for everything."

As soon as the elevator doors had opened, I had run out, wishing her a good day.

I had texted Tarek about it as soon as I had arrived at work.

At first I hadn't told him what I had said.

She asked me if I was your girlfriend, I had written.

What did you say? he had texted back.

I hadn't shown my card right away. What do you think I said?

I hope you told her that you were, he had replied.

That's what I told her.

Now, I laughed about it. "She was fine," I told him. "She didn't say anything other than what I told you this morning."

We got to International Law class and sat down. Zara was already there and said hi to us.

I had an idea and leaned over and whispered in Tarek's ear.

"Would she come if I invited her out with us tonight?" I asked him. Our entire conversation was in low tones so that no one else could hear.

"I don't know," he said honestly. "Ask her."

"*You* ask her," I said.

"Why me? It's your idea," he said into my ear. His goatee was tickling my face, and I almost giggled.

"Because you know her better than I do. And I think I intimidate her."

"You intimidate everyone," he said.

I sighed, rolling my eyes.

"But," he continued quickly, "it's nice of you to think of her. I don't think she has many friends here. So ask her." It was almost a command. Almost. He knew better than to give me orders.

"I don't like your tone," I said jokingly.

"What do you mean?"

"You can't tell me what to do," I retorted, still whispering. "I'm not your g—" I stopped, the words stuck in my throat.

"What? What was that? You're not my *what?*"

I huffed. "Jesus Christ! I'll ask her."

"Thank you, sweetheart," he said with sarcastic sweetness.

I glared at him.

I turned to Zara. She looked at me and smiled, uncertain.

I got straight to the point. "Hey, so—we're going out with my friends Josh and Eric tonight after class at 8 to have a drink and something to eat. I wanted to know if you would like to come with us."

"Where are you going?" she asked.

"Just to the place across the street," I said.

She hesitated for a second. "Sure. Thank you," she said.

After class that evening, we wandered downstairs near the law school's main entrance, where we met Zara. I noticed again how young she looked. She looked like she was twenty, but she was probably about twenty-five. Josh and Eric were there, and even Dinesh was coming with us.

"Your girlfriend let you go out tonight?" I heckled him.

"Yes, it only happens once a month, so let's get crazy," he laughed. I liked being around Dinesh because he was always positive.

And he didn't miss a beat. "So your boyfriend let *you* go out tonight?" he said to me.

"Are you kidding?" Tarek said then. "You think I could let her or prevent her from doing anything?"

"There's no way he could!" Josh agreed.

Then I saw Alyssa. I must have been feeling social that evening. Must be all the endorphins from the sex I'm having, I thought.

I motioned Alyssa over. "We're going across the street to have a drink. Do you want to come?"

She looked surprised, then smiled, and there was warmth in her smile. "Sure," she said.

Then I caught Eric's eye but he looked away quickly.

"Dude, are we going or not?" I called to him and Josh. "Some of us have to work tomorrow."

As we all walked over to the bar, I was remembering the last time I had been there. It had been the beginning of the semester, and I had been with Tarek, Josh, and Dinesh.

We sat upstairs. Tarek and I were on the sofa.

I had introduced Zara to everyone. I think everyone knew who she was, but didn't really *know* her. *I* didn't really know her, either.

Josh, Eric, and Alyssa were sitting across from us, with Josh in the middle. Dinesh was next to Tarek and Zara sat next to me. I tried to engage her in conversation.

She was nice but very shy. It turned out that she already had a law degree and was doing a Master of Laws in International and Comparative Law.

She drank a Coke and ate a little bit. Josh, Eric, and I had ordered a bunch of appetizers.

Alyssa leaned over and asked me how Melanie was. I told her that, unfortunately, I hadn't hung out with her recently except for at school. I made a mental note to catch up with Melanie soon.

Alyssa appeared relaxed around us, I was happy to note.

"Hey," I said to her then, raising my voice a little to be heard over Eric, "what are you going to do next semester? Did you end up taking an internship?"

She smiled a little, which made her look even younger.

"I'm doing an internship with a judge," she told me.

"That's awesome. Congrats," I said, and meant it.

Then I noticed something. I noticed that, although Eric was still chatting with Josh, he kept looking over at me and Alyssa, like he was half-listening to our conversation but trying not to let people know that he was.

Interesting, I thought.

We were all having a good time, relaxing, but the mood changed dramatically when I looked up and saw Sameer and Saul enter the room, with none other than Alicia, her long, straight hair hanging almost to her waist, making an entrance with a swagger.

"Aw, fuck," I said under my breath. Tarek leaned over to my ear.

"It's OK, don't worry," he told me. He didn't know the real reason why it bothered me, however.

Saul's black hair shone in the low light from the bar. He was quite muscular, and also vain. I remembered for a second how I had run my hands over his arms, and immediately shoved the image from my mind.

His eyes scanned over us and rested on Alyssa. Luckily, he didn't seem to fixate on me.

Saul went right over to Alyssa and began to chat with her, she still sitting down and he standing.

Sameer looked at me, then at Zara and addressed her directly.

"What are you doing with these people?" he asked her.

These people, I thought. What a jackass.

"Don't be a jerk to her," I said to him.

He looked at me, annoyed.

I was getting angry, but Tarek said something to Sameer then, in Arabic, and they went back and forth for a few moments. The conversation was more or less cordial, as far as I could tell.

I prayed to God right there that Sameer wouldn't tell Tarek about me and Saul. It was bad enough that Saul was here in my presence. I looked at Josh, who raised his eyebrows for a second at me; then I looked at Saul and Alyssa, curious.

Then I remembered the look that I had seen Saul giving Alyssa the other day, right before she had told me that she knew I liked Tarek. That was the day that I really knew that there was more to her than what she presented on the exterior.

Saul was coming on to her. He was trying to sleep with her. I was certain of it and didn't like it. In fact, maybe they had already slept together and he wanted more. I was going to have to get her alone to find out.

Then I noticed that Eric was looking at them, and decided to study him for a second.

What I saw on Eric's face floored me.

He was gazing at Alyssa, his eyes full of emotion and concern. His look alternated between that and loathing, when he looked at Saul.

He likes her, I thought. Eric likes Alyssa.

Eric and Alyssa, sitting in a tree.

Then I chuckled in spite of myself. Eric looked at me then, and I mouthed, "Holy shit" at him.

Then his eyes changed and they were telling me not to say anything.

Please, Isabel, his expression said, *I've never asked you for anything like this before.*

I nodded imperceptibly, agreeing to keep my mouth shut.

So that's why he's so pissed off this week, I thought. He likes Alyssa and Saul likes Alyssa and Saul is putting the moves on her. It was a difficult situation to be in, but it wasn't without resolution.

Tarek and I had been right. Law school *was* like high school.

I was too old for this shit.

Alicia called Sameer and Saul over then. I glared at her, and she wasn't liking it.

The three of them went to the bar together, but not before Saul touched Alyssa's shoulder.

Then Alyssa caught me looking at her, and looked away immediately.

She's embarrassed, I thought. She's still considering sleeping with him, or she has already, despite what I told her.

Amazing.

When Tarek and I were at his place later that night, I asked him what he and Sameer had talked about.

"Nothing important," he told me.

"I'll ask Zara," I said, half-joking.

He looked at me, narrowing his eyes a little, his mouth in a half-smile, half-smirk, as if he didn't like my retort.

"No you won't. Besides, like I said, it was nothing."

"Then tell me," I said. I was leaning over the counter as he was preparing tea. I couldn't shake the feeling that he wasn't telling me because Sameer had said something about me, something that Tarek knew I wouldn't like. I told him as much.

Tarek sighed. "That's right," he said, glancing at me, one eyebrow raised, "you always think the worst."

"At least tell me—" I was choosing my words carefully, "did he say something about me that would make you mad at me?"

Tarek looked at me, curious. "Like what?"

"Like—I used to sleep around, for example?" I hedged.

He shook his head. "Nothing he said changes anything," he said firmly. "Come here." He took my hand and led me around the counter to stand in front of him. Then he kissed me on the lips. "Don't worry about him."

I exhaled, letting my tension ease. He had kissed me the same way he always did. "OK," I said.

My phone blipped then, and I ignored it. It was late and I decided to let our conversation rest.

I put my arms around Tarek's neck and kissed him. "It's late. Let's go to bed."

He smiled and pulled me against him. "I like that idea." He kissed my neck.

"Hmmm, I knew you would."

Right before I went to sleep that night, I checked my phone to make sure my alarm was set, and saw a message from Eric.

Please don't say anything, not even to your man. We can talk later.

I wrote back.

OK, don't worry.

My life was getting slightly more complicated. Little did I know, this was next to nothing compared to how my life would be in a couple of weeks.

On Saturday afternoon, around lunchtime, Tarek and I were studying at his apartment.

We were planning to have dinner downtown with Lara and Patrick. It was one of Lara's rare free nights. I was a little nervous about it but figured that of everyone in my family, she was the least threatening. I was actually more worried about what Patrick would say than about what my sister would say.

I had also been a little on edge because the day before, Eric and I had been texting back and forth about his predicament. As far as he knew, Alyssa and Saul hadn't hooked up but it was only a matter of time. I told him that he needed to tell Alyssa how he felt, but his opinion was that if she was considering hooking up with Saul, then she didn't have any feelings for Eric.

But she won't know that you have feelings for her unless you tell her, I had told him. Regardless, you don't really know if she is actually considering hooking up with him or not, or whether she's just being flirty or nice.

I believed that Saul wanted to sleep with her, though, because of the looks I had seen him give her. My opinion was that Alyssa should listen to me and not hook up with him, but that in the end she was an adult and it was her business.

I had eventually cut Eric off since I had been at work.

I had been thinking about Eric this morning when Tarek had asked me what I was thinking about. I almost jumped. I didn't like keeping things from him.

"Nothing," I sighed. "Yesterday I was talking to Eric."

"Did you find out why he was upset?"

"He likes some girl."

"Really? Who?"

I exhaled. Eric had made me promise not to say anything. This sucked. "I don't know. Someone at school, apparently. He didn't say." I hated doing that, lying outright. For a second I thought that Tarek didn't believe me.

"Interesting," he said instead. I looked at him; his demeanor was fairly calm.

He must have believed me, I thought.

"But why is he upset about it?" Tarek asked me then.

"I think because—he thinks she may like someone else. Actually, it's all quite juvenile." I had chuckled. "I'm too old for this. Frankly, he should talk to someone his own age about this."

Tarek had laughed at that.

Now, this afternoon, feverishly outlining, I was thinking about how I would get everything done by exams. The end of the semester was fast approaching, and I was getting antsy. This was my *modus operandi*. I would start to worry and then start outlining like crazy. But you had to be careful. You didn't want to peak too soon. That is, there comes a time during the semester for law school students when they know all they are going to know for the exam, and they have all the information straight. If you overthought things, you wouldn't do as well on the exam. So, while I wanted to study, I had to be careful not to overstudy too early. If I peaked a week before the exam, that was bad because I would have to re-study and relearn during the coming week.

I chuckled. I was sitting at the dining table, outlining, and Tarek was sitting on the sofa, reading Property cases.

He looked at me and asked, "What's so funny?"

"I'm thinking that I don't want to peak too soon," I said, smiling.

"What?" he asked, the look on his face telling me that he was understanding it as a sexual innuendo.

I told him what I had been thinking about. "Get your mind out of the gutter," I told him.

"I thought you liked it there," he said suggestively.

"I do, I can't deny that." I looked at my computer screen again, but it was too late. I was already thinking about him naked. "Hey, stay on track," I told him then. "I need thirty more minutes to finish this section, then we can do whatever you want."

"*Whatever* I want?"

"Subject to my approval, of course."

"Oh good." He was smiling. "You're liberal with your approvals, anyway."

"No one's ever called me liberal," I joked.

"Maybe that's why I like you so much."

"Keep talking like that and I'll have to go over there and shut you up." I was sounding suggestive now.

"How would you do that?" he asked me.

"Oh, I can think of a couple of ways." I was still looking at my computer screen.

There was silence for a few seconds. Then Tarek said, "God, woman, you are making this impossible!"

"Look who's talking! I was here minding my own business, outlining!" I tried to sound as innocent as I could.

"You're the one who talked about *peaking*!"

I opened my mouth, then couldn't think of a witty retort. "I neither confirm nor deny that."

Tarek laughed and leaned back on the sofa. I couldn't stand it anymore and went over to him, straddling him on the sofa and kissing him. He held me to him, his hands on my back.

"You make me crazy," I told him.

"Hmm, I could say the same about you," Tarek murmured in my ear.

Then my cell phone rang.

"Jesus," I said. "Ignore that."

"You should see who it is," Tarek said. "Maybe it's an emergency."

"It's never an emergency," I sighed, frustrated. "No one ever calls me." Except, apparently, at the worst time.

My phone kept ringing.

"Come on, just answer it," Tarek told me, kissing me lightly on the lips.

I rolled off of his lap and stood up, grabbing my phone off of the coffee table.

"It's my sister," I said, wondering.

"Hey, do you want coffee?" Tarek was asking me.

"Um, yes please," I said, smiling at him.

He smiled back and went into the kitchen.

I answered my cell phone.

"Ariel?" I said.

"Isabel, I'm so glad I caught you!"

"What's wrong?" I didn't like how her voice sounded. The first thing I thought of was that maybe she and Javier had had a fight. I didn't think that was likely; he was really easygoing. But I couldn't think of why else she would sound like that.

"I don't know what to do!" she said.

"Hey, hey, calm down. It's OK." I needed to get her to tell me what was going on.

"Are you at home?" she asked me.

"No, I'm—I'm at Tarek's apartment," I said. I was thinking that I hadn't talked to her during the past two weeks, but Lara would have undoubtedly filled her in on what had happened between Tarek and me. They constantly texted each other. *Millennials.*

"Oh, Lara told me!" I had been right, apparently. "I'm really happy for you guys. She told me you stay over there like every night!"

Lara also couldn't keep a secret to save her life.

I felt myself blushing. "More or less," I told her.

"And you guys are going out with Lara tonight, right?"

"Yes, we are."

There was a pause.

"Sweetheart, what's wrong?" I asked her.

I knew it was really bad when she started to cry. Ariel hardly ever cried. She had thick skin, like her big sister.

"Isabel, I didn't know who to call!"

"It's OK. Tell me. What's going on?"

She started rambling, the pitch of her voice rising and falling. She sounded like she was trying to keep her voice under control, but wasn't doing a good job of it. The only thing I understood was at the end when she said she didn't know what to do.

"Ariel, Ariel, you have to slow down! I can't understand you." I tried to sound gentle but firm.

Tarek was looking at me from the kitchen with a questioning expression on his face, and I held up my free hand, as if to say I didn't know what the hell was going on.

I had to try and calm her down.

"OK, take a deep breath," I told her.

I heard her inhale and exhale over the phone.

"OK, now tell me, slowly, what's going on."

The pace of her speech was still rapid-fire, but at least I understood her. "Isabel, I took a pregnancy test and it was positive!"

I forced myself to remain calm. "OK," I said.

"But I didn't believe it, so I went to the doctor yesterday."

"Okaaaayyy . . ."

"And I *am*! I'm pregnant!!!"

She was starting to get hysterical again.

"Hey hey, calm down," I told her. "It's OK." I paused. "How far along are you?"

I saw Tarek's expression when I asked the question. He must have understood because he was raising his eyebrows.

I nodded and curved my hand over my stomach, pantomiming a big belly.

"Six weeks," Ariel told me over the phone.

"OK, you told Javier?" I assumed she had.

"No, not yet."

"Sweetheart, you should tell him. Is he home today?"

"No. He went out to lunch with his parents but I had to work. He's not back yet. I just got home from work, and I needed to call you!"

"OK, so—" I was trying to think of what to say to calm her down. "I promise, it's going to be OK." Then I instantly felt horrible because I couldn't guarantee that it would be OK. "First, you need to tell Javier. And what did the doctor say?"

"He said everything's fine. Everything looks normal. He says I'm about six weeks but we don't know for sure because I wasn't keeping track. So he's sending me for an ultrasound."

"OK, that's good," I said. "So—are you worried about telling Javier?"

I wasn't sure at first if the source of her anxiety was telling him or something else.

"I'm more worried about telling Mom!"

Like that.

I sighed. Our mother was a different story. "You let me handle Mom, OK? I mean, you'll have to tell her at some point but you can choose when. I promise that I will deal with her." I paused. "Javier will be ecstatic." I knew that it was the truth. He loved kids but, most of all, it was obvious to everyone that he loved my sister and would take care of her. He was also as much of a gentleman as Tarek was. I smiled then, thinking about how Ariel and I were so alike and that, interestingly, our significant others were also similar in some ways.

"You think so?" she was asking me.

"Absolutely. So—look, what else are you worried about?"

"Well, we're not married yet—"

"But you told me that you guys are planning to get married at some point, right?"

"Yes, of course."

"So there's no problem. Get married sooner if you want, or not. It's up to you."

"How am I going to be able to work with a baby?"

"Ariel," I began, "tons of women do that. You'll be able to. You'll see. And I can help you. And—" I was going to say, and Mom can help you too, but I wasn't sure if that would stress her out even further. "You'll see," I repeated. "This is great news, Ariel, honestly. Think of it, a little you or a little Javier. How adorable is that?"

She was almost chuckling. I considered that a mild success on my part. "Isabel—" she began.

"Tell me."

"It was incredible. I could already hear the baby's heartbeat—in the doctor's office."

I smiled, already thinking how I was going to spoil this child rotten, buy him clothes and books and toys and teach him how to cook and how to review a contract and be a good free-market capitalist and, when he was old enough, teach him to shoot.

"Life is always something to celebrate—you know that," I told her, still smiling.

"Yeah," she said. Then she said quickly, "Oh my God, Javier just got home."

"OK, take a deep breath and talk to him. Call me anytime, Ariel. I mean that—anytime." Then I had a thought. "And tell Lara!" That way I wouldn't have to keep my mouth shut tonight when I saw her.

We said goodbye and I hung up.

I stood there for a moment, pondering.

Then Tarek was standing in front of me. "Are you all right?" He touched my arm.

"Oh yeah, I'm fine," I said, looking at him. "I'm worried about my sister. She's freaking out."

He smiled. "I think you told her all the right things, though."

"Is that what you would have told your sister?"

"Yes, pretty much."

"OK, well, I trust your judgment, so—"

"Oh, I always like getting compliments from you." His smile became a grin.

"Yeah well, I'm becoming more liberal with them, at least where you're concerned." I kissed him on the mouth and he put his arms around me. I twirled one of his curls around one finger.

"Isabel, I know you're worried about her but she'll be OK."

"I know."

"And you're a good sister."

"I try. Thank you for saying that."

"It's true." He pulled back. "Let's take a break. Then you can do some more outlining before we go to dinner, if you want."

"OK."

"And I get to meet your sister tonight. I'm so nervous," Tarek said jokingly.

"Lara is the least crazy person in my entire family, so I figure we'll start with her." I chuckled.

I kissed him again, and could feel emotion welling up inside me, and my heart felt like it swelled to five times its size.

I was feeling things that I didn't quite understand. I would soon realize that it wasn't that I didn't understand them. It was that I hadn't remembered.

When we were getting ready, I realized that I was in fact a little nervous. I hoped that my sister didn't embarrass me too much. She usually behaved herself, for the most part. But Patrick was a wild card. Sometimes he was conservative, but sometimes he downright made fun of me. I didn't usually mind; I hoped that he was on his best behavior tonight.

I had decided to dress up a little, and wore a form-fitting black dress with long, fitted sleeves that I had worn to work earlier that week. I liked how it looked on me.

Even though Tarek had joked earlier about being nervous about meeting my sister, there must have been some truth in that statement. He had asked me what shirt to wear and kept changing his mind about it.

We were in front of his bathroom mirror. I was doing my eyes and then started laughing.

"What's so funny?" he had asked me, smiling.

"You changed your shirt again! Why?"

"I think I like *this* one for tonight."

"But I liked the other one." The other shirt had been a deep burgundy.

"Okaaaaaay," he said, sighing, "I'll go change again."

"Babe, wear whatever you want. You look good in everything." Make up your mind, I thought.

"Is this OK?" He was next to me again, and wearing a black blazer over the burgundy shirt.

"*Yes*, you look great. Honestly." I was putting on mascara and held very still.

"I love it when you call me that, by the way," he said then.

"What?" I was confused; my brows furrowed. I almost got mascara on my eyelid.

"When you call me—you know, when you call me babe."

"What? I didn't say that." Had I?

Tarek chuckled. "Yes, you did."

"Did *not*."

He looked at me. "Let me get this straight. You'll sleep with me, but you won't admit to calling me babe or sweetheart, or anything like that. Is that right?"

"You got it," I said, suppressing a smile.

"Amazing," Tarek shook his head.

"I'm going to use some of your hair gel, if that's OK," I told him.

He handed it to me.

"Thank you, babe," I said, smiling.

"Oh my God," Tarek said incredulously. "You're impossible."

I smiled. I would have winked too but didn't want to mess up my eye makeup.

I finished my hair and makeup without further incident. Then I began thinking again, and exhaled loudly.

"Are you worried about Ariel?"

"Yes. I'm worried about what my mother will say to her, but I really don't have any control over it." I paused. "So I guess it's pointless to worry about it."

Tarek turned his body to face me. "I'm sorry, Isabel."

"It's OK. I'm sure everything will be fine." I finished by putting on lip gloss, then turned and faced Tarek.

"It's exciting, though," I told him. "It's like having a little mini-me, someone that looks like you and that copies everything you do." I was reminiscing.

"How do you know so much about kids?" he asked me, curious.

"Oh, I wouldn't say that I know anything. But my cousins in Spain have a lot of kids, and when I'm over there I enjoy spending time with them. Sometimes I take care of them and stuff." Then I added quickly, "I know what you're thinking."

"What am I thinking?" Tarek was still curious.

"You didn't peg me for the maternal type."

"I didn't say that."

"Everyone thinks that," I said quickly.

"Well, they're wrong."

"What do you mean?"

"By maternal type, do you mean the kind of woman who cares about her friends and family and who shares her class notes with her friends so they won't be stressed about studying?" He was smiling knowingly.

I looked down, blushing. "Yeah, something like that."

"Well, I seem to remember you doing all those things."

I nodded. "Something like that," I repeated.

"Hey," Tarek said, lifting my chin up so that I faced him again.

"Yeah?" I asked hesitantly.

"Do not ever let anyone make you feel bad—for you who are."

I nodded.

"Don't let people make you think that you're a bad person, because you're not." He shook his head. "I won't let you think that about yourself."

I felt like my heart would burst. "Thank you."

After a few moments, I said, "Let's go. If we stay here any longer, I'll end up dragging you into bed."

"That wouldn't be so bad," he said.

"I know but I want to see my sister. So we'll have to wait a couple of hours."

"OK," he said, feigning impatience.

There was no doubt in my mind. Tarek was the best thing that had happened to me in a very long time.

We got to the restaurant before Lara and Patrick. I knew that would happen because my sister was almost always late. Like our mother, she ran on Argentine time.

We sat down at a square table and ordered wine. The restaurant my sister had selected served Mexican-Asian fusion cuisine. I was a big fan, but I pretty much ate everything.

The locale was large for a DC restaurant, with an upstairs, and the lighting was pretty low. That was also a plus for me, since I blushed really easily. It was easier to hide in the semi-darkness.

We were looking at the menu when I turned toward Tarek. I still sensed a little bit of tension.

"Hey, don't be nervous," I whispered.

"I'm all right," he said.

Then I laughed lightly.

"What's so funny?" he asked accusingly.

I leaned toward him and whispered in an even lower tone, "Maybe we *should* have had sex before coming here. That way you'd be more relaxed." We would *both* be more relaxed.

He chuckled, then changed the subject. "Do you think they'll want to go out after dinner?"

I considered for a second. "Most likely not. My sister will probably be tired from work." I raised one eyebrow. "Why? Did you want to go out? What did you have in mind?"

"I had in mind you without any clothes on," he said, grinning.

"Tarek!" I gasped, lightly punching him on the shoulder. "Behave yourself!"

He didn't have time to retort because at that moment my sister and her husband showed up.

"Hey hey!" Lara said exuberantly.

I stood up immediately and hugged her tightly. We always greeted each other effusively like this, even if we had recently seen each other.

"You look great!" I said to her.

"So do you!" she said back.

It was true. Her shoulder-length brown-blond hair hung in curls that framed her beautiful, flawless face. Her blue-gray eyes were alive, as always. She wore a flowing green dress with brown boots. For probably the thousandth time, I thought about how unfair it was for a woman to be so gorgeous and so intelligent at the same time.

By the time she and I were done greeting each other, Tarek and Patrick had already introduced themselves to each other and were chatting.

I introduced Lara to Tarek and she gave him a hug. My sister hugged everybody. You could not possibly be in a bad mood when you were with her.

"I've heard a lot about you," Lara told Tarek in her sing-songy voice as we all sat down. She had also picked up the Argentine tone of our mother.

"Well, none of it's true," Tarek said, smiling and glancing in my direction.

I tried to run through my memories to remember everything I had told Lara about him.

"Oh, she only says good things," Lara said, waving one hand.

"Really?" Tarek raised both eyebrows.

"Yeah, like, how much of a gentleman you are, and how smart you are."

"Order your drinks, dudes," I said then, trying to finalize this portion of the conversation. "The mojitos are pretty strong here."

"Oh, don't change the subject," Patrick said, smiling.

But then I was saved because the waiter came and took their drink orders. My sister and Patrick both ordered fru-fru mojitos.

Then I thought of something. I couldn't believe I hadn't brought it up already.

"Have you talked to Ariel?" I asked as I put my hand on Lara's arm.

"Yes!" she exclaimed, as if she had just remembered. "I can't believe she's pregnant!"

Another thing about Lara was that she was incredibly loud. Even with the chatter and the music in the restaurant, a few people turned and looked at us. I rolled my eyes.

"She was pretty shaken up when she called me," I said.

"I can't believe they're going to have a kid in New York," Patrick was saying.

"Has she told Javier yet?" I asked Lara.

"Yeah." Lara smiled. "He's thrilled."

"I knew he would be," I smiled, and looked at Tarek briefly. His eyes met mine.

I hesitated then. "Has she told Mom?"

"I don't think so. I mean, I talked to her a couple of hours ago and she hadn't told Mom yet."

I sighed. "OK."

"She'll be all right," Lara said then. She was also an eternal optimist. It was amazing that she and I had the same parents, but were so different.

I turned to Tarek for a moment, putting my hand on his. "Sorry, I don't mean to be talking about this now."

"It's OK," he said, squeezing my hand.

"So tell me how you guys are doing!" Lara said, looking at each of us in turn.

"All right," I shrugged. "School is taking up all of our time, you know, same old story."

"Isabel has practically all of our classes outlined already," Tarek said, smiling.

"She always does," Patrick said. His smile was a bit devious.

"Has she always been like that?" Tarek asked my sister.

"Like what?" I said. "You mean studious?"

"You mean like a nerd?" Patrick said.

I gave Patrick a smirk. "Look who's talking. Takes one to know one." It was true. Patrick owned more books than I did.

Tarek smiled. "I mean, like—" He was trying to find the right words. But I knew what he meant.

"He means like a machine, with my head buried in books all day," I clarified.

"She's very disciplined," Tarek said, looking at me.

"Yes, she's always been like that," Lara said. Then she asked, "You guys have all of the same classes, right?"

"Yes, except Tarek has one more class than I do, since he's in the full-time program."

"Oooo, a full-time student with no job and tons of free time," Patrick said jokingly.

I didn't say anything at first, because I always felt bad that I had an income and Tarek didn't. I hadn't shared my feelings on that with Lara.

I tried to maintain the jovial atmosphere. "That's right, so I'll expect your outlines *and* your grades to be better than mine," I said to Tarek.

"I don't see how that's possible," he told me.

"Oh, I'm sure there's grade inflation, so you'll be fine," Patrick said sarcastically.

"See," I turned to Tarek, "I'm trying to at least be on par with Patrick since he graduated his Master's degree with a 4.0. It's rough. I'm not sure if I can do it."

I winked at Tarek, and he smiled at me, his eyes smoldering. I was still holding his hand, and suddenly felt the need to take a deep breath.

After we had ordered, Tarek asked Lara about her medical residency and I told Lara that Tarek's mother was a nurse. They both regaled us with various stories about the ER while Patrick and I laughed.

After a while, when we were halfway through dinner, and everyone had had at least one or two drinks, I became more relaxed, leaning back in my chair. The topic for the moment was federal student loans.

"It's not a free-market system," I was saying, wine glass in hand. "I mean, how can it be, when it's propped up by federally subsidized student loans?"

"Right," Tarek agreed. "If the federal government didn't subsidize higher education, then no one could afford to pay for it, and the tuition costs would have to come down."

"Not only that," Lara chimed in. "The American Medical Association limits the number of places in medical schools and in residency programs. It's slow to respond to demand."

"Meanwhile, almost everyone at this table is saddled with at least six figures of graduate school debt," I punctuated. My sister would, more than likely, recoup her debt with her physician's salary. I doubted that I would be able to do that anytime soon.

"How are Josh and Eric—and Melanie?" my sister asked me then, changing the subject. She probably didn't want me to dwell on it, since I tended to dwell on everything.

I turned to Tarek to explain her question.

"She always asks about those three because they're my only friends. In fact—" I took a sip of wine, "when my sister can't get in touch with me she calls Josh first, then Melanie, then Eric, in that order." I looked at Lara. "You should be happy I only have three friends. That way I'm easier to keep track of."

"First of all," Lara said, scoffing, "you have more than three friends."

"Yeah, now you have four," Patrick butted in, "since I think a boyfriend counts as a friend."

"Oh, stop it!" Lara told him.

I smirked at Patrick and shook my head.

"You know why I have such few friends?" I asked Patrick, rhetorically, not expecting an answer.

"I know, I know," Patrick said. "People can't handle you." His tone conveyed that he had heard that explanation several times before.

"No—I mean, yes, that's technically correct, but there's a more significant reason." I continued. "People don't like honesty—"

"Or logic," Tarek concluded for me.

I looked at him and smiled. "You don't seem to mind either, though."

He half-smiled at me and his eyes were alive. "What can I say? I like to be challenged."

"You mean you're a sadomasochist," Patrick said, on the verge of laughing out loud.

"Shut UP!" My sister backhanded him lightly on the shoulder. "Be NICE!"

"Hey, did you just backhand your husband?!" I told her, feigning incredulity. But I was laughing too. Patrick was like a brother to me. No, in fact, he *was* a brother to me. And like siblings who loved each other, we ribbed each other constantly.

I glared at Patrick. "Be nice to my boyfriend, or I'll kick your ass."

"You'll do it, too," he said, chuckling.

"I *will*."

"When are you going to see Mom next?" Lara asked me.

I sighed a long sigh, partly to give myself time to dodge the question.

"I don't know," I shrugged. "The weekends are the only time I have to study, and—" I was going to say that the weekends were also the only time that I got to spend quality time with Tarek.

"I'll be here over Thanksgiving," Tarek said then.

"Are you guys going to Mom's for Thanksgiving?" Lara asked.

"I hadn't planned on it. Actually—" I looked at Tarek for a second. "I was thinking of going to see Ariel then, but—" I had wanted to mention that to him. "We can talk about it later," I told him, smiling.

"Here, I'll help you prepare," Patrick said, grinning mischieviously.

Confused, I said, "What are you talking about, you weirdo?"

"I'll help you prepare for when you take him to meet your mother. Let's role play. I'll be your Mom."

"Jesus, how old am I?!" I lamented.

Patrick put on his Mom face, trying to look all serious, but his blue eyes were twinkling. He rested his elbows on the table, and clasped his hands together. Then he turned to Tarek, who was already laughing.

"What are your intentions regarding my daughter?" Patrick asked.

Lara almost choked on her mojito.

"She's not going to ask that!" I protested. "Don't answer that," I said to Tarek. I didn't think he would, but wanted to head it off in case he did.

Patrick continued. "How do you feel about children?"

"How do *you* feel about children?" I asked Patrick. My mother was always on Lara's case about when she was going to have kids.

"Isabel loves kids," Lara said.

I glared at her, shocked. "That's not true!" I protested.

"You don't like kids?" Tarek asked me. "I thought you did."

I looked from him back to Lara, then opened my mouth. "I—don't like them, but I don't hate them."

My sister ignored me and looked at Tarek. "Did she tell you that she took care of our cousin's baby for an entire summer?"

"I didn't know that," Tarek was surprised.

"She needed help," I said defensively. "She couldn't get him into the free daycare, because there's a lottery system in Spain; there aren't enough places for all the kids. Gee, socialized daycare, paid for by the taxpayers, but there's not enough money for it. How surprising," I said with irony. Everyone at the table was still looking at me. I sighed. "She eventually put him in a private daycare, but I had the summer off, so—"

"You loved that little baby," Lara said.

It was true. In fact, I still did. He was fourteen years old now, and I spent time with him whenever I went back to Barcelona.

"Jordi," I said, sighing. I turned toward Tarek. "His name is Jordi; it's a typical Catalan name. He was—*is* a cutie," I continued. The truth was, I had really bonded with my little cousin. It had been him and me, all day. I had taken care of that little thing that had depended on me for everything from the moment my cousin put him in my arms and left for work.

I took a sip of my wine, then held my wine glass in both hands. "I *do* like kids," I admitted, looking at Tarek. "Is that a dealbreaker for you?"

He smiled warmly and touched my hand. "*Au contraire.*"

Lara went on. "You know our aunt still blames you for that, right?"

"For what?" I asked, not understanding.

"For the fact that Jordi is so right-wing," Lara smiled.

"Please," I said with annoyance, "like the fact that I took care of him when he was a baby has anything to do with that." My subsequent conversations with him when he was an older child may have had something to do with that, though. I smiled over my wine glass.

Lara continued. "He's had a picture of Jose Maria Aznar in his room since he was eight years old, and he dreams of coming to live in the U.S." Like that was *my* fault, I thought. Well, it probably was.

"Anyway, Jordi shouldn't bother coming to the U.S.," I said with a heavy heart, "the way this country is headed." Not that I wouldn't love it if he did.

Patrick nodded.

But I didn't want to put a cloud over tonight. "So what else will my mother ask me?" I said to him.

"She'll ask about his job prospects." Patrick raised his beer glass as he spoke.

"No, she won't!" I said. "Anyway, he's a CPA," I said proudly, "so that's not a problem."

Then I considered the implications of my statement, that that suggested that we would be together long-term. It made me embarrassed, because I wasn't sure if I wanted him to know that I was contemplating that.

"I didn't peg you for a CPA," Lara said. "I thought accountants were nerdy."

"Thank you!" I told her, then turned toward Tarek. "See?"

"Your sister is nerdy," Patrick said to Lara.

"Dude, that offends me," I said with mock seriousness.

"It shouldn't," Patrick said. "Nerds are cool now. Didn't you know?"

"Anyway, she's right," Lara said. "Mom won't ask that. She'll be more subtle."

"OK," Patrick changed his line of questioning. "How old are you?"

"Leave him alone, Pat," I said, annoyed.

"Twenty-nine," Tarek answered.

Patrick looked surprised, then turned to me and was himself again. "He's only twenty-nine?" His eyes widened.

"Yeah," I shrugged.

"You're dating a man in his twenties." It wasn't a question.

"Yes, so?"

"Oh, that's rich. You're dating a Millennial!" Patrick started to laugh.

"He's not a Millennial! He was born in—" I tried to do the math in my head, but the noise and wine were clouding my mental faculties.

"1981," Tarek answered for me.

"81," I repeated. "I think, technically, that makes him a Gen X'er, like me."

"No, I think he's Gen Y," Patrick nodded. "Hold on." He whipped out his smart phone. "I'll check Wikipedia."

"Yes, the source of all knowledge," I said sarcastically.

"He thinks it's funny," I explained to Tarek, "because—"

"You make fun of Millennials all the time," he finished.

"Yes," I nodded.

"And with good reason," Tarek said.

"Thank you," I winked at him.

"OK," Patrick said, " apparently, people born in the beginning of the 1980s on are considered Millennials, so," he looked at me, "he's a Millennial, ha!"

"So what?"

"Your Mom's going to think he's too young for you," Patrick said.

I smiled slyly. "Look around you, Patrick."

Patrick looked back at me, a confused expression on his face. "What?" he said.

"You see how many fucks I give about that?"

Everyone laughed.

We were back at Tarek's apartment. I was so full from dinner. Lara had insisted on sharing a dessert with me. I never ordered dessert, but she was a bad influence.

We made tea and sat down on the sofa.

"So why are you afraid to tell me things about yourself?" Tarek asked me.

His question was unexpected. I was caught off guard and didn't know how to answer.

"What do you mean?"

He said patiently, "You didn't want me to know that you like children."

"Because it's a stereotype that women in their mid-thirties have a biological clock that's ticking."

He chuckled. "Is yours ticking?"

"I am *not* talking about this with you now," I pouted, crossing my arms.

"OK, I'm sorry." He turned toward me on the sofa and kissed me, right on my jawline. "I was just joking." He put his arms around me.

"But tell me why," he said. As usual, he didn't let me off easy.

I decided to be honest.

"Because I'm afraid that eventually you'll find out something about me that you don't like."

"Isabel, I don't think that's going to happen."

"You can't know that."

"I *do* know that, because I know you."

I thought about our earlier conversation, when we had been getting ready to go to dinner. He *did* know me, at least, he knew some things about me.

"My sister asked about you the other day," he told me then, changing the subject.

"About *me*? Why?"

"Because I talk about you all the time."

"Jesus, what do you say?!"

"Not a lot. We talk about school, how smart you are, all the languages you speak."

I lay my head back on the sofa and twirled his curls around my fingers.

"Lara's really nice," he said. "She's really outgoing."

"Yeah, she's very different from me."

"Not that different. You're two independent women."

I nodded in agreement.

"Her husband is hilarious," Tarek continued.

"Oh my God, he makes me laugh so hard." I traced my index finger along his jaw. Then I shuddered.

"Are you cold?" Tarek asked me.

"No," I smiled, then leaned over to say into his ear, "I am totally hot for you right now."

He put his hand against my face and kissed me, and there wasn't much talking after that.

I had planned on Sunday being relaxing, but a phone call with my mother ruined that. She called me at around 10:30am. Tarek and I had finished breakfast, and I was on my second cup of coffee, so I answered it.

"Hi Mom," I sighed into the phone.

"Isabel, *aquí habla Mama.*"

"I know, Mom."

"Have you talked with your sister?"

"I saw Lara last night."

"I was asking about Ariel, but how's Lara doing?"

"She's doing really well. Her schedule is a bit rough, but she's handling it."

"You went out with her last night?" Her voice sounded hopeful, like maybe Lara had set me up with someone. I exhaled, trying not to let my mother get me worked up.

"We went to dinner with her and Patrick," I answered.

"We? Who's we?"

Oh no, I thought. Epic fail.

"Ummm . . . ," I stalled, trying to think of what to say.

"I can't—I can't really talk right now," I stammered.

"Are you at home?"

I was a rat in a maze with no visible way out.

"Nooooo," I said slowly.

"Well, where are you?" Her voice sounded concerned.

I heard Tarek chuckling, and glared at him.

I stood up and walked to the kitchen.

"I guess I was going to have to tell you at some point," I sighed loudly.

"I'm at my *boyfriend's* house," I said, emphasizing the word "boyfriend." Take *that*, lady.

"Isabel, don't joke."

Oh my God, she really didn't believe that I could ever have a boyfriend, could she?

"I'm not joking." I lowered my voice, but knew that Tarek could still hear me. "Remember? I mentioned him to you?"

There was a pause.

"That guy you're studying with?"

"Yes."

"*Oh, really?!*"

Here we go.

"Wait, how long—how long have you been seeing him?"

"Not that long." I knew what she was thinking. Not that long, but I was already sleeping at his house. Well, maybe she thought that I had gone over there for breakfast. Yeah, right.

"When do I get to meet him?" she asked.

"Soon, Mom." I would try to put that off as long as I could.

"Can't you come over this weekend?"

"I don't think so, Mom. We have a lot of studying to do."

"So you're at his house now?"

"That's what I said, Mom," I said resignedly.

"Where does he live?"

"Pentagon City."

"Does he live in a condo?"

No, he lives in a five-acre mansion right next to the mall. "Yes, Mom."

"What's his name?"

Tarek was in the kitchen now, washing dishes. But I knew it was an excuse to listen to my conversation with my Mom.

I sighed again.

"Don't you think I should know his name, if you're spending your weekends with him?" my mother insisted.

I broke down and told her his first and last name.

I steeled myself for what would come next.

"What kind of name is that?" she asked.

"His first name is an Arabic name, and his last name is French."

"Where is he from?"

"Miami," I smiled, imagining the confusion that would cause.

"Where was he born?"

"France."

"Why does he have an Arabic first name?"

"Because his mother is from Lebanon."

"Interesting." She was turning it over in her mind, I could tell.

"What does he look like?" she asked then.

"You can find out when you meet him," I said.

"Don't end up like your sister," my mother said. Her tone was as if she were talking to an eight-year-old. "Promise me you're using—"

"Mom!!" I practically shrieked into the phone. I was thirty-four years old, and couldn't believe she would say that to me.

"So you talked to Ariel?" I asked then, changing the subject as quickly as I could.

My mother sighed.

"It's not that bad, Mom," I said.

"You have always defended your sisters, over everything, even when you shouldn't have," Mom said firmly. "Even when they brought home bad grades, you defended them."

Of course I did. I wasn't their mother. I was their big sister. That was my job, as I saw it.

"Mom, I honestly don't see what the big deal is," I insisted. That was a half-truth. Of course, I got the point. Ariel was young and unmarried, living in a place that wasn't ideal for raising a child.

"The big deal is that she's not married! The big deal is that she just started her career! The big deal is how they will be able to afford it living in New York!"

"They have room," I told her. "The baby can sleep in their bedroom during the first year."

"Then they won't get any sleep," Mom insisted.

"Then they can get a bigger place," I said.

"They can't afford a bigger place, certainly not if they have to pay for a nanny."

"They can put the baby in daycare."

"Daycare!" Mom said, sounding mildly horrified. "The thought of putting a newborn in daycare makes me cringe!"

"Lots of people do it, Mom." My mother was a worry-wort; if she didn't have enough to worry about, she would make stuff up. Arguably, even I had to admit that Ariel's situation was cause for some concern. However, I honestly thought that it would turn out fine.

My mother had stayed at home to raise the three of us until my father had died, and at that point she had had no choice but to return to work. In Spain, it was the norm for either the maternal or paternal grandmother to babysit the children all day so that the couple could work. Typically, mothers from that generation hadn't had careers.

"Maybe one of our cousins from Spain could come as an au pair," I continued, trying to calm Mom down.

"But where would the au pair sleep? They only have one bedroom!"

This was going nowhere.

"Mom, what do you want me to do?"

"I can't believe that your sister let this happen! I mean, she's usually so responsible! Even *you* haven't gotten knocked up yet!"

Even me?! "Gee, thanks, Mom."

"Oh, you know what I mean!"

"So you think I'm—*loose?*"

"No, I meant, you're way older than she is—"

"Again, thanks, Mom."

"—and single. I mean, I imagine you're active in that way, especially now—"

"All right!" I was done. "Mom, listen," I said determinedly, speaking over her voice. "What's done is *done*. You can't change it. I can't change it. It's done. We all have to make the best of the situation now. Don't you agree?"

"Of course."

"There is *no point* in complaining about what's happened. She's pregnant. That's it. There's no going back. Don't you want her to have a healthy pregnancy?"

"Yes, of course I do."

"Then don't stress her out!" I lowered my voice. "Whatever you do, Mom, please don't stress Ariel out. Believe me, she's got enough to think about right now."

Mom finally calmed down enough to lower her voice too. She said that she was definitely going to New York to see Ariel over Thanksgiving.

"I'm going too," I said then.

"You are?" Mom sounded incredulous.

"Yes."

"Won't you have exams to study for?"

"Yes, but it's important that I see her."

"OK, good, then we could go together," Mom said.

"We'll see," I said. The idea of riding on a train for four hours with my mother, being her captive audience, was not altogether appealing to me.

Then I said that I had to go and, after telling her that I loved her, we hung up.

I turned to Tarek. "Are you *happy* now?!"

He was on the verge of laughing. "About what?"

"You *know*. There, she knows about you now. Now I'll have to suffer every weekend when she calls me." I mimicked my mother's voice as best I could. "Are you at *Tarek's* house? How is *Tarek* doing? When am I going to meet him? Blah, blah, blah."

He laughed then. "So what?"

"So what?!" I pointed a finger at him. "All right, a little *quid pro quo* here. Call your mother right now and tell her about me, my name, where I'm from, everything."

Tarek stepped toward me and looked at me with wide eyes. "She already knows all those things."

"Whatever." I waved a hand dismissively.

"Isabel, my mother has known everything about you for a while."

"Liar," I said, crossing my arms.

He handed me his cell phone. "If you don't believe me, then call her yourself."

I felt myself softening. "I believe you."

He moved again, standing in front of me, and took both of my hands in his. "You have no idea how long I've—liked you, do you?"

"Probably as long as I've liked *you*."

"Well, how long is that?" he asked.

"I don't want to tell you," I said, blushing. Then I whispered, "It's embarrassing."

He kissed me on the lips, slowly. I uncrossed my arms and put them around his waist, drawing him against me. It felt like my heart was expanding, like it was going to burst out of my chest.

"It's OK," he whispered back. "You don't have to tell me."

I took his face in my hands and kissed him tenderly. My fingers traced his cheekbones.

"I'm going to go shower," Tarek was saying, and I was broken out of my thoughts.

"OK," I dropped my hands from his face.

He stepped away, still holding onto one of my hands. Then he turned back to me for a moment.

"Aren't you coming?" he asked. His smile was devious and his eyes were all charm.

I was surprised for a second, then smiled back. "I'll be right there." Then I blushed again.

It was getting to be near the end of the semester and everyone was freaking out a little bit. I was trying more and more to stay away from campus, because the tension in the air was palpable, and I didn't need the full-time Millennial students affecting my mood.

Sunday had been an eventful day, mainly because of the many phone calls. Shortly after I had spoken with my mother, Ariel had called me, begging me to come to New York to see her over Thanksgiving because Lara couldn't come and she didn't want to be alone with my mother.

"And you handle Mom so well!" she had pleaded. "Please, Isabel!"

Her begging hadn't been necessary, I had told her, because I was already planning to go.

"You can bring Tarek if you want," she had told me.

"We'll see," I had said.

Afterward Tarek and I had talked about it.

"Look," I had told him, "Frankly, I would love for you to come with me. But I'm not sure that it would be a good time."

"Isabel, I understand," he had said.

"Ariel will be emotional, and I'm not sure how Javier is doing about it. My mother will be a tornado, cooking and cleaning up a storm and insisting on my sister doing this or that, and asking her every invasive question you can imagine."

Tarek had been really patient. He was always patient. "I would love to go with you, but it's OK."

"It's not that I don't want you to go—"

"I know," he had said, "I can meet them another time."

"I think that would be best," I had told him.

I couldn't tell if he was disappointed or not. I didn't like leaving him in DC by himself over the holiday, and told him so.

"Can't you go see your family? I'm sorry to leave you alone on Thanksgiving."

"I don't think it's worth the cost of the trip," he had said.

That made me feel awful. It must have shown on my face because he hugged me.

"Please don't feel bad," he had said. "I can use the time to finish outlining, and Josh and Eric will be here, and they said that we can hang out."

"OK." That made me feel marginally better. I began to mentally prepare myself for interacting with Ariel and, most of all, with my mother.

After that, Tarek's mother had called and he had spoken to her for a while. He told me that everything was fine with them, but that his uncles kept insisting for him to confirm that he was going to work for them after he graduated. If Tarek was upset about it, he hid it well. He told me that his plan was to borrow more money in student loans next year, and not accept any money from his uncles for living expenses. So he would have to take out loans not only for tuition, but for rent and living expenses as well. The tuition at our school was around $26,000 per year. Add living expenses to that over three years, and you would easily rack up at least $200,000 in debt.

"I can cook for you if you want," I had blurted out when we were talking about it. "I mean, I can cook so that we don't have to eat out so often. And we can go out less."

He had stared at me. I hadn't understood his expression at first.

"Tarek, I don't mind," I had continued. "We both have to save money."

Then he had smiled warmly. "That's so kind of you."

I had shrugged. "Well, I'd like to. I mean, I'm your—you know," then I was blushing. "I want to help. You know that, don't you?"

He had kissed me then, pressing his lips against mine passionately.

When we pulled away, a little reluctantly, I had told him, "I don't want you to be stressed out."

"Isabel, I—" he had begun.

"Tell me," I had said.

"I'm really glad that I met you." He had smiled shyly.

Today, I was still slightly concerned about studying for exams, but figured I could study on the train ride to New York, if I managed to take the train by myself, and not with my mother. I needed to get my ticket soon.

As soon as I got to campus and sat down with Tarek, I opened my laptop to search for train tickets and check our class calendar online.

"So we don't have class the Wednesday before Thanksgiving," I said, thinking out loud.

"Right, and our Crim Pro professor cancelled class on Tuesday," Tarek said then.

"Really?" I looked at him.

"Yes, it's on the syllabus." He showed me.

"Great! Then I'll try to get a train ticket for early Tuesday morning."

"When are you going to come back?" Tarek asked.

I sighed. "Probably Sunday, to be honest." I looked at him then. "I'll miss you."

He smiled at me, and I thought his eyes were a little sad. "I'll miss you too."

Josh and Alyssa approached us then and sat at our table.

"So I found out that we don't have Crim on Tuesday," I told them.

"Yeah, that's awesome," Josh seconded.

Alyssa looked at me briefly, then said softly, "Hey, Isabel," tilting her head in acknowledgement of my existence. I smiled, genuinely for once. Interestingly, our interactions were less and less chilly and more and more cordial.

"Hey, Alyssa," I told her. Then I thought of something. "I'm glad you're here, I have a question for you."

She looked at me sideways with slightly narrowed eyes.

She was right to be wary of me, I thought. We still weren't friends, exactly, but we certainly tolerated each other a great deal more than before.

"Yes?" she said to me slowly as she sat down.

I leaned forward, thinking about how to phrase the question precisely. "The case we read in Property the other day . . . ," I pretended to think about it. "*Vasquez v. Glassboro Service?*"

"Yes." She nodded, an inquisitive expression on her face.

"Well," I continued, "I don't understand what the problem is with the remedy requested. Did you get that?"

"Which case was that?" she asked.

I showed her my notes. "How can the Defendant argue that his tenant isn't a tenant?" I asked.

"Oh, I remember this case," she said then. "It's because the landlord is arguing that the Plaintiff is a licensee, not a tenant of his property."

"What's the difference?" I asked, although I knew the answer.

"Well, a licensee is different from a tenant. You see, a licensee is only granted the right to use a property, not to live on the property. A tenant has a possessory interest in the property, in other words, a right to live on the property."

She certainly knew what she was talking about. "Why does that make a difference here?" I continued my questions.

"Because the remedy is different based on whether the person is a licensee or a tenant. Here, the landlord evicted the Plaintiff. If the Plaintiff is a licensee, then when the Defendant breaches the contract he had with the licensee, the licensee can seek contract damages for breach. But if the Plaintiff is a tenant, then his remedy is specific performance. That means that if the tenant wins, the court restores his right of possession of the property, and he gets to live there again."

"Oh, OK. Thanks," I said. "That makes sense."

I stared at her, and felt my lips curving into a smile, but caught myself. I hadn't meant to trick her. I just didn't know why she hid the fact that she was so smart.

I didn't have too much time to gloat that I had confirmed my suspicions, or to question Alyssa further, because at that moment Saul showed up. It was odd that he would approach us without Sameer nearby. Those two were practically joined at the hip.

Saul seemed to have come out of nowhere, so much so that I almost jumped out of my chair. He said hi to Alyssa first, but was looking directly at me the entire time. His intense gaze unnerved me. I also noticed how clean-cut he looked today. His short hair was neatly trimmed and the skin on his face looked smooth, like he had just shaved. In that moment, I could understand why I had slept with him last year. His personality left a lot to be desired, at least in my opinion, but he was attractive.

Alyssa said hi back, a bit shyly.

"Hi, Isabel," he spoke melodically, his eyes half-closed. I was sure that everyone at that table noticed the way in which he had said it, or else they were totally tuned out. In fact, I could feel some tension from Tarek, and Josh's expression had changed, as if he were slightly bothered by it.

I completely ignored Saul, refusing to feed his fire.

"Hey," I said to Josh, "we have class the Monday before Thanksgiving, right?"

"Yes," he answered. "Why?"

"Because I might go to New York to see my sister, and I might leave that Monday, depending on tickets."

By this time, Saul was chatting with Alyssa. While talking to Josh, I was trying to eavesdrop on their conversation. If I had heard correctly, they were making plans for this weekend.

Saul finally left, and the tension around the table eased, especially from my end.

Once we got to Crim Pro class, I messaged Eric.

I thought I overheard Alyssa making plans with Saul this weekend.

Oh, yeah?

Yes. Then I continued. How are things going between you and her?

They aren't going.

You should tell her how you feel, Eric.

LOL. Look who's talking.

I told him eventually. I smiled to myself.

You never did tell me that story.

I will one day.

Who told who first?

I told him first.

I don't believe you.

Honest to God. I told him first, but technically he kissed me first.

Technically?

It's a long story.

I stand by my previous statement. You're much nicer now that you're getting laid regularly.

STFU.

Your grasp of Millennial-speak has also improved.

Jackass, LOL.

Then I needed to pay attention, since the guy in front of Tarek got called on, and that made me on edge, wondering whether the professor would call on me next. Sometimes the professors did that; they called on people in groups depending on where they were sitting in class.

The rest of the night passed without incident, which was saying something for this crowd.

Later that night, when Tarek and I were having dinner in his apartment, he looked like he wanted to ask me something.

"Hey, what's on your mind?" I asked him.

"What do you mean?"

"I keep having the impression that you want to tell me something, but you don't say anything."

He sighed.

"Are you mad?" I asked him quickly.

"No, no." He looked at me, and by his expression I knew I wouldn't like the question.

"What's up with you and Saul?"

It was the question I had been dreading, and I wasn't prepared for it. I had been fooling myself, thinking I could dodge it indefinitely.

"Nothing is *up* with us," I said carefully. "I don't like him."

"Why not?" He touched my hand, holding it loosely.

"First of all, he's a womanizer. And it makes me angry because—well, you know what Sameer thinks about me because of that day when he warned me not to go out with you. He obviously thinks I'm a—he thinks I 'sleep around,'" using air quotes. "But his best friend sleeps around, I mean, however you define that. My point is—" I rambled. "He and Sameer both criticize me for doing the same thing as they do, you get it?"

"I get it."

"It's a double standard, and it makes me angry."

Tarek didn't say anything for a few moments.

"Is that the only reason you don't like Saul?" he asked me, looking into my eyes.

I knew then that he wouldn't ask me directly, but the real question was whether I had been romantically involved with Saul. I had a decision to make, and took the path of least resistance.

"Yes," I said. "I mean, other than the fact that he occasionally looks at me like I'm a piece of meat."

"I noticed that."

"But he looks at a lot of women that way." That was true.

There was a pause. "Does that answer your question?" I asked, trying to appear calm.

All of a sudden Tarek seemed to deflate. "Yes, look—I'm sorry I asked. I'm kind of—protective of you. I don't want anyone to upset you."

I kissed him. "I know and I—like that about you." I had almost said, I *love* that about you.

He seemed like he believed me. And I felt terrible. I was a horrible person. I had never lied to him about anything. And if he found out the truth now, he would hate me.

I couldn't believe that it took me until mid-morning to remember what day it was. I woke up that Wednesday with my arms around Tarek. I kissed his back and breathed in the scent of him. I certainly didn't feel like going to work.

He turned around and kissed me. "Do you want to—?"

"I wish," I said, whining. "I have to get to work."

Then I had an idea.

"Hey, what are you doing on Friday?" I asked him.

He chuckled. "I'm going out with *you* Friday night, or we can stay in, if you want."

"No, I meant—what are you doing during the day?"

He looked at me, then grinned. "I don't have any plans."

"I was thinking—" I began. "If you want, I can take the day off from work, and maybe we could go to the range, and then do something else—I mean, if you want."

His grin broadened. "Sure," he said. "I would love to spend the day with you." After that, it was more difficult to leave him, but I was able to in the end.

I showed up for work relatively early. I had decided to go low-key and comfortable, and wore black jeans with a white blouse and blazer.

I still couldn't believe that classes were almost done. But I was a little more relaxed about exams.

I was fairly ahead of the game, since I had most of my outlining done, thanks, at least in part, to Tarek and his diligence. He was indeed studious, as he had initially told me months ago.

I had been at work for a couple of hours when I had to date a document. At that point, I realized what day it actually was.

"Holy shit," I murmured to myself. I didn't know if I was more surprised at the actual date or at the fact that I had almost forgotten.

This was always a difficult day for me. In the past, at best I would spend the evening with Lara or Ariel. At worst, I would be by myself at home, overthinking and remembering every last detail, unable to sleep all night.

Then I smiled a little. Tonight I wouldn't be alone. I would be with someone who cared about me. I again felt the familiar rush that was starting to be all too frequent. It was like an extra dose of something, adrenaline, maybe? When I felt like that, all I wanted to do was be with Tarek, and to hold him and have him hold me.

I'm getting too soft in my old age, I thought.

Even with Tarek, tonight would be difficult. I always dreaded it. It brought back memories that I hated, that made me hate myself. Even now, I still asked God why, why do this? Nothing was fair. Life wasn't fair.

For the briefest of moments, I thought about calling my mother. But I was delusional to even think about it. I was afraid that I would remind her of things she wanted to forget. She seemed to be good at that, forgetting things she wanted to forget. I wish I had that ability.

I pushed all those thoughts to the back of my mind, and concentrated on my work. It was, thankfully, a busy day. My coworkers didn't bother me too much, and I went to the gym during my lunch break. The post-workout shower felt really good, but I couldn't wash away all my negative thoughts like I wanted to do.

I was eating lunch at my desk when Lara called.

"Hey," she said.

"Hey, Punk," I said warmly. "How are you doing?"

"I'm good. Getting psyched for my late shift tonight. I hope the crazies stay home."

I said a quick, silent prayer that she would have an OK night and would be safe. "I'll be thinking about you, as always."

"I know. I'll be fine." Then she paused. "Isabel, will you be OK tonight?"

"Yeah, I'll be fine."

"Are you going to hang with Tarek?"

"Yes." I was smiling.

"Are you going to sleep at his place?"

"Yes."

"How often do you sleep over there?"

I was confused. "What do you mean?"

"I mean," Lara continued, "like, are you there on the weekends or—?"

"No."

"No, you're not there on the weekends?" Now she was confused.

"No, I mean—I'm there pretty much *all* the time." I spoke in low tones and in code to make sure no one at work understood what I was talking about.

"What do you mean all the time?" Then it must have dawned on her because she gasped. "You mean you sleep over there *all* the time? Like, every night?"

"Well, pretty much."

"Wait, wait, wait a minute." She knew I was at work, so she would try to ask me questions that required only one-word answers. "Are you telling me that you have slept at his place every night since you two started going out?"

"Not—quite to that extent, but practically."

"Oh my God."

"Why? Is that weird?" I finally walked outside the office, into the main corridor of the floor, so that I could speak more frankly. No one was around.

"No, it's—wow, then this is really serious!" She sounded happy.

"Really?" I was curious now. This was like a window to something I didn't really know about. "Is that what it means?"

"I would say so! It certainly sounds serious to *me*."

"What does that mean anyway, *serious*?" I thought it was a relative term.

"Like, you're definitely exclusive."

I told her then that we had already had that conversation.

"Ooo, the *talk*?" she giggled, making fun of me.

"No, not the *talk*," I said, half-annoyed. "It just came up."

"Well, Patrick and I approve," she said, still giggly, then added quickly, "not that you need our approval."

I realized then that I hadn't had much of a chance to speak to Lara since the four of us had gone to dinner.

"Well, he said you guys were really nice," I told her.

"Well, we know that's a lie," she joked.

"No, seriously, thanks for going out with us. And thank you for not being too hard on him."

She paused. "You know that Mom totally grilled me about him."

I sighed. I had figured that would happen. I didn't envy my sister at that moment, and was pretty sure that Mom had been relentless. "What did you tell her?"

"That he's really nice and seems to like you a lot."

"Well, thank you," I told her.

"It's *true*."

I told Lara that I loved her and that I had to go.

"Promise me that if anything comes up tonight, that if you're feeling really sad, that you'll call me," she said.

"I won't. You'll be at work."

"Call me anyway."

"Lara, I will be fine. I won't be alone."

"OK."

Then we hung up.

Once I was back at my desk, I started to think again, but the thoughts weren't all negative. As happened so frequently nowadays, they eventually drifted to Tarek.

I really liked him, but it was more than that. In fact, we hadn't really been officially seeing each other for that long, but I was starting to not like it when he wasn't around.

Later, I was walking downtown to campus when Ariel called.

"Hey," I answered, "are you all right?"

"Yes, I'm OK," she said. "How are *you*, Isabel? Are you going to be OK tonight?"

"I'll be fine." In the past, that would have been a lie. Now, however, I actually believed it.

"Is Tarek with you?" she asked then.

I guess everyone had the same thing on their minds, I thought and smiled to myself. "Not right now, but I'll see him in class."

"How are *you* doing?" I asked Ariel then. "How are you feeling?"

"I feel OK, tired but OK." She was smiling, I could tell. I knew she would be stressed, but the thought of her having a little mini-me must also be incredibly exciting. A part of me was jealous of her.

"Mom is still stressing me out," she continued. "But I flat out told her not to come up until you come up over Thanksgiving. She wanted to come visit this weekend!"

"Smart," I said. "Don't worry, I'll handle her."

"I know you will. I can't wait to see you, Isabel. I miss you so much."

It was difficult for us to be so far apart. And Ariel was the baby of the family. Lara and I were both protective of her. It was interesting that when we were younger, Ariel and I had had more of a mother-daughter relationship because of the age difference but also because of the situation.

Now, however, we had a sisterly relationship, and I was glad for it. "I will make Mom behave, and everything will be fine, I promise," I told her, and meant it. I could handle Mom. Ironically, just when I had been starting to be able to handle everything in my life, Tarek had shown up with his sexy eyes and his gorgeous smile.

We hung up and I reached the law school building.

No one else would call me today. Mom never called me on this date, and I never called her. I often wondered how she handled it.

I ran into Alyssa as I entered the law school building. She was alone.

I walked directly up to her. She looked taken aback for a second but quickly regained her composure, so much so that I was grudgingly impressed. Again, I thought that she must be more mature than she had appeared to be at first glance.

"I hope you know what you're doing," I told her.

"What are you talking about?" she asked, but she knew; I could see it in her eyes.

"You've either slept with Saul or are thinking about it," I whispered. "Remember what I told you. Also, he bangs Alicia regularly, as far as I know. So you're not going to be the only one."

"I'm a big girl," she told me.

"So—what then?" Now I was annoyed with her, throwing my arms out to the sides.

She shrugged. "I don't know. He's really nice."

"Alyssa, he's only nice when he wants something. In that, he and Alicia are perfect for each other."

"Like it's any of your business," she said, trying to be confident. But I saw uncertainty in her expression.

"Don't say I didn't warn you. And don't come crying to me afterward." My words were harsher than my tone. If Alyssa did sleep with him, I would know why. He was sexy and she was lonely. That had been me a year ago.

I sighed and dropped my shoulders. I wanted to tell her that I was sorry for bringing it up, that it was in fact none of my business, that I didn't want to see her get hurt. But I just shook my head quickly. "We'll talk later," I told her, then left to go find Tarek.

I found him where I always found him. I was still trying to sort out my feelings, but put all that out of my head for now.

I sat down next to him and gave him a lingering kiss.

"What's that for?" he asked, his eyes alive and sparkling.

"I don't know," I said, smiling shyly. "Happy to see you, I guess." I glanced at his laptop, which was open. He was reviewing his notes for class. "What are you working on?"

"The usual. Trying to figure out how to take over the world."

I laughed. "I can help with that. But I'll settle for taking over this city."

"That's enough," he told me. "This city is the center of the free world, so—"

"Agreed."

I looked around. There was no sign of Eric or Josh.

"How was work?" Tarek was asking me, and I was instantly brought out of my thoughts.

"OK. Busy. I talked to both my sisters."

"Really?" He seemed surprised. "Is everything all right with them?"

"Yeah, they always call me on this day." I shrugged, distracted.

"What do you mean *this day*?"

Oh yeah. He didn't know. I chuckled, but it wasn't a happy sound. "That's right. You don't know. I figured you already knew everything about me." I looked at him sideways. "It seems like it anyway."

He was waiting for me to tell him, but didn't say anything.

I sighed. "It's the day my father died, twenty years ago."

"Oh, Isabel, you should've told me." His brows furrowed.

"Well, I'm telling you now."

"I'm sorry."

"It's all right. Look." I put my hand on his thigh. "We'll talk about it later. I don't want to talk about it right now."

"OK," he nodded and kissed me quickly, but the look of concern didn't disappear from his face.

"I'm OK, really," I assured him.

The evening was fairly uneventful, except for the fact that Eric kept sending me messages during class. I told him about my earlier exchange with Alyssa.

Maybe you should go out with them this weekend, I said, meaning to keep an eye on Alyssa.

I don't know, he answered.

You should tell her how you feel about her. I was getting frustrated with him.

I don't know.

Then I told him that I had to pay attention to the lecture, and that he should too. Why I was getting wrapped up in these high-school dramas, I had no idea.

Later that evening, Tarek and I had finished dinner and I was sitting on the sofa at his place. I sighed, thinking about Eric and wondering why I was making his problem my problem.

Tarek must have read my mind. "Have you talked to Eric recently?" he asked me. He was in the kitchen, preparing tea.

"We were chatting during class, but I eventually told him that we both had to pay attention."

"What were you guys talking about, if I may ask?" He was trying to sound nonchalant, but his movements gave him away. It was almost like he was trying too hard to appear indifferent. I wasn't buying it.

"About what to do about this girl he likes." I was looking at him as I said it.

"Who does he like?"

"Babe, he made me promise not to say anything. I'm sorry."

"Is it someone I know?"

"Yes." I paused. "I told him to tell her how he feels about her. I don't see the point in dragging it out."

Tarek was chuckling.

"I know, I know," I said, then went to join him in the kitchen. "This is what happens when I have friends who are ten years younger than me. I get sucked into all the drama."

He stood in front of me and I pulled him to me, kissing him on the mouth. "If I didn't know any better, I'd think you were jealous."

Tarek looked down and sighed.

"Eric's having a hard time right now," I told him. Then I whispered into his ear, "So please, babe, don't be jealous."

In all honesty, I could not conceive of the idea of being with anyone other than Tarek right now. But I didn't say that. Maybe I should have.

When the tea was ready, we sat down on the sofa. I leaned back, one hand holding my mug and the other over the mug, feeling the warmth of the rising steam. I suddenly remembered again what day it was, then immediately became sad. I couldn't change what had happened to my father, and I couldn't change how my mother felt. My mind wandered.

"Hey." Suddenly, I was aware of Tarek's hand on my leg. I looked at him. "Are you all right?"

I sighed. "Yeah," I said, smiling weakly.

"Isabel, I know this must be a hard day for you."

"Well, you know what it's like." Except that he really didn't, because even though Tarek's father had died young, Tarek hadn't been responsible for his death.

"I'm sorry." He touched my face, brushing my hair back behind my ear.

"Look," he began, "I don't want to pressure you, but if you want to talk about it—"

Then I was shocked. Because I *did* in fact want to talk about it.

I turned and looked at him, incredulous. "Actually, I've never talked about it, but—do you mind if I did?"

"No, of course not." He half-smiled. "Why would you feel that you had to carry something like that all by yourself?"

"Because I always have." I shrugged.

He gave me a look of comprehension.

I took a deep breath.

"Isabel," Tarek said then. "I'm sure that whatever happened, you could not have prevented it. It was an accident, right?"

"No," I shook my head. "That's the story I tell everyone."

We sat in silence.

"Isabel, I don't—I don't want to cause you pain by having you relive it, but—sometimes it helps to talk about it. Whatever you want to do."

I waited, churning thoughts around in my head, then turned my entire body toward him, still sunk into the back of the sofa, and began speaking. Tarek listened.

"It was late, and my family was at home sleeping. Where we lived—it wasn't exactly the country, but there weren't many houses around—it was kind of isolated."

I took a breath, then continued.

"Someone broke in. My father heard him. He got up and woke me up. I slept in my own room and my sisters shared a room across the hall." I inhaled, then exhaled in one quick breath. "My father told me to call 911 and make sure my sisters were OK. He took his rifle and went downstairs. I called 911, and told my sisters to hide in the closet." I paused for a second. "That must have all happened in the space of less than a minute. Then I got another gun he had, a handgun, a 9 millimeter, from his gun safe. I figured that if something happened to my father, I would have to do something. So I went downstairs—I was scared shitless."

"He had confronted the guy in the family room. They both had their guns drawn. I didn't think that the guy could see me where I was. It was too dark there, but my father had turned on a light, and I could tell that that guy was—" I struggled with how to articulate it. "He was crazy,—feral. My father said something to him, like, 'Get out of here, we already called the police,' and when the guy didn't leave, my father fired at him, hitting him in the chest." I touched my own chest then. "But the guy kept coming. We learned later that he was totally high. That's why the first bullet didn't stop him."

I paused for about thirty seconds, then went on.

"Because he didn't stop, I fired at him, aiming for his chest, but hit his right shoulder instead. Even though he had the gun in his right hand, he still managed to shoot, not at me, but my father. I guess he assumed that my father had shot him again because where I was, he couldn't see me. At the same time as he shot my father, I shot him again, right in the chest. Then I shot him twice more. He wasn't moving. I took his gun away, like my father had shown me how to do, unloaded it, and went to check my father. He was dying on the floor. I went to him, and he—he died in my arms right there, looking at me."

As an afterthought, I said, "and the guy died too."

I stopped for a moment.

"And your mother was OK? Was she there?" Tarek asked, curious.

"She stayed with my sisters. She didn't want me to go downstairs. Maybe if I hadn't—maybe things would've turned out differently."

"Isabel," Tarek said then, touching my hair, "you can't blame yourself for killing that guy."

"I don't," I shook my head.

He understood. "You blame yourself for missing."

"Exactly. My aim was off, I was nervous, and I overcorrected. I had been shooting regularly for two years. There was no excuse for that, I mean, all you have to do is aim for center mass, right?" I hesitated for a moment.

"And do you know what my father said to me as he lay there? He said, *has hecho bien, hija*. I told him, *no, porque te ha disparado*. And he said, *eso no importa, porque tu madre y tus hermanas están a salvo, gracias a tí*." I told Tarek what the words meant. My father, even when faced with his own imminent death, was only thinking about his wife and his daughters.

"I've never told anyone that, not even my sisters," I said then. I was exhausted just talking about it.

Tarek took me in his arms. I was sad, but didn't cry. I had cried about it enough, and there came a point where I had accepted it for what it was, even if I hated it.

"You can't blame yourself for that."

"But why would God take him, and leave me? My mother wasn't the same for a long time. Sometimes, when she looks at me I see this look on her face, like she still blames me for it."

"That's not true."

"But how do you know?"

"Because I know. No mother would blame her child for that."

I wanted to believe him. I felt so safe in his arms and wanted to stay there like that all night. He was rubbing my shoulder, comforting me.

"Tarek, I feel bad unloading all this on you," I said into his chest.

"Why?" His tone conveyed that I was crazy for feeling that way.

"Because I'm not the only one who's lost a father."

"Isabel, you know there are no guarantees in life. Life is about what you do with the hand you're dealt. And I don't believe that God deals us things that we can't handle."

"I guess. I—" I was having difficulty articulating what I was feeling.

"I know," he said softly. "It's a lot to deal with—I mean, for your entire life."

"I think about him every day."

"Of course you do." His voice was barely above a whisper.

I didn't say anything for a little while. It was so soothing being here with him like this, even if the topic was so depressing.

All of a sudden, I exhaled and my shoulders relaxed. I sat up so that I could look at him. His expression was tender, and I kissed him.

"Thank you. It feels good to talk about it." Indeed, it felt like a huge weight had been lifted off my chest.

"Anytime. I—" all of a sudden he looked like he was on the verge of saying something, something important, something that made him shy to bring up. I didn't understand. "You can tell me anything." That couldn't have been it, I thought. It didn't matter, anyway.

I leaned against the back of the sofa. I felt like I couldn't move, and was suddenly so tired.

"I'm so sorry," he said softly.

"It's not your fault."

"I'm still sorry."

"You're so good to me," I said, in a voice so low that I wasn't sure he heard.

He smiled. "Honestly, Isabel, if—if I'd known you were here in DC I would have been here sooner."

He took my hand, and I squeezed his in response.

"I know, babe," I told him. I felt like he knew me. I felt like I never wanted to leave his side. "I know," I repeated.

On Friday morning we woke up lazily. I slept in since I had taken the day off. I was so cozy in bed, shielded from the cold world outside.

During the previous night, I had woken up out of a deep sleep, having heard a noise inside the apartment. I had sat up in bed in one rapid-fire motion, then rolled over to feel under the bed for my gun safe. I didn't find it because I wasn't in my apartment.

Then Tarek had his arms around me.

"Isabel, it's OK. It's OK," he had whispered urgently. "It's just the neighbor."

"No, it's from inside the apartment!" I was almost frantic.

"No, it's not. The walls are paper thin here. I swear it's the neighbor coming home and shutting her door."

I had taken a deep breath, forcing myself to calm down. Then I had checked the apartment just in case but, of course, Tarek had been right.

"Sorry," I had said to him, returning to the bedroom, "it sounded like it was right here."

"I know, but it's not."

I had gotten a glass of water, then gone back to bed, with my head against Tarek's chest and under the blanket. Then I had suddenly realized something.

"Oh," I had said aloud. "Oh!"

"What's the matter?" Tarek had asked me.

"That's why your neighbor was looking at me like that the other day!"

"Like what?"

I had proceeded to tell Tarek about the other morning, when his blonde neighbor Amber had told me that she had never seen me in the morning before, and had given me that knowing smile, like she knew something that I didn't.

"Tarek, she can hear us!" I was beyond mortified.

He had chucked.

"Did you hear what I said?" I had asked him.

"Isabel, who cares?"

"Who *cares*?! I can't believe that you let me—" I had stopped, embarrassed.

"Let you what?"

"Carry on like that!"

"Like what?"

"You *know*!"

"Isabel, so she knows we're—having a good time. Big deal."

I had huffed, annoyed. "Big deal!" I had muttered to myself. "I don't want everyone knowing my business!" Or my habits, I thought.

He had hugged me to him. It was embarrassing, but I figured there wasn't anything I could do about it now.

Then, as always when I was this close to Tarek, I began to get turned on. I had lifted his shirt and started kissing his chest.

"What are you doing?" he had asked in a way that conveyed that he knew quite well what I was doing.

"I'm awake now, so what are you going to do about it?" I had asked suggestively.

"Oh, I can think of a couple of things," Tarek had said, rolling over on top of me.

I had been much quieter than usual, however.

Luckily, weekday mornings and afternoons weren't too crowded at the range. We had no problem getting a lane, and we spent time shooting my 9-millimeter, revolver and AR-15.

On the way back to my place, I had my music cranked up. We were on the freeway that surrounded Washington, DC, and Boston was playing. One of my all-time favorite songs came on.

I looked out this morning and the sun was gone.
Turned on some music to start my day.
I lost myself in a familiar song.
I closed my eyes and I slipped away.

I started singing, and soon I was belting out the lyrics, while Tarek smiled at me, shaking his head slowly.

> *It's more than a feeling, when I hear that old song they used to*
> *play, more than a feeling.*
> *I begin dreaming (more than a feeling)*
> *'till I see Marianne walk away*
> *I see Marianne walkin' away*

I didn't hear the siren, but I saw the police car right as it was on top of us.

At the same moment I saw the car, Tarek said urgently, "Isabel, slow down! It's the cops!"

"I know! I know!" I told him.

"What did you do?"

"Nothing!" I said honestly. A thousand things were going through my head at that moment. Why would he stop me? When I filled out the application to take the bar, would I have to report this? Probably, but only if he issued me a ticket, or arrested me, right? Was that right?

Arrest me?! He wouldn't arrest me, would he? I didn't even know what he was pulling me over for.

I automatically slowed down. I was in the right lane, so I began to slowly pull over on the right side of the road.

"Why would he stop you?" Tarek was asking me.

"I don't know. I didn't do anything!" I stopped the car and put it in park. "This is an illegal stop because I didn't do anything. So anything he may find is an illegal search."

And I had guns in the car. No big deal. I mean, I had a concealed carry permit.

Wait, I thought then. I didn't have to tell the cop anything.

I was racking my brain. Think, think, I told myself. You're taking Crim Pro right now—

"Isabel?" Tarek's voice was neutral but slightly tentative.

"It's all right," I told him.

"But you have guns in the car!" he whispered urgently.

"Don't worry. It's all legit." I looked in the rearview mirror. The cop had opened his door and was getting out of his car slowly. "Don't say anything. Let me do the talking. And for God's sake, don't look nervous. I'm pretty sure that a nervous Arab man is probable cause for an automobile search." Tarek half-chuckled at my lame joke.

I finally ordered my thoughts. The Supreme Court had decided tons of criminal procedure cases. I knew this.

In doing the auto stop, the policeman had the authority to order both of us out of the car. He could do that, but I figured he wouldn't unless we made him nervous. If I had done something technically illegal such as speed, then the cop had probable cause to arrest me. But the police hardly ever arrested people for traffic infractions like that, although technically it was in their authority to do so. If he arrested me, then he would get the right to search me and the interior of my car. However, he couldn't search the trunk unless he had probable cause to think that the trunk contained evidence of a crime. And my guns were in the trunk.

If he didn't arrest me, which was the more likely scenario, assuming he had pulled me over for a minor traffic infraction, then he could only seize things in his plain view. He couldn't search the car or the trunk unless he had probable cause to believe that they contained evidence of a crime. I had to be very careful about what I said to him. I couldn't let him search the car or the trunk. I hadn't done anything wrong, and I legally owned my guns. But I didn't want any hassles. And it was the principle of the thing.

I watched him walk toward my car from my rearview mirror, and cracked my window a little. Tarek was still a little tense, but more relaxed than a few moments ago.

The policeman approached and stood by my window.

"Why did you stop me, officer?" I asked politely.

"Do you know why I stopped you, miss?" the policeman asked firmly but politely. His large size was intimidating. I had to crane my neck to look at him. I could tell that he asked the question by rote.

"Ah, no Sir," I answered. "That's why I asked." I kept both hands on the steering wheel, and felt my heart rate speed up.

"You changed lanes without using your turn signal back there," he said. It was definitely not a question.

That's not true, I thought. I always use my turn signal. You just didn't see it, Mr. Officer. But I said nothing.

"Do you dispute that?" the officer asked me.

"Yes, Sir, I do," I stated firmly. I felt tension from Tarek. Please don't freak out, Tarek, I prayed silently. "I did use my signal." Of course, if he wrote me a ticket, it would only be my word against his. And I would pay the ticket, of course. There was no point in sweating it out all day at the Fairfax County Courthouse for the judge to end up believing the officer over some arrogant law student.

"No, you didn't," the officer said.

Again, I was silent, since he hadn't asked a question.

Then the officer spoke again. "You don't have anything illegal in the car, do you?"

"Sir, I do not consent to any searches," I said slowly and deliberately.

"Are you an attorney?" he asked suddenly, surprised.

"We're law students, Sir."

"Both of you?" he asked. Then he glanced at Tarek for the first time.

"Yes, Sir."

I noticed then that he hadn't taken his ticket pad out yet. I guessed that might be a good sign. I was trying hard not to be too optimistic.

The officer started to smile a little. I would have missed it if my eyes hadn't been glued to his face in anticipation of whether or not he was going to write me a ticket.

"Well, that's a first," he said, and the smile that tugged at the corners of his mouth was a bit more noticeable now.

I looked at him, confused. "What's that, Sir?"

"Well, that's the first time I've seen a woman, law student no less, with conservative bumper stickers and a Middle Eastern boyfriend."

I laughed. I couldn't help it. Then I also felt myself blushing, as the tension from everyone eased. "Yeah, we get that a lot," I said, glancing at Tarek, who appeared more relaxed.

I looked back at the policeman and could see it in his eyes when he decided not to write me a ticket.

"OK," he said, "I'll let you go with a warning this time, but please use your turn signal from now on."

I *had* used my turn signal, I thought, but didn't say anything in response.

"Thank you so much, Officer," I told him, smiling.

We wished each other a good day and he left. I waited until his car left the shoulder, then started my engine. I looked at Tarek. He sighed, relaxed his shoulders, and looked back at me, smiling and shaking his head.

The usual suspects, and by that I mean Tarek, Josh, Alyssa, and me, were sitting in the downstairs area of the law school, trying to find something to talk about other than exams, which were on everyone's minds.

Josh looked at me then. "Are you going to the minority corporate counsel conference?" he asked.

"I'm not sure," I answered, running a hand through my hair. "Frankly, I'm not sure how useful it will be." Seeing as how I had not had any luck interviewing with law firms.

"Why would you go to a minority conference?" Alyssa asked me.

I stared at her, already thinking of something snarky to say. But the look on her face told me that it was actually a genuine question.

"What do you mean?" I asked, my brows furrowing.

"Why would you guys go to a minority conference? You're not minorities," Alyssa said, shrugging.

"We're Hispanic," Josh said.

Alyssa looked at Josh's light brown hair. "But you're not Hispanic, you're white—both of you," Alyssa responded.

"I speak Spanish," Josh told her, by way of explanation.

"Hispanic does not mean 'dark-skinned,'" I told Alyssa. "Under the federal definition, 'Hispanic' means someone from a Spanish-speaking country."

"So all you guys," Alyssa insisted, motioning to Tarek as well, "totally take advantage of that."

"What do you mean 'take advantage'?" I asked her. "Why shouldn't we? We're being rational." Then I motioned toward Tarek. "And he doesn't 'take advantage' of minority statuses," I said, using my air quotes, "because he's not a recognized minority under federal law."

"What do you mean?" Alyssa appeared to be genuinely confused.

"The only recognized minority groups," I explained patiently, "at least for affirmative action purposes, are African-American, Hispanic and Asian/Pacific Islander. There's no 'Middle Eastern' or 'Indian' minority group, although maybe someone from India could make an argument that he or she is 'Asian.' As far as I know, people of Middle Eastern backgrounds are considered Caucasian."

"Really?" Alyssa was incredulous.

"The purposes of minority preference is to right past wrongs regarding those groups traditionally discriminated against," Josh clarified.

"At least, theoretically," I agreed.

"Well, you guys don't *look* Hispanic; you look white, and you don't even speak English with any accent," Alyssa insisted.

I could understand her point, but she was setting an arbitrary definition of 'minority,' which was different from the ones the schools and employers used.

"Alyssa, that is not the definition of 'minority' under federal law," I repeated. "That is a definition that you are imposing, and Josh and I don't have to follow your arbitrary standards."

"Look, I'm sorry," Alyssa answered, holding up her hand, "but I don't think it's fair of you guys to designate yourself Hispanic."

"Why not?!" I was getting worked up. "My parents were discriminated against, I have been discriminated against for speaking Spanish in public, so why shouldn't I self-identify as Hispanic?"

"Because—" her words failed her, and I was tired of making the same point. I opened my mouth once again to protest, but Tarek beat me to it.

"Look, Alyssa," he said, peering directly at her, "whatever your opinion on this, they have the right to self-identify as Hispanic. You don't have to like that fact, but it's allowed and, frankly, it makes logical sense to do so. A person would be crazy not to distinguish himself as a minority if he can, since it's definitely advantageous in many ways."

Alyssa tried to protest again, but Tarek cut her off. "And, by the way, you have to accept that the opinions of other people are also valid. If you are as tolerant as most people say they are, then you will be tolerant of other people's opinions."

Josh chimed in then as well. I opened my mouth and then realized something. Like an idiot, I sat there, mouth half-open, frozen. Luckily, everyone else was still arguing and I didn't think that anyone had noticed that I had been about to say something.

I had realized something, something so obvious but earth-shattering, and it made me so afraid.

He was always defending me, and he didn't care who he had to defend me against.

And he was always concerned about me, taking care of me, wondering how I was doing.

And I loved him for it.

I *loved* him. I was completely in love with him.

I couldn't imagine my life right now without him in it.

This was what I had been afraid of, since basically the first moment I saw Tarek. But honestly, what had I thought would happen after we started being together like we were?

I knew the answer to my own question. I had always known that it would come to this. In fact, I had been in love with him for a while. I knew that now. All those feelings I had, I hadn't known what they were, but it was because I hadn't remembered, until now.

Subconsciously, I knew then, and had started seeing him because I wanted that, even though, consciously, intellectually, I didn't want it.

Because it always ended up being too painful.

The end of the semester was fast approaching, but I was looking forward to tonight. We were all going out dancing. I hadn't been out dancing with Tarek since the beginning of the semester. Whenever I thought of that night, I smiled.

I still hadn't told Tarek how I felt about him. In fact, I hadn't told anyone, not even my sisters. It was the prisoner's dilemma all over again.

And after tonight I would have to wait to see him, since tomorrow morning I was going to take an early train to New York to see Ariel. I would have the long weekend to think it over.

Tarek appeared to know that something was going on with me. He kept telling me how quiet I was, and that I seemed lost in my thoughts all the time. I could not deny that that was indeed the case.

I tried to put those thoughts out of my head so that I could enjoy tonight.

I was at Tarek's place, in front of the bathroom mirror. We had had dinner and were almost ready to head downtown to meet Josh and Eric at a club.

Out of nowhere, Tarek appeared in the bathroom doorway.

My chest tightened immediately. I managed a smile at him.

"Isabel, when are you going to tell me what's bothering you?" he said. His arms were crossed and he had that intense look in his eyes.

"Nothing is bothering me," I answered, but didn't look at him. Instead, I focused on applying my mascara.

He sighed slightly. "Did I do something?" he said then.

Yes, I thought. You made me fall in love with you. "No," I said instead, half-chucking. "You didn't do anything."

He didn't seem convinced, but I didn't volunteer anything else.

I hated this. I hated being so closed off from him. I had a knot in the pit of my stomach. Part of me wanted to tell him right there. And part of me wanted to cry. Instead, I sighed, turned around and kissed him.

"I'm all right, thinking about my sister," I lied.

Tarek smiled warmly. "You're going to see her tomorrow."

"I know." Then, without thinking, I said, "I'll miss you."

"I'll miss you too," he told me, touching my face.

Upon arriving at the club, my mood brightened instantly. Even though we would be taking final exams in a couple of weeks, we had time to enjoy ourselves for a little while. Tarek also seemed a little more relaxed.

I hugged Eric and Josh. Eric appeared to be feeling more confident about finals; he was less stressed in general. Well, he was less stressed about law school stuff in general. He was still stressed about Alyssa.

"So are we ready to get crazy?!" Eric shouted at us over the din of music.

"You know it!" I told him, smiling.

Indeed, it was a great night, in fact, a memorable night, for many reasons. The alcohol started swirling, we started dancing, and I danced so closely with Tarek that we might as well have been in bed together.

The place was packed, which was surprising since the next day was the biggest travel day of the entire year. At some point, well past midnight, the four of us went back to the bar for more drinks. And that was when the night started going to hell.

The bar had cleared out a bit. I was trying to get around a tall guy with a broad back. With him was a short girl with long, blonde hair. When the guy turned around, I about had the shock of my life.

Saul was standing in front of me. He grinned a broad grin, then looked at Tarek and back at me. The blonde girl who was with him was Alyssa. I didn't know why I was surprised. Alyssa was reminding me more and more of myself. And when someone told me not to do something, it was a given that I would do it.

And, of course, on the other side of Saul stood Sameer.

"Hi Isabel," Saul said, looking me up and down. I felt Tarek tense up at my side.

I smirked and shook my head. What could I possibly say to him?

Sameer greeted Tarek but ignored me.

To her credit, at least Alyssa looked sheepish. I quickly pulled her aside.

"Don't say that I didn't warn you about him," I shouted in her ear, trying to make my voice rise above the music.

"Jealous?" Saul shouted at me. I gave him a look that said not to be crazy.

"So you'll both have shared the same man," he continued.

"Shut the fuck up!" I told him, sticking my finger threateningly in his face and taking a step toward him.

The situation was unraveling quickly.

Sameer opened his mouth then. I shot him a look of hatred. Unfortunately, it wasn't enough to stop him.

Sameer looked directly at Tarek and said, "I can't believe you don't care," while shaking his head incredulously.

"What are you talking about?" Tarek asked him, not understanding.

"Don't say anything!" I said to Sameer, and my voice betrayed my desperation.

And at that moment Sameer understood that Tarek didn't know, that I had been bluffing all along. I saw the realization in his eyes, and the smirk on his lips that accompanied it.

Sameer ignored me and looked at Tarek. "She slept with Saul!" he said, motioning toward me.

Alyssa jumped in then, God bless her for trying. "That is none of your business!" she shouted to Sameer.

"Wait," Tarek said, looking at me. I crossed my arms and stood there open-mouthed like an idiot. "Isabel, is that true?"

There was literally no way out. The moment of truth had come, and I couldn't hide it. I was tired of doing that anyway.

I looked at him sadly. "Tarek, it was a long time ago, before I even met you."

"But I asked you if you had and you said no!"

"I know, but—" I had no response to that, to the lie.

Tarek's eyes widened. Of course he was shocked. He had trusted me, and I had lied to him.

The worst part was that Saul and Sameer seemed to be enjoying this.

"Let's talk about this outside," Tarek said then, with a voice like ice.

He took my elbow to lead me away from the group.

I stopped for a moment, turned around, and looked at Alyssa.

"I'm not leaving you here with them," I told her in a tone I only reserved for when I talked to my sisters, when I would take absolutely no argument from them.

She seemed to deflate and, amazingly, allowed me to lead her toward the exit.

Tarek led me, in a daze, toward the main entrance of the club. Eric and Josh were at my heels, along with Alyssa.

Suddenly we were all outside, and although usually the cold air felt good and refreshing to me, this time it chilled my mood. It didn't matter. I deserved this, I thought. Whatever hit was coming, I deserved it.

Tarek walked quickly away from the club's entrance, and I followed, next to him, my arms crossed and hugging my sides, fingernails digging into my ribs. I felt as though I were literally holding myself together. When we were clear of the end of the line, he turned to me, upset. I felt horrible, like everything good in my life was ending.

"So tell me," he said, his hands on his hips.

I opened my mouth, but nothing came out. I felt so alone.

"I—" but I couldn't go on.

"So you slept with him." It wasn't a question. His eyes were piercing mine.

"Yes," I said, nodding. My voice was a whisper.

"Why didn't you tell me? Did you date him?"

"No, I—it was just a hookup." I reconsidered, because it had been more than one time. "Well—"

"Well, *what?*"

"I slept with him." This was going to be painful. "Three times." I saw the shock in Tarek's eyes and continued at a rapid-fire pace. "It was three weekends in a row. I was out with Josh and Eric, and Saul and Sameer were there, at the same club. And I hooked up with him that night—"

"You mean you slept with him that night." Again, it wasn't a question. Tarek's voice was hard.

"Yes, and the following two weekends. He called me." Saul had called me for a booty call. "And I was lonely. And he was just there. But then he kept calling me, and I didn't want to see him anymore, because it wasn't—" It wasn't fulfilling, I thought. It wasn't what I was looking for. It wasn't like it was with Tarek. "It meant nothing!" My voice rose, and I wondered how much longer I would be able to keep it together.

I noticed that Josh, Eric, and Alyssa were there beside me, and I didn't feel quite as alone now.

"And you can do that?! Sleep with someone you don't care about?" Tarek was angry now, and I didn't blame him.

"Tarek," I raised my voice, "you knew that a long time ago! I told you I had done that in the past! What's the—" I stopped abruptly, because at that moment I understood.

"I see," I continued, the timber of my voice falling all at once. I was instantly sad as I looked Tarek right in his eyes. "You've always thought that—that I was—" I paused so that my voice didn't break. "You've *always* thought badly of me for that. You've *always* thought I was that kind of girl." I paused again. "Wow." I didn't know why I was surprised. I mean, the evidence strongly suggested that I *was* that type of girl.

"Isabel, I don't—" he started quickly, and his anger faded a bit.

I heard Eric suck in air. Josh didn't say anything.

My voice came out just above a whisper. "But it didn't stop you from screwing me, did it?"

"Damn." Eric's voice was accusatory.

Tarek looked hurt. I didn't know if it was because he was upset that I had guessed his thoughts or for some other reason. At that moment I didn't care.

He also wasn't saying anything.

"Your silence says it all," I told him. "Well, it's good to finally know what you really think about me."

"Isabel, I don't care what you did before you met me."

"Tarek, that's a fucking lie! You obviously do. Why else would you be so mad right now?"

"Because you lied to me! I asked you to your face what had happened between you and Saul and you said nothing! A relationship cannot be built on lies—"

"You can't blame her for that!" Alyssa said in my defense, but I waved a hand toward her, as if to say, thanks but it's not worth it.

People were turning to look at us. It made me even angrier. People around here loved a show like this.

"No," I said firmly. "You asked me whether there was any *other* reason why I didn't like him, and there wasn't." That was a true statement. I wasn't mad at Saul because he and I had slept together. I was mad at myself for that.

"Don't be a lawyer, Isabel! You know what I meant! Don't you think I would have wanted to know that?"

"Would it have made you break up with me?"

He paused, and his eyes changed. I thought maybe for a second that he understood why I hadn't told him.

"That's not the point and you know it," he said, sticking his finger in my face.

Neither of us said anything for a few seconds. I didn't know what else to say. I felt lost, like I was losing the only really good thing I had in my life except for my sisters.

"Why do you think you have the right to know about my life before you came into it?" I asked, articulating each word carefully.

"Why do you hide things about yourself?" Tarek shot back.

Then Eric spoke directly to me. "Come on, Isabel. I'll take you home."

"Like hell you will," Tarek growled at him. "I'm taking her home."

Now Eric was getting angry. He again addressed me.

"I'm not going to let him take you home if he's going to be an asshole to you!" Eric was raising his voice.

I wanted nothing more than to hide in a corner right now, embarrassed out of my mind.

I opened my mouth to say something, but Eric continued.

"*I'll* take you home." He had lowered his voice. I looked at him and his expression was one of concern.

"That's not going to happen," Tarek stepped closer to Eric.

"I'm not going to let you yell at her!" Eric raised his voice.

"I won't! And why do *you* want to take her home? So you can try to take advantage and hook up with her?!"

Then Eric got beyond pissed off. "Like I would fucking do that!"

"Tarek, he wouldn't do that," I said, my arms unfolding. I wanted to put my arms around Tarek, to tell him that I loved him, that whatever had happened with Saul had been over a year ago, that it had meant nothing, that I wanted to be with him and only him.

Tarek faced me. "So why the hell is he calling you all the time, Isabel?!" He said, irate and pointing at Eric. "I told you he's crazy about you, and I'm not going to let him try anything!"

The testosterone level here was suddenly way too high. "You don't understand," I told him. "He doesn't feel that way about me." I looked at Eric, then sideways at Alyssa.

"Eric," I began, pleading with him, "you have to tell him what's been going on, why you and I have been talking so much lately. Either you tell him or I'll tell him. But I don't like keeping things from him."

"Well, you kept your past with Saul from me!" Tarek was still raising his voice, this time at me. I guess I deserved that. I glanced at his eyes briefly and saw the anger there. After that, I couldn't look at him.

My voice cracked when I spoke. "I didn't like keeping that from you."

"Why did you then?!"

Even though I wasn't looking directly at him, I could feel his eyes burn through me, trying to understand why I hadn't told him, and trying to figure out if I was telling the truth now. I hated it. Except for the thing with Saul, I had always been truthful with him.

Eric apparently wasn't done. He got right in Tarek's face. I had never seen Tarek this angry, and had rarely seen Eric like this. I thought for a second that there might be an altercation, and was trying to figure out what I should do if it came to that.

"She was *petrified* of telling you!" Eric's voice had gone down a notch, I was relieved to notice.

"Why?" Tarek was still looking at me, but I was avoiding his eyes.

Eric sighed, shaking his head. In that moment I knew that he knew me. He really knew me. I hadn't told him any of this.

"Because she was afraid you would act like you're acting now." Eric's voice was almost at normal volume now.

I was holding in tears like nobody's business, *uber* determined not to cry in public. Most of all, I was determined not to cry in front of Tarek. I had never cried in front of any man, except for my father, and I would be damned if I were to start now.

Eric sighed, a sigh of resignation. He didn't say anything for a few moments.

"I'm crazy about Alyssa," he said. Tarek and Josh both looked at him and I chanced a look in Tarek's direction. He was surprised. However, no one was more surprised than Alyssa.

Eric continued. "Saul is after her. I don't know if she's slept with him."

"I haven't," Alyssa chimed in then, and appeared to only be talking to Eric.

Eric went on. "Nobody knows how I feel about her, but Isabel figured it out because—well, that's how she is." Eric and I looked at each other, and I made a sorry attempt at a smile.

"Eric, why didn't you tell me?" Alyssa said.

Eric continued, directing his conversation at Tarek. "Isabel has been cheering me up, or trying to, and has been trying to figure Alyssa out since—oddly, Isabel is her only real female friend at school, if you can call them friends. And for what it's worth, Isabel tried to warn Alyssa a while ago about Saul."

"You knew about this?" Tarek said to Alyssa then. "About Isabel and Saul?"

When no one answered right away, Tarek said, "So everyone knew except for me?"

He looked at me and I cast my eyes downward. That was enough of an answer, I guess.

Josh spoke up then. He had been on the sidelines, observing the events up until this point. "Isabel didn't tell anyone. But people know; people talk. It's law school. Hell, Alyssa knew Isabel was crazy about you even before Isabel knew! And those two were hardly even talking at that point."

"Well, that's fantastic!" Tarek said with bitter irony. It was getting more difficult for me to hold in the tears, but I was still determined. "You left me in the dark, Isabel! Not only that, but when I asked you what your problem was with him, you lied to me. I can forgive anything, but I can't forget a lie."

He was so angry. And now I was angry. He hadn't really given me a chance to explain. But I was done with this. I couldn't take any more and saw no reason to stand here and be a lightning rod.

I faced Tarek. "I'm not going to stand here and take this shit," I told him, "not from you."

I turned and walked away, and didn't look back.

Eric called out, just loud enough for me to hear. "Isabel, if he really cared about you, he wouldn't care who you slept with a year ago!"

I knew that he was right. And I also knew, or at least hoped, that Tarek didn't really care who I had slept with. He cared about the fact that I had kept it from him when he had asked me.

I began to walk more quickly. I heard Josh and Eric calling but ignored them. Then I blocked everything out, people chatting and hollering, cars honking, homeless people asking for change, everything. I could feel my own breath and hear my own heartbeat. I was aware of how cold I felt and how much my feet hurt in my heels.

I was walking so fast that if I had been walking any more quickly, I would have been running. In fact, it was a wonder I didn't fall over in my heels. I looked ahead and saw the entrance to the metro station not too far away.

Then I felt a hand on my arm, but continued walking, not caring whose hand it was.

Tarek stepped in front of me.

"God, you walk fast!" he said, and for a moment, I thought that maybe he would smile.

"Look who's talking," I said. "And, for that matter, I never hear you approaching. It must be because you weigh so little that your feet hardly touch the ground when you walk."

His mouth curved slightly.

I looked at him. "Tarek, I don't have anything else to say." That was patently untrue.

"I'll drive you home," he said.

"I know you don't want to look at me right now—"

"Isabel," he said, taking a deep breath, "I'll drive you home." He was still tense but his eyes weren't as angry as before. "I'm not going to let you go on the metro by yourself late at night."

I paused. I didn't think that I could win this argument, even if I wanted to. And I didn't want to, because I wasn't ready to be away from him. "OK," I said softly.

We walked to the metro station together in silence. We waited on the platform in silence. In fact, the entire metro ride back to Pentagon City was pretty much in silence.

I had my arms crossed. I wanted to take his hand, but if he rejected me I would break down, and I couldn't face that right now. So instead, on the metro I sat down and leaned my head against the glass window and closed my eyes. I tried to pretend that it had all been a nightmare, hoping that when I opened my eyes I would be in bed with him.

However, once we were in his car, the talking started. I had been dreading it like the plague.

Once he had the car started, I sank down in the front passenger seat and let the heat wash over me.

But, as usual, Tarek didn't let it go.

"So are we going to talk about this or not?" he said then, glancing sideways at me.

"Tarek, I don't have anything more to say. I screwed him. It was over a year ago. It was before I met you. It didn't mean anything. I was—lonely."

"So that's the kind of guy you liked to screw?"

I had never heard him use the word "screw." It made me so sad that I almost started crying right then.

"He was at the right place at the right time."

"Isabel, he didn't care about you at all!"

"I know!" I said, pissed off now. "And I didn't care about him! It was just sex. Like I said, I was lonely. Maybe you don't know what's it like to be truly lonely, to crave intimacy with someone, even if it's a false intimacy," I spat.

"And you can do that?"

"Look, if I were a man, nobody would say anything! Nobody says anything about Saul and how he sleeps around. When people talk about somebody 'sleeping around,'" using air quotes, "they're always talking about a woman. Why is that?! Men are expected to sleep around and women are—"
I left it hanging. Women who did that were called "sluts." Men who did that were called "normal guys."

"Well, I don't care about what other people say and I don't care what other people do!" Tarek continued. "I only care about *you*. And the fact is—Isabel, you lied to me. You had the perfect opportunity to tell me about it, and you didn't!"

I was losing it. I knew then that I wasn't going to make it home without crying and it was going to suck. I would look so weak in front of him. That thought made me want to cry even more.

We were still on the highway. We had maybe ten more minutes to get to my apartment. It was too long.

"Eric told you why I didn't tell you!" I said, but my voice was breaking already. I looked out the car window into the dark. It was as black outside as I felt inside. I felt my chest began to heave. Oh, Jesus—

"Well, that's not good enough!" Tarek was angry again. I didn't know how to calm him down. I didn't know how to calm myself down. "Are there any other men you haven't told me about?!"

"Notice that I've never asked *you* about any of the women *you* slept with in the past because I don't care!"

"I mean, anyone else I *know*?!" he clarified.

The implication was too much. I had tears down my face now, and could hardly see for them. My chest heaved and I covered my face with my hand and continued to face the window.

"I get it, Tarek! Congratulations! You're better than me!" My voice cracked on the very last word.

"Isabel?" I heard Tarek's voice and the sobs came like a waterfall.

I put my hands over my face and my face toward my lap. I felt the tears come through my hands and onto my clothes. God, if I could only have made it a few more minutes!

I couldn't say anything, and couldn't think of anything. I sobbed and sobbed. There were enough tears here for my whole life, for everything I had ever lost.

All of a sudden the atmosphere in the car changed. I felt the tension ease a little every time my chest heaved. On some level, it felt good to cry like this because I never did. It was a tension release. But the tension that was slowly dissipating wasn't entirely on my end.

"Oh, Isabel, I made you cry! I'm sorry! I'm so sorry." Tarek's voice was calmer, and I heard concern in it. But I still couldn't look at him. He continued. "I'm a jerk, I'm sorry! Please don't cry. It's OK." His hand was at my ear, brushing back my hair.

But I couldn't stop crying on demand. The floodgates had been unleashed.

I finally spoke between fits of sobbing. "I didn't tell you—because—because I didn't want—didn't want you to think I was a slut. And I—I feel like one. I—I feel like one now!" The pitch of my voice was so high that I didn't think anyone would have recognized it.

"Isabel, don't think that—"

"And—and you obviously think I'm one." I felt everything slipping away from me. I loved him and he was slipping away.

"I have never thought that about you and I don't think that now."

"I—I told you before," I continued. "I told you that I don't—don't do relationships—because it's too hard. I—I end up like this. What's the fucking point?!" I should just become a nun, I thought to myself, because the hook-ups weren't fulfilling anyway. Sure, it felt good for a minute, but in the morning you had to face the fact that you had been that vulnerable with a guy you didn't really feel anything for and, worst of all, who didn't care about you.

"Hold on," he told me.

We were finally out of the highway and close to my apartment building. The only reason I knew that was because I had felt the car decelerate and make the turn on the exit ramp. I couldn't see for all the tears, and kept my face covered.

After a couple more minutes the car came to a stop and I chanced a look through the passenger window, through my fingers. We were parked in the parking lot in front of my building.

As quickly as I could, I unbuckled my seatbelt and tried to open the car door but it was locked. I still wasn't thinking straight.

Tarek took my arm and then drew my face to his and kissed me on the cheek, near my ear. Then he stayed there like that. My entire face was wet and I was sure that my makeup had run.

"Isabel, I'm so sorry," he said. "Don't hate me. I didn't mean to make you cry."

"This is the worst day of my life," I said, and meant it. When my father died, I had had to live with that. Now I would have to live with that and losing Tarek. It was too much. "Tarek, I was so lonely when I did it. I was so lonely—"

"Sssh, I know."

"I was always so lonely until I met you. And I should have told you but—I didn't know how or when. And I bluffed Sameer; I told him that I had told you about it because I hoped that then he wouldn't say anything to you. I was so embarrassed about it. If I could undo it, I would."

"I know. It's OK." He sighed and brushed my hair away from my face. "Isabel, I'm sorry. I've handled this—really badly."

When I didn't say anything, he said, "Come on, let's go talk upstairs. It's cold."

I kind of took that as a good sign, the fact that he wanted to go upstairs with me instead of kicking me to the curb in the parking lot. Then I realized that that was what an optimist would think, and I wasn't an optimist.

Thank God we didn't see anyone on the way to my apartment because I would have been mortified. I was shaking and couldn't fit my key in the door lock, so Tarek carefully took it from me and unlocked and opened the door. When we got inside I went straight to the bathroom because I refused to talk to him looking all ugly with melted makeup.

But it turned out that my makeup wasn't as bad as I had thought. The areas around my eyes were a little black due to the mascara, but it wasn't horrible. I took all of my makeup off and washed my face.

I was so nervous. If he broke up with me now, I didn't know what I would do. The realization that I would still have to see him next semester, and the year after that, made me nauseous. What if he started seeing someone else? What if he started seeing Dalia? I still had a bunch of my clothes at his apartment. I would have to go get them at some point.

Most of the emotionally difficult things in my life, I had run from. It was easier that way. I wished I could run right now. I wished I could disappear from my apartment and get on the train to New York to see my sister. But it wasn't that easy.

Nothing worth anything is easy, Ariel had told me countless times.

I thought about my sister and how she was undergoing a life-changing event at the moment. My predicament seemed so much less dramatic right now.

I couldn't stay in the bathroom forever, so I left.

Tarek was in the kitchen and had made tea. I approached him but couldn't look at him.

"I—I should've told you," I stammered, with my arms crossed. "I'm sorry I didn't. I was afraid that maybe you wouldn't take it well." I paused. "I guess I was right. I usually am, and it sucks." I sighed. "Just once I would prefer not to be right, and to be pleasantly surprised instead." He didn't say anything so I continued. "If you don't want to be with me anymore, that's fine. I mean, I would hate that but—I wouldn't blame you. You can walk out of here right now and—" and I would die inside, I thought. "And I would be fine. I mean, I wouldn't—I wouldn't be fine. But I would move on."

He walked over to me, very slowly, and took both of my hands in both of his. He leaned his face against mine and said, "You think you can be rid of me that easily?"

"I don't want to be," I said.

"Isabel, I swear to God, I don't care what you did before you met me," he told me. "I was surprised when I found out tonight." He sighed. "I would've preferred to hear it from you, that's all. It doesn't change how I feel about you."

"How *do* you feel about me?" I couldn't believed I had asked that.

He looked surprised at the question. "Well how do *you* feel about *me*?"

I wasn't sure if he actually expected an answer, and I wasn't ready to give one. I felt weak, emotionally drained, like I was at the end of my rope, holding on by a thread. I didn't like feeling this way.

"Look," I said, dodging his question, even though he hadn't answered mine either. "It's late, and I have to catch an early train, and I'm keeping you up, so—" I left it hanging.

"OK," Tarek said softly. "Are you all right?" His hands were at my waist and his mouth was at my ear.

"Yes," I lied. *No*, I thought. I want you to stay here with me. I want you to tell me that you love me.

"I'm not sure if I believe you," he said.

"I'll be fine." I tried to make my voice sound much more stoic than I felt.

Tarek looked at me then. "I'll pick you up Sunday." I guessed that he figured that there was no point in forcing me to talk if I didn't want to.

"OK," I said, looking down.

He kissed me and I kissed him back, and the kiss lingered for a little while. Then he hugged me to him and I breathed him in, hoping that everything would be all right. I still wasn't convinced.

He kissed me again at the door, and then left. I felt like my heart left with him. Once he left, I felt instantly depressed, as if I could be more depressed.

I took a sip of my tea, then hung my head in my hands, with my elbows on the kitchen counter. I didn't like how I had left things unsaid.

I don't know why, but my thoughts went to Santi. I always felt that Santi had understood me, or the person I had been thirteen years ago, like he knew me, and he cared about me. And he knew that I loved him, even though I had never told him.

I paused. Didn't he?

All of a sudden, it hit me like a freight train. My pulse quickened and I was beginning to get breathless.

I am a first-class idiot, I thought.

I had never told Santi that I loved him. I had never told him. Why hadn't I? Maybe there had been a good reason when I was twenty-one years old, but damn it, I was too old for that shit.

I ran out the door with no regard for whether I tripped and fell in my heels. At least I had the presence of mind to grab my apartment keys.

I ran down the stairs, holding onto the railing for dear life. There was no point in falling and breaking a leg now. I pressed both hands against the double doors downstairs and ran outside.

I desperately looked around the parking lot. Where had he parked his car? I didn't remember. Ugh, I was so bad at remembering where I parked my *own* car!

Then I saw him, two rows away, getting into his car.

"Hey!" I shouted, loudly, emptying all the air from my lungs.

He looked up and saw me. I walked over to him, hugging my sides because of the cold. I could see my breath in front of me; my pulse was still elevated.

It was a clear night; I even saw some stars. And there was a full moon. I figured it was as good a night as any for beginning the rest of my life.

The walk over to Tarek's car seemed to take forever. When I was about five feet away from him, I stopped. I was getting cold feet, figuratively, not literally, but I was too far in to turn back now. Go big or go home, I told myself.

"So that's how you greet me now?" he asked me, half-smiling. Was it my imagination or did he look glad to see me? I must be delirious, I thought.

"No *Tarek*? No *babe*? Just hey you?" He was trying to be lighthearted, and I tried to read his eyes but it was difficult in the semi-darkness.

"Sorry, I didn't mean to be rude," I told him.

Then he became serious. "Isabel, you're shivering! It's too cold to be out here."

I waved a hand dismissively, as if saying, how can you think about that right now?

I paused, gathering all the courage I had. "Can—can I tell you something?" I stammered, partly due to the cold but mostly due to nerves.

His brows furrowed. "Of course. Come here."

I approached and he held my upper arms lightly. "Tell me," he said.

Then it occurred to me that I had decided to do this but hadn't thought about what to say. How could I say this and not sound like an idiot?

"You asked me how I felt about you," I said, my tone tentative and guarded.

He nodded.

"I mean, I—I always figured you knew."

"So you think I'm a mind reader?" I could see a smile tugging at the corners of his lips.

"Aren't you?" I said, with a hint of sarcasm.

We looked at each other for a few moments. Then he spoke.

"So tell me," he said gently.

"Tell you what?"

He almost chuckled, and I could feel any remaining tension start to ebb slowly.

"You know, Isabel," he said slowly, deliberately.

I smiled weakly. "You never let me off easy."

"If I did, then you would be forever alone in your head."

I smiled a little more broadly. "Are you afraid that I'll drive myself crazy, become a raving lunatic?"

"No, it's not that. I—everyone should have someone to talk to." He paused, and appeared to be thinking about what to say. I thought that it was ironic how alike he and I were in that way. That was exactly how I was, weighing everything before I said it. More accurate, I thought, was that I *used* to be that person, until I had met Tarek and started to spill everything without thinking.

"But don't change the subject," he said then, smiling a little. He sighed and began to rub my upper arms. "Look, I know it's difficult for you to talk about your feelings—"

I jumped in quickly. "But that doesn't mean that I don't have them. It doesn't mean that I don't have them—for you." I looked down.

He leaned forward and touched his face to mine. I could feel the heat from his body. I thought about the fact that I was five years older than he was, but that somehow he always seemed older, in that he seemed more mature, at least emotionally.

He kissed me lightly on the lips, and I almost died. He had kissed me like he had that first time, a little hesitant at first, then soft and very gentle. When he pulled away, I thought it was too fast.

"Isabel, don't be afraid. Tell me, please." His eyes were pleading. It occurred to me that this might be a turning point in our relationship, in that if he felt the same way about me, then this was going to turn out to be something very serious. And if he didn't, well then, I guess this would be the end of things. I didn't see how we could go on with me in love with him and he not in love with me.

"OK," I said, my voice heavy. "I will."

I looked at him then, at his lean shoulders, his dark eyes, his long lashes, his curly black hair that framed his face, falling around his ears. I couldn't believe that God would permit this man to fall in love with me. I didn't deserve how he had treated me all semester, when I had tried so hard to distance myself from him at first. But he was my friend, my best friend other than my sisters.

"I'm going to do something I don't usually do," I told him. "I'm going to tell you exactly how I feel."

He closed his eyes for a second and then opened them again, inhaling deeply.

"That is all I ever hoped you would tell me." He shook his head; he looked tired. It made me feel bad.

"Can you handle it, whatever it is, can you—?" my voice started to break.

"I can handle anything you tell me."

"OK," I said.

Then I started to think again. I was trying to think about everything that had happened between Tarek and me since the semester began. I was thinking that Tarek must love me, given all the things that he had done for me, right? Then I was thinking that maybe he really cared about me, but only the way you deeply cared about a good friend, one who has helped you through tough times. Or maybe he really did love me, but couldn't be with me in that way for some reason. Maybe it was his family. I knew very little about them. His father had passed away a long time ago, and what if his mother and his uncles wouldn't approve of me? And if that were the case, and we couldn't be together, then I would have to see him several times a week for the next year! It would be horribly upsetting, like having your Freudian id taken out and displayed in the law school for everyone to see, even the baby Millennials!

I was overanalyzing again. I had to put an end to the brain chatter and focus.

I looked at Tarek hard, and was suddenly aware of my pulse. My chest rose and fell faster than usual. He must have seen the look of sheer panic on my face, because he was looking intently at me and said, "Just tell me, please, just tell me."

I could do this. It was like a law school exam. I would freak out for the first five minutes, then once I started writing, I wouldn't stop writing until time was up. Once I started writing, everything would be all right. I had to open my mouth and start speaking, and the words would come out, and it would be all right. Despite the intensity of my current situation, I still laughed inwardly at my own lame comparison.

I looked at Tarek again, who was waiting patiently, and I played my last card.

"I—I love you," I told him. It was a statement of awe. "You made me fall in love with you." My voice lowered to a whisper. "How could you do that to me? How could you *do* that?"

His eyes widened. I had never seen him look so surprised. Actually, shocked was a better word.

And as I had thought, once I opened my mouth, the floodgates were unleashed.

My voice sounded like I didn't believe what I was saying. "I'm completely in love with you. You're all I think about, all the time. I'm always counting down the hours until I can see you again. You're the only man

I can really be myself around. And for some bizarre reason, you seem to tolerate my company. No one else does. The first time I saw you, the only thing I could think about was how sexy you were. And the more you and I talked, I couldn't believe how a man so gorgeous could be so selfless, and so intelligent. You were like a gift from God, only for me. I couldn't believe how lucky I was."

He had opened his mouth. I wasn't sure if he was going to speak or not but I wasn't done yet.

I continued quickly. "I tried so hard not to fall in love with you. You have to believe me, Tarek." I felt the tears starting to form at the corners of my eyes, but held them in for now. "But you made it impossible for me! I didn't want to fall for you. But the harder I tried not to, the more quickly I fell for you."

I kept going, because I knew that as soon as I stopped talking, he would talk, and this moment would end.

"Look, I know I'm older than you. And I'm super negative—" I took a break to look at him, take a breath and hold in the tears.

He kept looking at me, speechless.

"And God knows, I'm not perfect—" I stammered.

He finally spoke. "Isabel," he said quietly. "It's OK, it's OK." He ran a hand down my cheek. You *are* perfect. You are perfect—for me."

I looked down, embarrassed. I felt stripped to my bare soul. On some level, it was cathartic, but it was also terrifying for another person to see me like this.

Tarek took me into his arms, hugging me close. "Oh, Isabel, oh my God," he said into my hair. I thought I heard a smile in his voice. Again, I must be unhinged.

He continued to hold me, and I hugged him back, my arms around his waist and my face buried in his shoulder.

I was crying again, but softly this time.

Tarek held my face in front of him. I thought I must look ugly, with no makeup and a face puffy from crying and my eyes red. He started to stroke my hair, from the crown of my head down the side of my face, very slowly. With his other hand he gently wiped the tears from my face. And with his simple gesture, it was suddenly clear to me.

Tarek was stroking my hair the way I had always stroked my sisters' hair when they were sad or upset or sick. This was how I had comforted Lara and Ariel all the time when they were younger, holding them and stroking their hair and wiping away their little tears from their little faces. When Dad had died I held both of them for days; they slept in my bed sometimes because they were so scared. I would stroke their hair until they fell asleep (a real feat with two of them). Lara came home with a C in high school and was afraid Mom would be mad at her, and as she cried I told her that it would be OK. When Ariel came home from college crying uncontrollably when her boyfriend broke up with her, I held her and dried her tears and told her he didn't deserve her. And I remember when I came back from Spain, having left Santi in Madrid, Lara let me cry to sleep every night for a week, holding me and brushing the wet hair from my face.

Just as Tarek was doing right now.

Everything that had happened between Tarek and me flashed before my eyes again, but with new meaning this time. Everything he did for me was no less than what I would do for my sisters.

"Oh my God," I said then. "I don't believe it."

"What?"

"I can't believe how lucky I am."

"Why?" His face was closer to mine.

I put my hands over my mouth in shock. "Oh my God, you're in love with me."

He nodded. "Isabel, for someone who is so intelligent, you can be so dense." He smiled broadly.

He took my hands in his and put his forehead against mine. "You are all I ever wanted, don't you know that?

I lost it then. I didn't care about anything at that moment except for how we felt about each other. I put my arms around his waist and drew his body against mine, my breasts crushing against his chest.

"Why didn't you tell me?" I said breathlessly.

He looked at me, and his eyes told the whole story. "I tried to—several times. I don't know—I couldn't take it if you didn't feel the same way."

I hugged him to me again, burying my face against his neck. "Stay with me tonight, please," I breathed into his ear.

"I wouldn't leave you for anything right now."

He kissed me and I took his hand and led him upstairs.

Once we were in my apartment, we couldn't stop kissing. My face was still wet from tears, but I didn't care anymore. I was surprised that I had had any left.

I was holding his face in both hands and he held me around the waist, pulling me toward him. I shivered, then opened my mouth to speak. There were so many things to say.

"Tarek, I'm sorry about Saul. I'm sorry. I'm sorry for not telling you."

He shook his head. "I want you to forget about it. It doesn't matter—"

"I haven't wanted to be with anyone else since I met you. I only wanted to be with you—"

"I know, Isabel. I know." He kissed me again. "I love you so much."

"Why didn't you tell me?!" I asked again, more urgently this time, as if his previous explanation weren't sufficient.

He opened his mouth but took a little while to speak. "I was afraid. I didn't want to freak you out."

"Oh, I'm freaking out right now," I giggled, and he laughed too. "But in a good way, I promise."

Then he was serious. "Did you think I would sleep with you if I didn't feel that for you?"

"Those two things are not always mutually inclusive," I said.

"Well, they usually are for me," he said.

We kissed, then he pulled away all at once. "Isabel, there's something else I have to tell you."

"Tell me," I said, kissing his neck.

"I don't think badly of anything you did in the past, I—it doesn't change the way I feel about you—not at all."

I was looking at him. Again, there was hurt in his eyes.

"I—" he went on. "It hurts me to know that you were so lonely, that you could be so lonely. I don't blame you. But it makes me feel horrible to think that you felt alone like that."

"It doesn't matter now," I told him. "Nothing about the past matters."

I should have known, I thought then. He had treated me so well, even knowing about my past. If I had been more honest with myself about reading his actions—

Then our hands were all over each other's bodies. I didn't waste any time. I took his hand and led him to my bedroom.

Then I remembered my manners, and turned to face him. "Are you OK? Are you cold? Can I get you anything?"

He was grinning, and his eyes were on fire. "No no, I'm all right."

I was a little cold, so I turned the heat up on the thermostat two degrees.

"Isabel," he said, "I'm sorry that I made you cry before. I didn't mean to—"

"I know, babe. It's OK."

"But I feel like a jerk."

"Tarek, it's OK. Please—it's OK."

I took him over to my bed and turned on the lamp on the night table. It gave just enough light.

We undressed each other quickly, kissing and laughing the entire time.

The sex was urgent, almost frantic, like we would die if we weren't connected right at that moment.

He was leaning over me on my bed, kissing me, and our connection this time was slightly different. We didn't hold anything back. I hooked one leg around his waist and flipped over, so that I was sitting on top of him. He smiled and brought my head down to his face to kiss me.

"Isabel, I love you," he told me. "And don't ever think anything else."

I smiled, then gripped his shoulders and he gripped my hips and I rode him hard until we both cried out.

Afterward, he pulled me to him so that I was lying on top of him, with his arms tightly around me. He was kissing my arm, then my shoulder and my neck.

I raised my head enough to look at him. "Promise me that you'll always tell me how you feel," I told him.

"I promise if you will."

"OK." I smiled.

After a few minutes I rolled over lazily so that I was on my side next to him. We were looking at each other. I felt myself blushing furiously. I put my hand against his face and he took it and kissed it.

I closed my eyes for a second and was on the verge of falling asleep, exhausted, when I suddenly remembered something.

I sat up quickly and reached for my cell phone, which wasn't on my nightstand, where it usually was.

"What's the matter?" Tarek was asking me.

"I have to set my alarm for tomorrow, I mean—for later this morning." I had almost forgotten that I was going to catch a train in a few hours.

I retrieved my phone from my purse, which was on the kitchen floor, and set the alarm.

"I'll drive you to the station," Tarek said.

"OK, thank you." I kissed him, my hand in his hair and his arms around me. Then I looked at him, questioning. "So—this is—I mean—so this is something very serious, isn't it?"

He smiled, and there were a whole range of emotions all over his face. But I could tell that he was happy.

"Yes," he said. "Are you all right with that?"

"Yes," I told him.

He kissed me again, and in a matter of minutes, I was asleep, elated.

The alarm on my phone sounded after what seemed like only a few minutes. However, we had slept for almost four hours. I woke up with Tarek's arms around me and my face against his chest, and I hated to move. But I had to.

I got up quickly and kissed him, but he didn't stir. I showered and brewed coffee. I was hungry and grabbed a couple protein bars to stick into my purse. I could eat them on the train.

By the time I was drinking my coffee, Tarek was getting out of the shower. I went to stand at my bedroom door, ogling him.

I giggled and he turned and looked at me.

"Good morning," he said, and his grin was devious. He walked over to me and kissed me, his lips still wet from the shower.

"Good morning," I said back. "Can I get you anything?"

"Just water."

I turned and went to the kitchen. We were ready to go a few minutes later. I made sure that my apartment was locked up, and we took the elevator to the first floor, since we were dragging my suitcase. I had tried to pack light, but I was bringing a couple of gifts for my sister.

The drive wouldn't take that long to the train station in downtown DC, since at this time of day there would be virtually no traffic.

Tarek started his BMW and before he pulled it out of the parking lot, he leaned over and kissed me. The kiss lingered and, before I knew it, our tongues were in each other's mouths and I had my hands all over him.

When we pulled apart, I told him, "Kiss me like that again and I won't go to New York."

"Ooo, I was hoping you'd say that."

Once the heat kicked in in the BMW, I relaxed.

The mood in the car was happy, content, but a little bittersweet because after what had happened last night, we would be apart for several days. I hated that, but I couldn't leave my sister when she needed me.

I put my left hand on Tarek's thigh as he drove. "You know I hate leaving you now."

"I know," he said, briefly squeezing my hand before returning his to the steering wheel. "But your sister needs to see you, you know that."

"You won't be alone, will you?"

"No, on Thursday I'm going with Josh and Eric to Josh's sister's house."

"That's still the plan?"

"Yes."

"All right." I looked ahead.

"And I'll pick you up on Sunday."

"OK."

We pulled in front of the train station and got out of the car. He helped me with my suitcase.

Then we exchanged a look, one of longing and connection and other intense feelings that I could not even begin to articulate.

"Come here," Tarek said, taking me into his arms. He kissed me like he didn't want to let me go.

"I'll miss you so much," I told him.

"I'll miss you too," he said.

"Tell me that last night really happened," I said.

He smiled. "It really happened. And I love you."

"I love you too. You know that."

"Let me know when you get there," he said.

"OK, and let me know when you get home now. You must be so tired."

"I'll be OK."

We stayed there talking and holding each other for several minutes. Neither one of us wanted to leave. But soon it was getting late.

"Isabel, you need to go or you'll miss your train," he said, brushing my hair back. "Be safe and I'll see you Sunday." Then he added, "I'll be waiting—" He dropped his eyes for a second, "very impatiently." Then he smiled at me.

I kissed him one last time, then took my suitcase and left, letting his hand go only when I had to.

He waved to me and waited there until I was deep into the train station, out of sight. When I didn't see him anymore, I concentrated on finding my track.

The train was packed with people going to visit family and friends over the Thanksgiving holiday. I had to push past everyone to find my seat; then I put my suitcase up, with the help of the elderly gentleman who was sitting next to me.

I sat down in my seat, giddy, unable to suppress the sly smile that kept popping up on my lips.

"Well, you're in good spirits at this godforsaken hour," the man next to me was saying, looking at me and smiling.

"Yeah, well, there's a first time for everything, I guess." I grinned at him.

Once the train was moving, I sank back in my seat, exhausted from the emotions over the past twelve hours. It still seemed like I was moving in a dream, like the life I was living couldn't be my own. It was too good.

My phone blipped. It was Tarek.

I'm home, thinking about you. Call me when you arrive. I love you.

I wrote back.

I will. Love you too, babe.

Then I noticed that I had text messages from both Josh and Eric. They both asked the same question.

Is everything OK?

I responded to both of them.

Yes, actually, things have never been better :) And don't be mad at Tarek! We made up.

Apparently, Eric was still up, whether partying or doing something else, I didn't know. I had a response from him a few minutes later.

I bet you did!

I grinned a huge grin, the kind that was going to stay with me all day. Then the train started pulling away from the station.

I leaned back in my seat, put my earbuds in and looked out the window. I thought that maybe I should sleep but I couldn't. I was too wound up.

So I continued to look out the window, even though everything was still dark. A little while later, the sky began to become more gray than black, and the buildings became more visible. Then the sun began to peek over the horizon line, spilling orange-red rays over everything.

It was a new day.